Globalisation, Economic Inclusion and African Workers

This book addresses the question of whether greater inclusion in the global economy offers a solution to rising unemployment and poverty in contemporary Africa. The authors trace the connection between global demographic change and new mechanisms of economic inclusion via global value chains, digital networks, labour migration and corporate engagement with the bottom of the pyramid, challenging the claim that African workers have become functionally irrelevant to the global economy. They expose the shift of global demand for African workers from formal to increasingly informalised labour arrangements, mediated by social enterprises, labour brokers, graduate entrepreneurs and grassroots associations. Focusing on global employment connections initiated from above and from below, the authors examine whether global labour linkages increase or reduce problems of vulnerable and unstable working conditions within African countries, and consider the economic and political conditions needed for African workers to capture the gains of inclusion in the global economy. This book was originally published as a special issue of *The Journal of Development Studies*.

Kate Meagher is an Associate Professor at the Department of International Development, London School of Economics, UK. She specialises in African informal economies and real governance, and has published widely on contemporary dilemmas of informality and economic inclusion, including *Identity Economics: Social Networks and the Informal Economy in Nigeria*.

Laura Mann is an Assistant Professor at the Department of International Development, London School of Economics, UK. Her research and publications include work on political economy of development, African higher education and labour issues, and critical approaches to new information and communication technologies in Africa.

Maxim Bolt is a Reader in Anthropology and African Studies at the University of Birmingham, UK, and a Research Associate at the University of the Witwatersrand, South Africa. His first book – *Zimbabwe's Migrants and South Africa's Border Farms* – explores wage labour in a place of transience and informal livelihoods.

Globalisation, Economic Inclusion and African Workers

Making the right connections

Edited by
Kate Meagher, Laura Mann and Maxim Bolt

Routledge
Taylor & Francis Group
LONDON AND NEW YORK

First published 2017
by Routledge

2 Park Square, Milton Park, Abingdon, Oxfordshire OX14 4RN
52 Vanderbilt Avenue, New York, NY 10017

Routledge is an imprint of the Taylor & Francis Group, an informa business

First issued in paperback 2018

British Library Cataloguing in Publication Data
A catalogue record for this book is available from the British Library

ISBN 13: 978-1-138-21894-9 (hbk)
ISBN 13: 978-0-367-07591-0 (pbk)

Typeset in TimesNewRomanPS
by diacriTech, Chennai

Publisher's Note
The publisher accepts responsibility for any inconsistencies that may have arisen during the conversion of this book from journal articles to book chapters, namely the possible inclusion of journal terminology.

Contents

Citation Information

The Journal of Development Studies is a Routledge journal published in collaboration with Global Development Institute (GDI), School of Environment and Development, University of Manchester, UK.

The chapters in this book were originally published in *The Journal of Development Studies*, volume 52, issue 4 (April 2016). When citing this material, please use the original page numbering for each article, as follows:

Introduction
Introduction: Global Economic Inclusion and African Workers
Kate Meagher, Laura Mann and Maxim Bolt
The Journal of Development Studies, volume 52, issue 4 (April 2016) pp. 471–482

Chapter 1
The Scramble for Africans: Demography, Globalisation and Africa's Informal Labour Markets
Kate Meagher
The Journal of Development Studies, volume 52, issue 4 (April 2016) pp. 483–497

Chapter 2
'Integration' or 'Selective Incorporation'? The Modes of Governance in Informal Trading Policy in the Inner City of Johannesburg
Antonio Pezzano
The Journal of Development Studies, volume 52, issue 4 (April 2016) pp. 498–513

Chapter 3
Remaking Africa's Informal Economies: Youth, Entrepreneurship and the Promise of Inclusion at the Bottom of the Pyramid
Catherine Dolan and Dinah Rajak
The Journal of Development Studies, volume 52, issue 4 (April 2016) pp. 514–529

Chapter 4
The Domestic Turn: Business Process Outsourcing and the Growing Automation of Kenyan Organisations
Laura Mann and Mark Graham
The Journal of Development Studies, volume 52, issue 4 (April 2016) pp. 530–548

Chapter 5

Do Transnational Links Matter after Return? Labour Market Participation among Ghanaian Return Migrants
Mary Boatemaa Setrana and Steve Tonah
The Journal of Development Studies, volume 52, issue 4 (April 2016) pp. 549–560

Chapter 6

Accidental Neoliberalism and the Performance of Management: Hierarchies in Export Agriculture on the Zimbabwean-South African Border
Maxim Bolt
The Journal of Development Studies, volume 52, issue 4 (April 2016) pp. 561–575

Chapter 7

Resilient Labour: Workplace Regimes, Globalisation and Enclave Development in Swaziland
Vito Laterza
The Journal of Development Studies, volume 52, issue 4 (April 2016) pp. 576–590

Introduction: Global Economic Inclusion and African Workers

KATE MEAGHER*, LAURA MANN* & MAXIM BOLT**

*Department of International Development, London School of Economics, London, UK, **Department of African Studies and Anthropology, University of Birmingham, Birmingham, UK

ABSTRACT *This introductory article explores the transformative potential of global connections for African workers. It challenges recent claims that African workers have become functionally irrelevant to the global economy by examining the shift of global demand for African workers from formal to increasingly informalised labour arrangements, mediated by social enterprises, labour brokers and graduate entrepreneurs. Focusing on global employment connections initiated from above and from below, we consider why global labour linkages have tended to increase rather than reduce problems of vulnerable and unstable working conditions within African countries, and consider the economic and political conditions needed for African workers to capture the gains of inclusion in the global economy.*

1. Introduction

Economic resurgence in sub-Saharan Africa raises new questions about who benefits from inclusion in the global economy. Over the past decade, donors and investors have scrambled to take part in the rise of the African Lions, associated with average annual growth rates pushing 5 per cent, improvements in governance and talk of an expanding middle class (African Economic Outlook, 2014; August, 2013; Economist, 2011; Roxburgh et al., 2010). Yet rapid economic growth has not trickled down to the majority of African populations. Nearly 50 per cent of Africans still live below the poverty line, more than two-thirds of non-agricultural workers earn their living in the informal economy, and youth unemployment is rising, particularly among university graduates (African Economic Outlook, 2010; Garcia & Fares, 2008; Vanek et al., 2014). Closer integration into the global economy through global value chains, digital networks, innovation hubs and inclusive business models is viewed as essential to turning growth into job creation in a region in which escalating unemployment is compounded by the highest population growth rates in the world. This special issue examines the positive and negative effects of global economic inclusion for African workers, with attention to the terms of inclusion fostered by globalising economies.

Clarifying the way in which globalisation affects African labour dynamics requires an engagement with debates about the meaning of global economic inclusion. Market-led approaches identify economic inclusion with greater participation in global markets (African Economic Outlook, 2014; de Haan & Thorat, 2013; de Mello & Dutz, 2014; World Development Report, 2013). Addressing poverty and economic exclusion involves reducing the barriers to participation by enhancing labour market flexibility and bridging market failures that limit access to resources and employment opportunities among the poor and unemployed (African Economic Outlook, 2014; London & Hart, 2011; Mendoza & Thelen, 2008; World Development Report, 2013). An emphasis on 'inclusive markets', 'financial inclusion' and 'inclusive growth' seeks to address economic exclusion by connecting the poor more directly into the global economy.

Conversely, structuralist perspectives define economic inclusion, not just as inclusion in global economic systems, but as inclusion in the *benefits* of the global economy (Heintz, 2009; UNRISD, 2010). They note that inclusion in global markets can increase rather than reduce the vulnerability of workers in developing countries. As Phillips and Sakamoto (2012, p. 288) explain, 'contrary to orthodox assumptions that "inclusion" in global economic activity (through employment) is the key to poverty reduction or "social upgrading", the terms of this inclusion can instead create and perpetuate poverty for a large part of the world's labour force'. The central issue is not just the presence or absence of connections to the global economy, but the economic and power relations embedded in those connections. Greater attention to the terms of global inclusion for rural and urban workers in developing countries has triggered a proliferation of research on processes of 'adverse incorportation', defined as 'inclusion on worse terms' (Barrientos, Kothari, & Phillips, 2013; Hickey & du Toit, 2007; Meagher & Lindell, 2013; Phillips, 2011).

Understanding the implications of global economic inclusion for African workers has been complicated by the complex changes in the nature and organisation of employment. Amid processes of globalisation, economic restructuring, diversification and informalisation, African workers have been forced into a range of new labour categories, including graduate micro-enterpreneurs, informal workers in formal firms, and modern forms of bonded labour. These arrangements often blur traditional distinctions between formal and informal, skilled and unskilled, free and unfree labour. Indeed, some scholars argue that these binary distinctions obstruct the task of understanding the dynamics of labour transformations in the context of globalisation. Lerche (2011) and Barrientos et al. (2013) have called for the varieties of vulnerable labour to be represented as a continuum of 'unfreedoms' with decent work at one end and extremes of forced and child labour at the other. They argue that examining gradations of informal and unfree labour as a continuum facilitates a clearer understanding of the impact of globalisation on promoting or undermining the creation of decent work.

Yet a similar continuum of labour quality outlined in the World Development Report on Jobs (2013) puts forward a very different interpretation of the boundary between decent and indecent work. According to the authors:

> Jobs are activities that generate actual or imputed income, monetary or in kind, formal or informal. But not all forms of work can be deemed jobs. Activities performed against the will of the worker or involving violations of fundamental human rights should not be considered jobs.

This account excludes as illegitimate forms of work only forced and child labour, while asserting that 'informal jobs can be good jobs for development in less developed countries' (ibid.m p. 33–34). The process of global economic inclusion does not only involve the incorporation of workers, but unleashes new struggles over the boundaries of legitimate and illegitimate forms of work.

This special issue seeks to advance the analysis of how global inclusion is reshaping opportunities and terms of employment for African workers in the context of resurgent growth. What kinds of new economic opportunities are being created by global connections, and how are they reshaping formal as well as informal labour markets? How do they affect the scope for agency and livelihood security among African workers, entrepreneurs and professionals? What are the implications of these transformations for employment, poverty alleviation and economic transformation within African societies? To what extent do these processes of economic change signal a new era of rising incomes and opportunity for African workers, and in what contexts do they represent novel forms of exploitation and adverse incorporation, characterised by expanding employment on disadvantageous terms?

To address these questions, the articles presented here draw on fresh empirical material from a number of globalising African countries to interrogate contemporary debates about economic inclusion. The scholars involved were initially brought together in a panel on African workers and globalisation at the 2013 European Conference for African Studies, with one outside addition.

Articles cover East, West and Southern African cases, focusing on some of Africa's most globalised economies, with a view to examining how workers are affected in best-case scenarios of dynamic global inclusion. Particular attention is paid to the refashioning of linkages between the local and the global, formal and informal, and the mediation of these interfaces by state policy, local associations and an ethically styled business infrastructure of enlightened capitalism, social enterprise and corporate social responsibility. The objective is to explore how African workers engage with new openings from below in the face of competing agendas of incorporation from above. While some have suggested that 'African Lions' might be poised to have their day in the sun, this special issue examines who will be the lions and who will be the gazelles as Africa's footloose labour, striving graduates and intrepid entrepreneurs engage with the opportunities and demands of the global economy.

This introductory article will set the scene by reflecting on the wider historical, structural and theoretical issues informing the global inclusion of African workers. It will focus on two broad questions: how has engagement with the global economy affected African workers over time, and what is the transformative potential of global connections in the current era? The next section will place the continuities and transformations of African workers' engagement with the global economy in historical context. This will be followed by a consideration of the contemporary context, involving a brief outline of the seven articles in this special issue, and an examination of the structural realities of global connections in the twenty-first century. The final two sections examine the effect of global connections on the terms of inclusion, firstly by focusing on the factors leading to adverse incorporation, and secondly by focusing on alternative possibilities for promoting economic transformation and long-term improvements in the livelihoods of African workers.

2. Incorporating African Workers: Transformations and Historical Continuities

When thinking about the developmental role of global connections, it is important to remember that the engagement of African workers in the global economy is nothing new. Historians and anthropologists have traced a long history of African engagement in global systems of production and exchange as traders, as slaves, as migrant workers in mines and plantations, and as peasant farmers producing export crops (Austen, 1987; Cooper, 2001; Hopkins, 1973). What is novel in the current conjuncture are the specific mechanisms and terms on which African workers are being incorporated into globalised systems of accumulation. This is not so much a question of the presence or absence of transnational linkages, but of how workers are defined as valuable in relation to the global economy. Global linkages have always involved more than just connecting with African labour; they play a central role in fashioning and refashioning the definition of legitimate work and the terms on which Africans are recognised and rewarded as workers.

From the outset, global connections have not necessarily offered African workers a path out of vulnerability. One of the earliest engagements of African workers with the global market economy involved the intensification of vulnerable labour through the slave trade. In the early colonial period, interests shifted to the creation of a system of free wage labour, involving new struggles over labour control and the boundaries of legitimate work. On the one hand, the colonial authorities had to uproot labour from indigenous systems of labour control (Brown & van der Linden, 2010; Guyer, 1993). On the other hand, viable labour markets had to overcome the existence of an 'exit option' which allowed African workers to flee or withdraw into subsistence or informality if wages or working conditions in the colonial economy were unattractive (Ferguson, 2013; Hyden, 1983; Lemarchand, 1992). Strategies of outlawing local slavery, coercive taxation systems, destroying and criminalising competing local activities, and inculcating Christian work ethics were used to drive African workers into labour markets and cash crop production to make them useful to the needs of colonial capital (Arrighi, 1970; Comaroff & Comaroff, 1991; Cooper, 1992; Freund, 1988; Watts, 1983; Wrigley, 1957). As the articles in this special issue demonstrate, new forms of labour discipline, religious ethics and regulatory change continue to play a role in redefining the boundaries of labour control and legitimate work in contemporary efforts to adapt African workers to the demands of globalising economies.

The formalisation of African waged employment from the late colonial period improved terms and conditions of employment, and made permanent jobs in formal sector firms or public administration into important markers of economic modernisation and personal economic success, particularly in the emerging middle classes (Ferguson, 1999; Freund, 1988). However, as Brass (2009, 2011) and others have detailed, colonial export production also continued to make significant use of non-waged and unfree labour, including peasant labour, forced labour and coercive forms of labour contracting, wherever free waged labour proved costly, disruptive or unavailable (Brown & van der Linden, 2010; Freund, 1988; Martino, 2012). Although forced labour was regarded as morally and legally unacceptable by colonial and metropolitan governments, its continued practice in many parts of West, Central and Southern Africa by way of chiefs, labour contractors and other intermediaries, allowed forms of work deemed illegitimate within market economies to play a lasting role in global production systems. As many of the articles in this special issue reveal, the role of brokers and intermediaries is echoed in contemporary labour practices for integrating formally unacceptable labour arrangements into global value chains.

Despite the persistence of informal labour systems, ideologies of modernisation converged with legal regulations and local aspirations to support a trajectory of labour formalisation during the independence period. This was abruptly reversed by crisis and economic restructuring in the late 1970s and 1980s. Once again, the economic and regulatory demands of the global economy radically restructured African labour systems. Trade and currency liberalisation, the downsizing of the public sector and consequent processes of retrenchment and deindustrialisation forced labour out of formal labour markets into burgeoning informal economies in a process Marxist scholars refer to as 'deproletarianisation', and others simply call 'informalisation' (Brass, 1994, 2009, 2011; Meagher, 1995; Rogerson, 1997; Vandemoortele, 1991). In many parts of the continent, real wages fell by over 90 per cent between the early 1970s and the early 1990s among professionals as well as unskilled labour, and informal economies swelled to an average of 72 per cent of the non-agricultural labour force, unravelling local 'expectations of modernity' (Ferguson, 1999; ILO, 2002; Jamal & Weeks, 1993; Mkandawire & Soludo, 1999; Rogerson, 1999; Vandemoortele, 1991).

Unable to absorb their own labour force within formal or informal economic systems, African economies were turned 'from a people-scarce system to a people surplus one', haemorrhaging workers into petty informal activities and transnational migrant networks (Ferguson, 2013, p. 230). In the intervening decades, the boundaries of legitimate work have been reshaped by ideologies of survival rather than modernisation, morally revalorising informal forms of work denounced as backward or illicit in an earlier era. Whether the widespread informalisation of African economies in the 1980s and 1990s is regarded as a return to cultural practices, as a means of cheapening and disciplining labour, or as a barometer of Africa's 'structural irrelevance' to the global economy, what is clear is that over time, global connections have been as much as source of vulnerability for African workers as a solution to it (Brass, 2011; Castells, 1997; Rogerson, 1997).

3. New Global Connections: Conduits, Siphons and Intermediaries

In the new era of 'Africa Rising', we are witnessing a global revaluation of African workers as productive economic actors. Global engagement with African workers offers welcome employment prospects for expanding pools of unemployed and informalised labour, along with new access to skills, capital and technology. Contrary to Ferguson's (2015) argument that African workers are not so much exploited as functionally irrelevant to global capital, international development agencies and global firms are keen to re-engage with African workers. However, global promises of access to jobs come with a further reshaping of the nature of employment. International development discourse is increasingly marked by an inversion of value hierarchies between formal and informal employment (World Development Report, 2013; African Development Bank, 2013). In the recent World Development Report on Jobs (2013), informal employment is celebrated as 'inclusive', 'transformational', and 'good for development', while formal employment is denigrated as a source of job shortage, economic stagnation, and social exclusion. While formal workers have always represented only a small fraction of the African labour force, the articles in this special issue consider whether global economic engagement with the informal economy represents a new horizon of opportunity for African workers, or a reversal of the developmental commitment to expanding decent employment.

Answering this question requires a closer examination of the structure of global connections that link African workers into the global economy. Understanding how, or whether, global economic inclusion can improve the opportunities and working conditions of African workers, calls for an examination of the actors, processes, institutions and disciplinary techniques through which global linkages operate, and a consideration of how benefits are distributed within them. While global connections can act as conduits of investment, skills and employment opportunities, they also have a potential to serve as siphons, tapping local labour, social knowledge and structures of collective action for the benefit of external investors (Dolan & Roll, 2013; Elyachar, 2012; Meagher & Lindell, 2013; Meagher, 2013). More specific questions need to be asked about how global linkages mediate access to the benefits of globalisation, and how they interact with the agency of African workers and entrepreneurs.

Examining the technical and institutional dynamics of global value chains, fibre optic cables, transnational kinship or religious networks, and corporate linkages with the bottom of the pyramid, we can begin to grasp the variety and complexity of networks linking African workers to the global economy. Far from constituting smooth direct channels of opportunity, these networks are structured by a range of intermediaries that link global firms and international development actors to the intricate institutional ecosystems of African workers, consumers and entrepreneurs. Reflecting on the rising importance of brokerage in contemporary South Africa, Deborah James (2011) notes its role in linking otherwise incompatible regulatory frameworks of state, market and local civil society. Proponents of bottom of the pyramid initiatives have emphasised the need for 'honest brokers' such as NGOs and social enterprises to mediate the gap between formal corporate institutions and the varied and often informal local arrangements encountered on the ground in African countries (Rivera-Santos, Rufin, & Kolk, 2012; Rivera-Santos & Rufin, 2010; Webb, Kistruck, Ireland, & Ketchen, 2010). Linkages between African workers and global sources of opportunity are often indirect.

This demands a stronger focus on how brokers and intermediaries alter regulatory arrangements in the process of connecting global labour demand to local labour supply. Some commentators highlight the role of communal or philanthropic intermediaries in bypassing publicly sanctioned systems of labour regulation. Gavin Smith reflects on how the apparently Polanyian re-embedding of economic activities in communal and societal networks may actually serve to 'shift regulation to new forms and social spaces' – in the process, acting to 'justify forms of labour regulation hitherto deemed unethical by all parties involved, and to delegitimise collective action by people in their capacity as workers' (Smith, 1994, pp. 80–82, see also Corrigan, 1977). Similarly, commentators on global value chains have noted that brokers and multiple tiers of intermediaries play a key role in evading labour regulations and squeezing labour in ways that are deemed legally and morally unacceptable in developed and developing countries (Barrientos, Gereffi, & Rossi, 2011; Lerche, 2011, p. 22; Theron, 2005). As James (2011) and others have noted, some intermediate workers may consolidate their positions by actively producing others' informality and vulnerability, such as local notables, educated rural fixers, or graduate SMEs, who facilitate global access to diverse informal labour systems (Avle, 2014; Bolt, 2013; Teglskov Nielsen, 2012). While intermediaries help to link local labour supplies to global labour demand, they can also be used to bypass legal and moral obstacles to intensified labour exploitation.

The articles presented here examine the mechanisms of labour inclusion through a focus on three broad contexts. Articles by Meagher, Pezzano, and Dolan and Rajak focus on workers in the informal economy experiencing globalisation from above; Mann and Graham, and Setrana and Tonah trace the experience of skilled workers engaging with the global economy from below; and articles by Laterza and Bolt examine experiences of globalisation by rural workers in dependent labour relations. From the perspective of informal workers, Meagher's article investigates the potential for Africa's rapid population growth and expanding informal economies to generate a 'demographic dividend' capable of fuelling rapid development. Drawing on evidence of Africa's stalled demographic transition and its interaction with processes of informalisation, she examines who is best placed to reap a dividend from global linkages with informalised pools of African labour. Far from resolving problems of employment and economic inclusion, she shows that the developmental benefits for African countries and African workers are likely to be limited. By contrast, Pezzano focuses on the capacity of informal street traders to resist global economic imperatives. He traces how struggles between informal traders, traders associations and various levels of state authorities in Johannesburg thwart efforts to incorporate informal actors on terms set by powerful global imperatives and formal sector officials. The selective regularisation of the right to the city for some informal traders produces a complex intersection of co-option and resistance among excluded traders, blurring the boundaries between informality and state recognition. While the ensuing struggles lead to a legal victory for excluded informal traders in the South African Constitutional Court, they also trigger a political backlash grounded in the organisational imperatives of the global city.

Dolan and Rajak's article examines how informal workers in Nairobi slums are being repurposed through an encounter with corporate Bottom of the Pyramid initiatives. Through the intermediary of a social enterprise, unemployed youth are trained to become entrepreneurs using regimes of corporate discipline normally reserved for wage labour. Discourses of inclusion and empowerment are deployed alongside training and performance metrics that use 'technologies of the self' to impose rigorous labour control on vulnerable informal workers restyled as entrepreneurs. Dolan and Rajak examine the implications of using poor youth to meet the requirements of the corporate bottom line at the bottom of the pyramid. While the allure of entrepreneurship responds to youthful ambitions for social advancement, the realities of insecure informal work frustrate aspirations and demonstrate the limited capacities of BoP initiatives to transform economic conditions.

Mann and Graham, and Setrana and Tonah, explore the efforts of skilled African workers to engage with the formal sector in search of more advantageous avenues of global incorporation from below. Mann and Graham examine the efforts of the Kenyan state and local IT sector to engage with global circuits of hi-tech, professional employment through strategic investments in infrastructure, skills and business linkages in the Business Process Outsourcing (BPO) industry. However, they show how latecomer disadvantage combines with political pressures in developed economies to undermine Kenya's access to high-value jobs in globalised hi-tech activities. Ideologies of seamless connections to the global economy by way of fibre optic cables were forced to confront real world hierarchies of lead firms, first movers and experience-based barriers to entry. In Setrana and Tonah's article, we encounter the individual efforts of Ghanaian return migrants to convert connections to skills and resources abroad into livelihood opportunities after their return to Ghana. Despite favourable economic conditions in Ghana – a country blessed by political stability, rapid growth and new oil discoveries – return migrants grapple with narrowing opportunities abroad and fragile labour market conditions at home. While some migrants are able to parlay global connections into successful livelihoods, they fall short of generating wider dynamics of employment generation and economic transformation within Ghana, leading to calls for state assistance to promote migrant-led processes of globalisation.

Articles by Laterza and Bolt examine how participation in global value chains and international charitable initiatives affects rural labour relations in Southern Africa. Laterza deconstructs the inclusive vision of a transnational Pentecostal social enterprise that combines donor resources with timber exports in the operation of an orphanage in Swaziland. Beneath the rhetoric of charity, arrangements rely on cheap, highly racialised labour relations based on white management and black workers disciplined through segregation, unfree labour practices and stark economic inequality. The demands of charitable financing and global timber markets reinforce rather than dissolve coercive colonial systems of labour brokerage and exploitative working conditions. Similarly, Bolt examines how the engagement of South African white farmers in global agricultural value chains perpetuate racialised relations of dependency between farmers and agricultural labourers in response to competitive global price pressures. White farmers use discourses of compliance with labour laws and corporate social responsibility aimed at an audience of state institutions and international supermarkets, while doing little to change the vulnerable conditions of black farmworkers. Instead, senior black farmworkers, tasked with connecting their subordinates to the institutional necessities within their reach, reinforce established paternalist conceptions of workforce hierarchy. In both articles, discourses of corporate and charitable governance often disguise rather than transform the social logics of dependency and racial inequality that endure below the radar of global economic values.

The wide range of global connections and African workers explored by these articles highlights the significant role played by intermediaries in structuring global connections. They offer valuable insights into the ways that that intermediaries and brokers not only connect, but reconfigure, global labour linkages and the distribution of benefits. The complex array of commercial or community-based labour brokers, social enterprises, NGOs and skilled graduates provide insights into the regulatory transformations taking place within these connections, and allows closer analysis of the use of efficiency concerns or charitable cover to mask unstable and often exploitative labour relations. A focus on intermediaries provides a more nuanced analysis of the dynamics of global inclusion by exploring the specific institutional mechanisms through which African workers are included in global circuits of capital, and the embedded regulatory arrangements that define access to the benefits of global inclusion.

4. Economic Inclusion or Adverse Incorporation?

A central question raised by this special issue is whether integration into global markets creates genuine inclusion in the economic benefits of global markets, or traps African workers in processes of adverse incorporation. The articles presented here confirm that global connections are transforming African labour relations, but not always in the interest of African workers. Collectively, they contribute to a more nuanced understanding of the dynamics of global economic inclusion, and the processes that lead to adverse incorporation. In particular, they highlight the selectivity of processes of inclusion, the limited organisational power of African workers to defend their interests within global linkages, and the tendency to focus on the quantity of employment created while obscuring questions of work quality.

Attention to the selective character of global economic inclusion highlights the reality of winners and losers among African workers. As several of the articles show, inclusion fosters simultaneous processes of differentiation and exclusion among workers, dividing Johannesburg street traders into regularised or irregular operators, black farm workers into regular or undocumented workers, and Kenyan slum dwellers into dynamic BoP entrepreneurs or unproductive hawkers and street youth (Pezzano; Bolt; and Dolan and Rajak, this issue). In the process, 'usable Africans' are identified, and 'unusable Africans' are deselected, delegitimised, even criminalised (Dolan & Roll, 2013). Far from creating channels for benefits to trickle down, such selective and partial forms of inclusion may exacerbate rather than stem the risk of ongoing poverty and political unrest (Meagher 2015).

Even among the included, many of the articles highlight the limited organisational power of African workers to translate global connections into meaningful improvements in incomes and working conditions. For many, global inclusion simply means a transition straight from the informal economy into the equally vulnerable 'precariat' (Standing, 2011). Transformative discourses of entrepreneurship and poverty alleviation disguise rather than alter conditions of low wages, unstable employment and harsh working conditions. From below, articles by Laterza and Bolt draw attention to the 'institutional, ideological and geographical barriers' that militate against real economic inclusion. From above, articles by Meagher, and Mann and Graham show how the competitive dynamics of global value chains drive risks and costs down the chain, creating 'nodes of poverty' and processes of 'social downgrading' for workers in the lower tiers (see also Barrientos et al., 2011; Goger, Hull, Barrientos, Gereffi, & Godfrey, 2014; Nadvi, 2004). Scope for realising gains is limited to the more skilled, connected and organised workers. For the rest, rather than gaining access to the advantages of global markets, global markets appear to be gaining access to African workers on terms that offer limited opportunities for improving their economic condition.

Indeed, many of these articles indicate that global economic inclusion is more strongly associated with informalisation and adverse incorporation than with improvements in incomes and working conditions. Globalising discourses of market integration tend to draw on notions of inclusion to remaster vulnerable and unstable employment as a source of economic opportunity. There is a tendency to focus attention on the regularisation and re-moralisation of informal employment, often aided by intermediaries such as social enterprises, Pentecostal religious networks and CSR initiatives that blur the lines between charity and cheap labour. In analysing the implications of globalisation for African workers, greater attention is needed to the quality as well as the quantity of work, and to the structural as well as the individual processes that contribute to the expansion of decent work opportunities. More also needs to be known about how processes of legal, corporate and charitable recognition of informal workers affect prospects for achieving decent work. Do calls for the recognition or regularisation of casualised workers, street traders and ersatz entrepreneurs in BoP initiatives precipitate a normalisation of their vulnerable status or open the way to addressing the economic realities of low and unstable incomes? Closer attention to issues of work quality are needed if the flurry of global connections is to move beyond the illusion of inclusion to deliver concrete gains to African workers.

5. Making Connections for Economic Transformation

Collectively, these articles invite further reflection on how globalisation can promote more equitable opportunities for African workers. Natural resource windfalls, booming foreign direct investment and expanding pools of skilled labour offer openings for investment in technological leapfrogging and upgrading to higher value sectors. The spread of fibre optic connectivity is transforming a growing number of African economies from 'black holes of informational capitalism' (Castells, 1997, p. 161) and promising to turn African producers into participants in a digital revolution (Graham & Mann, 2013). As Mann and Graham demonstrate in the case of Kenya, reaping the benefits of these global connections is not automatic, with firms struggling to attract work even after substantial investments have been made. Nevertheless, Kenya's experience may offer important lessons for future African entrants seeking to reap greater benefits from digital connections. Equally, the demographic slowdown in advanced economies draws attention to the rising importance of Africa as a source of labour for the global economy, suggesting policy openings for securing a better deal for African workers (Meagher, this issue). As commodity prices once again take a turn for the worse, Africa's growing workforce may become a key resource in relations with the rest of the global economy. More questions need to be asked about the linkages, alliances and policy strategies most conducive to ensuring that African workers reap their share of the gains.

African states play an important role in promoting effective avenues for the global integration of their workers. But states have responded in different ways to these incentives. At one end of the spectrum, articles by Bolt, Laterza and Pezzano in this issue highlight the complicit role of the Swazi and South African states, variously allying with international corporate interests in order to attract flows of foreign investment, or turning a blind eye to immigration infractions and labour violations in white commercial farms, except for periodic raids that only serve to intensify the vulnerability and docility of workers. However, parallel efforts by the South African state to use legal rulings to protect informal workers demonstrates the complex and often contradictory role of the state in mediating global engagement with African workers. The case of Kenya's entry into the globalised IT sector shows that African states can also take a leading role in building more advantageous global connections from below, with a view to fostering more productive and remunerative employment linkages (Mann & Graham, this issue). However, the state's efforts to forge global connections in response to local development needs rather than global labour demand can be thwarted by limited experience, as well as by the power of global market forces and incumbent global firms.

Whatever the response of African states, the articles in this collection highlight the crucial role of local institutions and collective organisations in mediating how global investors engage with workers and local entrepreneurs (Coe, Hess, Yeung, Dicken, & Henderson, 2004). Attention to the role of interests, economic pressures and power relations in shaping the quality of job opportunities reveals both the importance of and the constraints on constructive state involvement in ensuring that linkages with the global economy provide decent employment for Africa's expanding population. It remains to be seen whether the emergence of potential 'developmental states' in Botswana, Mauritius, Rwanda and Ethiopia (Kelsall, 2013; Mkandawire, 2001) and the identification of successful government-led upgrading of agro-processing sectors in Mozambique, Uganda and Ghana (Whitfield, Therkildsen, Buur, & Mette Kjaer, 2015) will open the door to the expansion and upgrading of local employment opportunities, or whether these states will be drawn into incentives for the cheapening and informalisation of labour in the quest for global competitiveness.

Ultimately, the articles in this special issue raise questions about the implications for African labour of contemporary discourses of inclusive growth (de Mello & Dutz, 2014; United Nations Development Group, 2013). In the era of the Social Development Goals, replete with promises of greater attention to equity and inclusion, there is a need to look beyond global connections to the nature of the economic transformations that they promote. As Cooper (2001, p. 203) reminds us, to understand what the global economy can do for Africa, we need to look at how production is organised rather than just focus on the existence of linkages to a wider spatial system. There is a need to look beyond the mere creation of global employment connections to consider the patterns of connections necessary to generate rising incomes, increased productivity and local economic transformation (Chang, 2002). Simply linking African labour to global demand provides little scope for the kind of strategic agricultural and industrial transformation needed to provide access to dignified livelihoods for Africa's growing population, skilled as well as unskilled, from poor as well as middle class backgrounds. Indeed, global labour linkages may weaken national organic links between agriculture and industry, and lock in incentives for free market policies of liberalisation and globalisation that encourage cheap labour strategies and trajectories of immiserising growth (Kaplinsky, 2000; UNRISD, 2010; Whitfield, 2012).

This prompts us to question whether the use of global connections to resolve Africa's employment problems stimulates the right kinds of labour demand. Evidence of 'jobless growth' and tendencies of inclusive initiatives towards casualisation and informalisation of African labour suggest otherwise. As James Heintz (2009, p. 32) argues, 'Progress in terms of poverty reduction will be far slower if informal employment expands and the returns to labour in these forms of precarious employment do not improve.' From a social as well as an economic perspective, policy initiatives to address youth unemployment by celebrating informal entrepreneurship sit uncomfortably with the aspirational climate of Africa's expanding middle class – as starkly revealed by the death of some 16 Nigerian graduates in a desperate stampede to apply for government jobs in 2014, and the ongoing saga of African migrants fleeing across the Mediterranean in search of better opportunities.

Finally, there is a need to consider the impact of global employment linkages on broader political transformations. Several articles in this special issue signal the dangers of casualisation for collective organisation. Dolan and Rajak echo Bauman's (2004, p. 90) observation that workers at the bottom of the pyramid are being encouraged to seek 'their own *individual* solutions to the *socially* produced troubles'. Other articles note the tendency of precarious conditions at the bottom of global value chains to throw traders and skilled as well as unskilled workers back into paternalistic relations and individual survival strategies. Yet Pezzano's account of informal street traders in Johannesburg speaks to the potential of collective organisation, showing that even informal organisations can sometimes circumvent processes of adverse incorporation. It also suggests that, for African workers, making the right connections for improved livelihoods may have as much to do with political alliances, state–society engagement and effective use of the law as with global economic linkages.

Acknowledgements

We are grateful to Deborah James and Ken Shadlen for helpful comments on earlier drafts of this introduction.

Disclosure statement

No potential conflict of interest was reported by the authors.

References

African Development Bank. (2013). *Millennium development goals (MDG) report: Assessing progress in Africa toward the millennium development goals.* UN/AU/ADB/UNDP.

African Economic Outlook. (2010). *Promoting Youth Employment.* AfDB/OECD/UNDP/UNECA.

African Economic Outlook. (2014). *Global Value Chains and Africa's Industrialisation.* African Development Bank, OECD Development Centre, UNDP.

Arrighi, G. (1970). Labour supplies in historical perspective: A study of the proletarianisation of the African peasantry in Rhodesia. *The Journal of Development Studies, 6*, 197–234. doi:10.1080/00220387008421322

August, O. (2013, March 2). Africa rising: A hopeful continent. *The Economist.*

Austen, R. A. (1987). *African economic history: Internal development and external dependency.* London: James Currey.

Avle, S. (2014). Articulating and Enacting Development: Skilled Returnees in Ghana's ICT Industry. *Information Technologies & International Development, 10*(4), 1.

Barrientos, S., Kothari, U., & Phillips, N. (2013). Dynamics of unfree labour in the contemporary global economy. *The Journal of Development Studies, 49*(8), 1037–1041. doi:10.1080/00220388.2013.780043

Barrientos, S., Gereffi, G., & Rossi, A. (2011). Economic and social upgrading in global production networks: A new paradigm for a changing world. *International Labour Review, 150*(3–4), 319–340. doi:10.1111/j.1564-913X.2011.00119.x

Bauman, Z. (2004). *Wasted lives. Modernity and its outcasts.* Cambridge: Polity.

Bolt, M. (2013). Producing permanence: Employment, domesticity and the flexible future on a South African border farm. *Economy and Society, 42*(2), 197–225. doi:10.1080/03085147.2012.733606

Brass, T. (1994). Some observations on unfree labour, capitalist restructuring, and deproletarianization. *International Review of Social History, 39*(02), 255–275. doi:10.1017/S0020859000112593

Brass, T. (2009). Capitalist unfree labour: A contradiction? *Critical Sociology, 35*(6), 743–765. doi:10.1177/0896920509343059

Brass, T. (2011). Unfree labour as primitive accumulation? *Capital & Class, 35*(1), 23–38. doi:10.1177/0309816810392969

Brown, C., & van der Linden, M. (2010). Shifting Boundaries between Free and Unfree Labor: Introduction. *International Labor and Working-Class History, 78*(01), 4–11. doi:10.1017/S0147547910000086

Castells, M. (1997). *The Power of Identity.* Malden, MA: Blackwell.

Chang, H.-J. (2002). *Kicking Away the Ladder: Development Strategy in Historical Perspective.* London: Anthem Press.

Coe, N. M., Hess, M., Yeung, H. W., Dicken, P., & Henderson, J. (2004). 'Globalizing' Regional Development: A Global Production Networks Perspective. *Transactions of the Institute of British Geographers, 29*, 468–484. doi:10.1111/j.0020-2754.2004.00142.x

Comaroff, J., & Comaroff, J. L. (1991). *Of Revelation and Revolution I: Christianity, Colonialism and Consciousness in South Africa.* Chicago: University of Chicago Press.

Cooper, F. (1992). Colonising time: Work rhythms and labour conflict in colonial Mombasa. In N. Dirks (Ed.), *Colonialism and Culture.* Ann Arbor: University of Michigan Press.

Cooper, F. (2001). What is the concept of globalization good for? An African historian's perspective. *African Affairs, 100*(399), 189–213. doi:10.1093/afraf/100.399.189

Corrigan, P. (1977). Feudal Relics or Capitalist Monuments? Notes on the Sociology of Unfree Labour. *Sociology, 11*, 435–463. doi:10.1177/003803857701100302

de Haan, A., & Thorat, S. (2013). *Inclusive Growth: More than Safety Nets* (SIG WORKING PAPER 2013/1). Ottawa, ON: IDRC.

de Mello, L., & Dutz, M. A. (2014). *Promoting Inclusive Growth: Challenges and Policies.* Paris: OECD/World Bank.

Dolan, C., & Roll, K. (2013). Capital's New Frontier: From 'Unusable' Economies to Bottom-of-the-Pyramid Markets in Africa. *African Studies Review, 56*(3), 123–146. doi:10.1017/asr.2013.82

Economist. (2011, January 6). A more hopeful continent: The Lion Kings? Retrieved from http://www.economist.com/node/17853324

Elyachar, J. (2012). Next Practices: Knowledge, Infrastructure, and Public Goods at the Bottom of the Pyramid. *Public Culture, 24*(1 66), 109–129. doi:10.1215/08992363-1443583

Ferguson, J. (1999). *Expectations of Modernity: Myths and meanings of urban life on the Zambian Copperbelt.* Berkeley: University of California Press.

Ferguson, J. (2013). Declarations of dependence: Labour, personhood, and welfare in southern Africa. *Journal of the Royal Anthropological Institute, 19*(2), 223–242. doi:10.1111/jrai.2013.19.issue-2

Ferguson, J. (2015). *Give a man a fish: Reflections on the new politics of distribution.* Durham, NC: Duke University Press.

Freund, B. (1988). *The African Worker.* Cambridge: CUP.

Garcia, M., & Fares, J. (Eds.). (2008). *Youth in Africa's labour market*. Washington, DC: World Bank Publications.

Goger, A., Hull, A., Barrientos, S., Gereffi, G., & Godfrey, S. (2014). *Capturing the Gains in Africa: Making the Most of Global Value Chain Participation*. Durham, NC: Duke University Centre on Globalization, Governance and Competitiveness.

Graham, M., & Mann, L. (2013). Imagining a Silicon Savannah? Technological and Conceptual Connectivity in Kenya's BPO and Software Development Sectors. *The Electronic Journal of Information Systems in Developing Countries*, *56*(2), 1–19.

Guyer, J. I. (1993). Wealth in people and self-realization in Equatorial Africa. *Man*, *28*, 243–265. doi:10.2307/2803412

Heintz, J. (2009). *Employment, Economic Development, and Poverty Reduction: Critical issues and policy challenges*, Commissioned for the UNRISD Flagship Report on Poverty. Geneva: UNRISD.

Hickey, S., & du Toit, A. (2007). *Adverse Incorporation, Social Exclusion and Chronic Poverty*. (CPRC Working Paper 81). Manchester: Chronic Poverty Research Centre, University of Manchester

Hopkins, A. G. (1973). *An economic history of West Africa*. London: Longman.

Hyden, G. (1983). *No Shortcut to Progress: African Development Management in Perspective*. Berkeley: University of California Press.

ILO. (2002). *Decent Work and the Informal Economy*. Geneva: International Labour Organization.

Jamal, V., & Weeks, J. (1993). *Africa misunderstood: Or whatever happened to the rural-urban gap?* London: Macmillan.

James, D. (2011). The return of the broker: Consensus, hierarchy, and choice in South African land reform. *Journal of the Royal Anthropological Institute*, *17*(2), 318–338. doi:10.1111/jrai.2011.17.issue-2

Kaplinsky, R. (2000). Globalisation and Unequalisation: What Can Be Learned from Value Chain Analysis? *Journal of Development Studies*, *37*(2), 117–146. doi:10.1080/713600071

Kelsall, T. (2013). *Business, Politics, and the State in Africa*. London: Zed Books.

Lemarchand, R. (1992). Uncivil states and civil societies: How illusion became reality. *The Journal of Modern African Studies*, *30*(02), 177–191. doi:10.1017/S0022278X00010673

Lerche, J. (2011). *The Unfree Labour Category and Unfree Labour Estimates: A Continuum within Low-End Labour Relations*. Manchester: Manchester Papers in Political Economy, CSPE.

London, T., & Hart, S. (Eds.). (2011). *Next generation business strategies for the base of the pyramid: New approaches for building mutual value*. Upper Saddle River, NJ: Financial Times Press.

Martino, E. (2012). Clandestine Recruitment Networks in the Bight of Biafra: Fernando Pó's Answer to the Labour Question, 1926–1945. *International Review of Social History*, *57*(S20), 39–72. doi:10.1017/S0020859012000417

Meagher, K. (1995). Crisis, Informalization and the Urban Informal Sector in Sub-Saharan Africa. *Development and Change*, *26*(2), 259–284. doi:10.1111/dech.1995.26.issue-2

Meagher, K. (2013). *Unlocking the Informal Economy: A Literature Review on Linkages Between Formal and Informal Economies in Developing Countries*. (WIEGO Working Paper No. 27). Cambidge, MA: WIEGO.

Meagher, K. (2015). Leaving no-one behind?: Informal economies, economic inclusion, and Islamic extremism in Nigeria. *Journal of International Development*, *27*(6), 835–855.

Meagher, K., & Lindell, I. (2013). Engaging with African Informal Economies: Social Inclusion or Adverse Incorporation? Introduction. *African Studies Review*, *56*(3), 57–76. doi:10.1017/asr.2013.79

Mendoza, R., & Thelen, N. (2008). Innovations to Make Markets More Inclusive for the Poor. *Development Policy Review*, *26*(4), 427–458. doi:10.1111/j.1467-7679.2008.00417.x

Mkandawire, T. (2001). Thinking About Developmental States in Africa. *Cambridge Journal of Economics*, *25*(3), 289–314. doi:10.1093/cje/25.3.289

Mkandawire, T., & Soludo, C. (1999). *Our continent, our future: African perspectives on structural adjustment*. Dakar: CODESRIA.

Nadvi, K. (2004). Globalisation and poverty: How can global value chain research inform the policy debate? *IDS Bulletin*, *35*(1), 20–30.

Phillips, N. (2011). Informality, Global Production Networks and the Dynamics of 'Adverse Incorporation'. *Global Networks*, *11*(3), 380–397. doi:10.1111/j.1471-0374.2011.00331.x

Phillips, N., & Sakamoto, L. (2012). The dynamics of adverse incorporation in global production networks: Poverty, vulnerability and 'slave labour'in Brazil. *Studies in Comparative International Development*, *47*(3), 287–315.

Rivera-Santos, M., & Rufín, C. (2010). Global village vs. small town: Understanding networks at the Base of the Pyramid. *International Business Review*, *19*(2), 126–139. doi:10.1016/j.ibusrev.2009.07.001

Rivera-Santos, M., Rufín, C., & Kolk, A. (2012). Bridging the institutional divide: Partnerships in subsistence markets. *Journal of Business Research*, *65*(12), 1721–1727. doi:10.1016/j.jbusres.2012.02.013

Rogerson, C. M. (1999). Small enterprise development in post-apartheid South Africa. In K. King & S. McGrath (Eds.), *Enterprise in Africa. Between Poverty and Growth* (pp. 83–94). London: Intermediate Technology Publications.

Roxburgh, C., Dörr, N., Leke, A., Tazi-Riffi, A., van Wamelen, A., & Lund, S. (2010). *Lions on the Move: The progress and potential of African economies*. McKinsey Global Institute.

Smith, G. (1994). Towards an Ethnography of Idiosyncratic Forms of Livelihood. *International Journal of Urban and Regional Research*, *18*(1), 71–87. doi:10.1111/ijur.1994.18.issue-1

Standing, G. (2011). *The Precariat: The New Dangerous Class*. London: Bloomsbury Academic.

Teglskov Nielsen, S. (2012) *The Jua Kali Connection - Young Professionals Straddling Nairobi's Informal Networks* (Masters thesis). Roskilde University, Copenhagen.

Theron, J. (2005). Intermediary or Employer-Labour Brokers and the Triangular Employment Relationship. *Industrial Law Journal, 26*, 618–649.

United Nations Development Group. 2013. *A million voices: The world we want.* New York: United Nations.

UNRISD. (2010). *Combatting poverty and inequality: Structural change, social policy and politics.* Geneva: Author.

Vandemoortele, J. (1991). Labour market informalization in Sub-Saharan Africa. In G. Standing & V. Tokman (Eds.), *Toward Social Adjustment: Labour Market Issues in Structural Adjustment.* Geneva: ILO.

Vanek, J., Chen, M. A., Carré, F., Heintz, J., & Hussmanns, R. (2014). *Statistics on the Informal Economy: Definitions, Regional Estimates and Challeneges* (WIEGO Working Paper No. 2). Cambridge, MA: WIEGO.

Watts, M. (1983). *Silent violence: Food, famine, and peasantry in Northern Nigeria.* Berkeley: University of California Press.

Webb, J. W., Kistruck, G. M., Ireland, R. D., & Ketchen, D. J. (2010). The entrepreneurship process in base of the pyramid markets: The case of multinational enterprise/nongovernment organization alliances. *Entrepreneurship: Theory and Practice, 34*(3), 555–581.

Whitfield, L., Therkildsen, O., Buur, L., & Mette Kjaer, A. (2015). *The Politics of African Industrial Policy: A Comparative Perspective.* Cambridge: Cambridge University Press.

Whitfield, L. (2012). Immediate versus Sustainable Poverty Reduction? Supporting Agro-Industries in Africa DIIS Policy Brief, September 2012. Retrieved from: http://www.diis.dk/files/media/publications/import/extra/pb-immediate-versus-sustainable-poverty-reduction-lindsay-whitfield_2.pdf

World Development Report. (2013). *Jobs.* Washington, DC: World Bank.

Wrigley, C. C. (1957). *Buganda: An outline economic history.* Economic History Review, 69–80. doi:10.2307/2600062

The Scramble for Africans: Demography, Globalisation and Africa's Informal Labour Markets

KATE MEAGHER
Department of International Development, London School of Economics, London

ABSTRACT *Images of an 'African Boom' have presented us with labour markets full of dynamic potential: a declining dependency ratio; low levels of unemployment; and a vibrant middle class. This buoyant view of African labour markets conceals a less encouraging reality of catastrophic youth unemployment and expanding informality. How has the continent known for the world's highest share of informal labour become a beacon of prosperity? This article will explore the reality beneath the outbreak of informal economic optimism, and consider why African labour markets are being painted in such rosy colours.*

Introduction

The resurgence of growth in African economies since the early 2000s, coupled with leaner prospects in OECD countries and rising competition from Asia, has encouraged investors and development experts to look at Africa with new eyes. Dubbed the 'hopeless continent' by the Economist (2000, p. 17) at the turn of the millennium, Africa is now seen as a cornucopia of wealth, entrepreneurial energy and consumer demand (The Economist, 2011). Investment possibilities have expanded beyond the traditional focus on natural resources to wider interests in the development of infrastructure, industry, services, and a new focus on the quality and quantity of African labour. Africa's young and growing labour force, not so long ago associated with a 'coming anarchy' of 'scarcity, crime, overpopulation, tribalism and disease' (Kaplan, 1994), is increasingly viewed in a more constructive light by development agencies as well as investors.

In particular, two aspects of African labour markets previously regarded as a sign of economic failure are now celebrated as resources for development. These are Africa's rapid population growth and her large informal economies. Sub-Saharan Africa has the highest rate of population growth in the world, at double the global average of 1.1 per cent per annum, putting heavy strains on per capita economic growth rates (Ranis & Gollin, 2013, p. 19). But warnings about overpopulation and the threat of environmental degradation have given way to talk of a 'demographic dividend' (Garcia & Fares, 2008). Similarly, Africa is home to a vast informal economy and hosts the world highest vulnerable employment rate, estimated at 77.4 per cent (ILO, 2014, p. 68). Attitudes to these realities have shifted from alarm to enthusiasm, as the informal economy is hailed as a source of entrepreneurship and job creation for Africa's expanding population (African Economic Outlook, 2012; Jütting and de Laiglesia, 2009).[1]

Reassessing African growth prospects through the lens of the 'African Boom' has highlighted new possibilities, but it also seems to be glossing over important realities. Buoyant views of African labour markets conceal more worrying realities of catastrophic youth unemployment, expanding informality and a rising tide of vulnerable and increasingly disaffected labour, creating a 'youth bulge' that seems more of a threat than an opportunity (Cincotta, 2010; DIAL, 2007; Eastwood & Lipton, 2011). How can Africa's rapidly expanding population cope with the contemporary realities of 'jobless growth'? How does the continent with the largest share of informal labour in the world become a beacon of prosperity? Whose prosperity are these optimistic analyses talking about? Current discussions about how best to unlock the dynamic potential of African labour markets have encouraged a focus on linkages with international business and global value chains (GVCs) to foster more inclusive arrangements for job creation and economic development. Questions need to be raised about whether enthusiasm for greater integration of African labour markets into global production and distribution structures heralds a welcome movement away from decades of global economic marginalisation, or represents a new turn in the 'adverse incorporation' (Hickey & du Toit, 2007) of African labour into the global economy.

This article will explore the reality beneath the increasingly optimistic assessments of African labour markets, and consider whether we are being urged to look at African labour markets through rose-coloured glasses. The analysis will begin with a consideration of how rapid population growth and expanding informal economies have been transformed from problems into resources. The next section will consider current efforts to link African informal labour markets into the global economy, with a view to addressing lack of labour demand, and raising informal incomes and productivity. This will be followed by two sections that examine more worrying trends beneath this rosy picture of informal employment as an engine of growth. The first will focus on the misreading of African demographic trends that obscures the realities of a stalled fertility transition, rising dependency, and a growing demographic liability rather than a demographic dividend. The second will zero in on informal labour market dynamics, which show that formal sector linkages with informal labour have been more closely associated with the intensification of vulnerable employment rather than with rising incomes. The main argument is that the twists in global economic integration that have redefined African informal labour markets as a resource have tended to encourage economic strategies more geared to the extraction of value than a redistribution of benefits to African economies or African workers.

Turning Problems into Resources

Africa's economic resurgence has yielded a decade of buoyant growth rates, averaging 5 per cent per annum across the continent since 2004 (International Monetary Fund, 2012). However, encouraging growth rates have been confronted with a catastrophic rise in youth unemployment. Youth unemployment rates are double adult unemployment across most of the continent, rising to 38 per cent in Nigeria and just under 52 per cent in South Africa (National Bureau of Statistics, 2011, p. 10; World Bank, 2014). This has drawn attention to the problem of 'jobless growth' plaguing Africa's fast-growing economies, and closing down opportunities for new entrants to the labour market. Part of the problem lies with the notoriously low employment-generating capacity of natural resource extraction, on which many African economies are heavily dependent. The faltering progress of economic diversification (some may say deindustrialisation), and the closing of the land frontier in many African countries has exacerbated pressures on employment. To compound the problem, most African countries face a population tsunami, which puts an estimated 8 million new entrants into the job market every year (World Development Report, 2013, p. 48).

Yet, the rapidly expanding policy literature on youth unemployment is representing Africa's young and growing labour force, not as a problem, but as a resource. A number of sources have argued that, with the right policies, African countries can turn their burgeoning youth population into an engine of growth (Garcia & Fares, 2008, p. xxvi; Ranis & Gollin, 2013). A recent report by the African Development Bank (2013, p. 1) claims that, 'Demographic trends are thus likely to provide an opportunity to reduce poverty and yield a demographic dividend that will lead to economic success as it did in the Asian emerging markets: as much as one-third of East Asia's economic "miracle" is attributed to demographic change.' Similarly, a report on African youth employment by the Ibrahim Forum (2012, p. 1) represents Africa's growing population as an asset for development: 'Africa is the only continent with a significantly growing youth population. In less than three generations, 41% of the world's youth will be African. By 2035, Africa's labour force will be larger than China's. How do we ensure that Africa benefits from this imminent demographic dividend?' Africa's expanding youth population is described as a 'precious resource', 'the most abundant asset the region has or will have in the near future' (Garcia & Fares, 2008, p. xxvi; Ibrahim Forum, 2012, p. 1). The core issue is how to turn this asset into a source of economic growth, rather than allowing it to become a source of instability.

A critical dimension of the policy mix recommended to reap this 'demographic dividend' involves supporting self-employment in the informal economy, and linking informal labour markets with formal sector firms and the global economy in order to increase demand for labour and access to resources and technology (African Economic Outlook, 2012; Garcia & Fares, 2008; Ranis & Gollin, 2013). This represents a reversal of long-standing concerns that an expanding informal economy represents a 'drag on growth'. Growing awareness of the astonishing size of informal economies across Africa since the turn of the millennium was initially greeted with alarm and embarrassment. The ILO's 2002 report on Decent Work revealed that African economies are the most informalised in the world, with 72 per cent of the non-agricultural labour force working outside the formal economy. As recently as 2009, a joint report on informal employment by the WTO and the ILO contended that expanding informal economies 'have prevented developing countries from fully benefiting from the dynamics of globalization' (Bacchetta, Ernst, & Bustamante, 2009, p. 9). The authors maintain that large informal economies reduce productivity, undermine export diversification, and weaken resilience to economic shocks, costing countries up to two percentage points in average growth rates.

Yet, new trends in the policy community are reconsidering whether the informal economy is a drag on productivity or a potential engine of growth. In a challenging new take on informality in developing countries, Jütting and de Laiglesia (2009, p. 17) note that, under some conditions, expanding informal economies can undermine growth, but 'informal employment is sometimes seen as ... an engine of growth ... informal employment growth since the early 1990s has been the main driving force of job creation in China and is seen as extremely flexible, dynamic and innovative'. The recent World Development Report (2013, p. xiii) emphasises the developmental role of all forms of employment, informal as well as formal: 'Critically, these jobs are not only found in the formal sector; depending on the country context, informal jobs can also be transformational.' Focusing more specifically on the African context, the African Economic Outlook (2012, p. 30) report, *Promoting Youth Employment*, asserts that 'The informal sector, long seen as a problem, is turning out to contain entrepreneurial talent that can foster job creation if adequately enabled by government policies.'

Reaping the Growth Potential of Africa's Informal Labour Markets

Worries about the threats posed by 'jobless growth', which have abandoned the bulk of Africa's expanding youth population to seek their livelihood in the burgeoning informal economy, have been turned around by a shift of focus from supply-side problems of excessive population growth and inadequate skills, to demand-side solutions emphasizing more creative approaches to employment generation. As the World Development Report on Jobs (2013, p. 18) points out, 'Many of these countries have large youth bulges, which can put downward pressure on employment and earnings. ... On closer inspection, the problem is often more on the demand side than the supply side.' The African Economic Outlook Report on Youth Unemployment (2012, pp. 26–27) concurs that 'Lack of demand for labour is the biggest obstacle to youth employment in African labour markets; supply factors are important too but less so.' This is substantiated by a survey of 37 African countries, where lack of labour demand is cited as the most important barrier to youth employment, far outweighing skills problems, information or regulatory obstacles. A growing literature on youth unemployment in Africa now argues that what is needed is greater integration of Africa's expanding informal labour markets into local and global value chains in order to increase demand and income opportunities for the vast stores of under-employed labour building up in African economies (Ranis & Gollin, 2013, pp. 99–100;

WDR, 2013, p. 76). Far from becoming functionally irrelevant to the global economy as James Ferguson's (2015) suggests, African workers are increasingly viewed as a potential solution to the need for a plentiful supply of cheap labour in the ageing societies of OECD and East Asian countries (Eberstadt, 2010).

A closer look at factors driving the explosive growth in China and India tend to reinforce the notion that linking informal labour markets into formal and international labour demand offers a mechanism for addressing unemployment while increasing competitiveness. Jütting et al. (2008) celebrate the ability of China to harness the flexibility and low cost of informal labour to improve the competitiveness of Chinese exports, turning informal economies from a drag on growth into an engine of growth. They note that:

> informal labour markets in China are subject to competitive forces, more so than the formal labour markets ... In China, the development of informal employment is a somewhat recent phenomenon related to the surge in the demand for labour in the booming parts of the country. It is thereby also quite closely linked to migration and the informal sector is quite integrated into the economy acting as a huge labour reservoir. (Jütting et al., 2008, p. 32)

Similarly, Siggel (2010) and Marjit and Maiti (2006) contend that linkages between formal firms and informal labour markets in India, particularly in manufacturing and services, can increase productivity and incomes in both the formal and informal sectors, and improve global competitiveness. While expanding Chinese and Indian informal economies continue to generate alarm in some quarters (Breman, 1996; Cook, 2008; Harriss-White & Gooptu, 2001), others have come to regard them as innovative models of how to harness informal economies for development (Jütting, Parlevliet, & Xenogiani 2008; Siggel, 2010).

This more favourable attitude to informal economies has been accompanied by growing interest in how to create effective linkages between formal sector firms and informal labour markets. This is particularly evident in the literature on 'inclusive markets' or 'bottom of the pyramid' approaches, which start from the premise that large informal economies constitute both valuable untapped consumer markets, and useful sources of low-cost labour and organisational infrastructure. Commentators on inclusive markets highlight the importance of building up a 'new business infrastructure' of social networks, NGOs, social enterprises and labour brokers to connect formal businesses to the consumer and labour resources of the informal economy in a cost effective manner (London & Hart, 2011; UNDP, 2008; Webb, Kistruck, Ireland, & Ketchen, 2010). The UNDP (2008, p. 21) report, 'Creating Value for All', represents informal economic systems as an important source of value creation in low income markets: 'informal rules can make inclusive business models viable ... by supplying an infrastructure of savings, credit or institutional mechanisms. Business can count on these communal processes to fill gaps in the markets of the poor'.

Yet, gaining access to the networks and institutions of informal actors is constrained by problems of poor infrastructure, extreme social fragmentation, and lack of formal regulations – referred to by Webb et al. (2010) as 'formal institutional voids'. Within this context, formal sector and international firms require the assistance of intermediary organisations to bridge the institutional distance between the formal and the informal economies. As Webb et al. (2010, p. 567) note:

> Through alliances with NGOs, MNEs can access the resources needed to overcome their own weaknesses and reduce the risks resulting from formal institutional voids. ...NGOs understand both the institutions within which the MNEs developed and the institutions of the local context. While perhaps not necessarily internalizing either context's institutions fully, NGOs can appeal to both sides' needs, as well as serve as an 'honest broker' to provide legitimacy and trust to both.

In addition to NGOs, a range of other types of intermediary organisations facilitate linkages between formal firms and the informal economy, including microfranchising arrangements, labour brokers and social enterprises (Christiansen, Parsons, & Fairbourne, 2006; Henriques & Herr, 2008; London & Hart,

2011). Microfranchising involves the linkage of multinational firms into distributive networks of informal operators, as evidenced by the rise of Coca-cola kiosks, mobile phone card distributors and ice-cream cycles across the cities of the developing world (Dolan & Roll, 2013). This is seen to provide jobs through nominal self-employment for less entrepreneurial informal operators, while giving them access to credit, ready-made business models, brand recognition and vicarious legal standing through association with the formal sector parent firm. However, studies of microfranchising emphasise the need for intermediaries, such as NGOs or local government, to manage links between parent firms and informal distributors (Henriques & Herr, 2008). Similarly, social enterprises are also coming into play as important intermediaries in microretailing or the outsourcing of simple IT tasks to informal workers in slums and other difficult to serve areas of Africa (Kistruck, Beamish, Qureshi, & Sutter, 2013; Sheth, 2013; Van Rensburg, Veldsman, & Jenkins, 2008). Through the activities of social enterprises, unemployed women and youth in rural as well as urban areas are linked to the labour needs of multinational corporations such as Unilever, Amazon and Google without the complexities and cost of formal employment relationships.

Labour brokers offer another model for linking formal sector labour demand to informal sector labour supply (Barrientos, 2011; Theron, 2005). Also known as labour contractors or temporary employment agencies, these are private sector firms that match employment demand and supply, often operating across the formal–informal divide in developing countries. The WDR on Jobs (2013, p. 48) notes 'a sharp rise' in the number of temporary employment services and labour brokers in some parts of Africa, and points out that they now facilitate outsourcing of service as well as manufacturing work, and of unskilled as well as skilled work, linking informal workers into the global economy:

> Transnational companies have built integrated value chains and can tap into national skill pools around the world... Technology itself is changing the way workers and firms connect, through their access to much larger, even global marketplaces for employment. Some of these marketplaces operate through the Internet; others use mobile phone technology. These changes are affecting workers in developing countries and not just those in high-skilled occupations. (World Development Report, 2013, p. 55)

In South Africa, labour brokers have tripled in number between 1995 and 2002, and provide 6.8 per cent of total employment in the country (Kotze, 2011). They are also expanding in Namibia, and beginning to gain a foothold in other parts of Southern and Eastern Africa, though their growth has been accompanied by growing concerns about their negative impact on labour and social welfare (Theron, 2005).

These various hybrid formations for linking markets across the formal–informal divide allow international firms to tap into African informal economies to access labour and consumer markets, and to unlock the resources of African informal economies for growth. This has fundamentally altered perspectives on the expansion of informal labour in Africa. Instead of regarding rapid population growth, weak employment capacity and expanding informal economies as a threat to economic development and social stability, they are now associated with a demographic dividend and new approaches to productive labour absorption. These developments raise two fundamental questions: Does linking African informal economies into the global economy turn population growth into a demographic dividend? And if so, who is likely to reap it?

Demographic Misunderstandings

Understanding Africa's potential to reap a demographic dividend from current trajectories in population growth requires a closer look at basic demographic realities on the continent. Garcia and Fares (2008) observe that 'By 2010 youth will account for 28 per cent of the population, making Sub-Saharan Africa the "youngest" region in the world. ... With good policies and institutions in place, the potential to reap a dividend from a larger, younger work force with fewer dependents is great.' Yet, references across the literature to enthusiastic expectations of an African demographic dividend misrepresent the demographic realities across much of sub-Saharan Africa. In particular, they gloss over the evidence that many African countries are suffering from a stalled fertility transition, which fundamentally alters the prospects of a demographic dividend, and has very different implications for growth.

To clarify, a demographic transition refers to a shift from high birth and death rates associated with poor countries, to low birth and death rates associated with higher levels of development. The 'youth bulge' created in stage three of the standard demographic transition model yields a large working-age population with a reduced level of young and elderly dependents. The resulting swell in productivity and savings arising from this situation is known as the demographic dividend, and provides a potentially valuable boost to productive development (Caldwell, 1986; Dreze & Sen, 2002). However, this can only occur with a significant decline in fertility rates and productive employment to absorb the working age population. Unless there is a decline in fertility to narrow the base of the population profile, there can be no 'youth bulge'; there is only a youth stratum atop an even larger population of children, yielding the triangular population profile typical of low-income countries.

In the case of sub-Saharan Africa, rosy assessments of Africa's demographic future rely on UN population projections while ignoring important changes in Africa's current demographic realities. A number of studies have noted that recent UN projections have over-estimated trends in African fertility decline owing to a failure to recognise that Africa's demographic transition has 'stalled' since the 1990s (Bongaarts, 2008; Bongaarts & Casterline, 2012; Eastwood & Lipton, 2011; Shapiro & Gebreselassie, 2008). UN population projections base their predictions on a country's past total fertility rate fitted into standardised global trajectories of fertility decline. This tends to gloss over recent deviations in the path of fertility decline owing to country- or region-specific factors. As Eastwood and Lipton (2011, p. 14) explain: 'If these [determinants of future fertility rates] are worse, or slower-improving, than the global norm, the UN model will project implausibly rapid accelerations of that country's fertility decline.' In the case of many African countries, the HIV/AIDS pandemic coupled with the high social cost of market reforms during the 1980s and 1990s have led to significant reversals in key drivers of the fertility transition, raising concerns about the accuracy of existing population projections. The problem is not the soundness of existing UN population data – indeed, UN population data have been used to demonstrate that the demographic transition in many Africa countries has stalled. The fault lies in the over-reliance of policy-makers on population projections despite anomalies in the actual data, and uncritical aggregation of demographic trends across Africa.

The possibility that Africa's demographic transition was not proceeding as expected was raised in 2008 in a seminal paper by John Bongaarts (2008). Using panel data from demographic and health surveys (DHS), Bongaarts points out that two-thirds of sub-Saharan African countries on which there are data (15 out of 22) have experienced no significant decline in fertility since the 1990s. He attributes this to reversals in socio-economic development during the 1990s, and to the low priority accorded to family planning programmes in recent years. Eastwood and Lipton (2011, p. 17) argue that falling infant and child mortality rates are key drivers of declining fertility rates, and note that these have stalled or even reversed in a number of African countries, particularly in West and Central Africa. In fact, they point out that of 17 African countries with two demographic and health surveys between 1990 and 2000, infant mortality rates actually rose in nine of them.

Optimistic interpretations of Africa's demographic transition are exacerbated by the tendency to aggregate population growth rates across sub-Saharan Africa. In fact, trajectories of fertility decline vary considerably across African subregions. The total fertility rate (TFR) in Southern Africa, estimated at 2.6 children per woman in 2005–2010, is about half the level in East, Central and West Africa, estimated at 4.7, 5.2 and 5.2 children per woman, respectively (African Development Bank, 2013, p. 7; Bongaarts & Casterline, 2012, p. 162; Marsden, 2013). Moreover, Marsden (2013) points out that the West and Central African countries, where political and economic instability are more pronounced, have a higher share of stalled transitions. Averaging fertility rates across the whole of

Africa give an impression of moderate decline, glossing over evidence of serious deviations from this path in many African countries.

Analysts contend that the stalling of the demographic transition is a result of declining GDP during the 1990s, along with reversals in life expectancy, infant and child mortality, and education (Cincotta, 2010; Marsden, 2013; Shapiro & Gebreselassie, 2008). These factors are central to reducing the demand for children within family units, which, in conjunction with access to family planning, is crucial to reducing fertility rates (Bongaarts & Casterline, 2012; Caldwell, 1986). Shapiro and Gebreselassie (2008) warn that unless long-term improvements in education and infant and child mortality occur throughout the African region, the stalling of the fertility transition is likely to spread. The upshot is that most of Africa is 'worse placed than was Asia to provide the preconditions for reduced TFR' (total fertility rate), and hence to move through the demographic transition as predicted (Eastwood & Lipton, 2011, p. 17). Efforts by a number of sources to dispute the evidence were unable to reject the possibility of a stalled fertility transition in African countries (Schoumaker, 2009; Sneeringer, 2009).

The implication of a stalled demographic transition in Africa is that there may be no demographic dividend to be reaped. The issue is not whether African countries have implemented appropriate policies to realise the economic gains of a youth bulge (Birdsall & Sinding, 2001, pp. 10–11), but whether demographic change is on course to create a youth bulge in the first place. African countries have a median age less than or equal to 25, which creates a pyramidal population structure rather than a youth bulge, entailing a high dependency ratio along with a rapidly growing youth workforce (Cincotta, 2010; Mo Ibrahim Foundation 2012). The Mo Ibrahim Foundation's (2012, p. 11) African Youth report notes that Africa's dependency ratio is currently the highest in the world, and a stalled transition means this situation will continue for the foreseeable future.

Moreover, the combination of HIV/AIDS and high youth unemployment have put further upward pressures on the dependency ratio in ways that are difficult to predict from the standard data (Eastwood & Lipton, 2011, p. 16). On the one hand, HIV/AIDS has 'hollowed out' the core working age population in a number of Southern, Central and East African countries. Indeed, Eastwood and Lipton (2011, p.16) point out that between 2000 and 2005, despite declines in the total fertility rate, the dependency ratio actually rose in Malawi from 96 to 99, and in Mozambique from 88 to 90. On the other hand, the realities of high youth unemployment and under-employment have delayed social autonomy for young adults, trapping many members of the working-age population in an ongoing state of dependency. Studies from West and Southern Africa found a sharp decline in the percentage of youth leaving the parental household by the age of 25, while evidence from Ethiopia and Rwanda found a similar pattern in rural areas (DIAL, 2007, p. 16). The result is that a significant proportion of the youthful labour force in many African countries is adding to the high dependency burden rather than alleviating it.

The upshot is a demographic profile across much of Africa that looks more like a demographic liability than a demographic dividend. Indeed, a number of commentators have expressed concerns about the anti-developmental potential of Africa's demographic profile. Far from creating a potential engine of growth, Bongaarts (2008) suggests that the demographic profile of African countries 'will likely have adverse effects on the region's prospects for social and economic development'. Others have noted that Africa's pyramidal population structure, low median age and high dependency ratio is not associated with a demographic dividend as in East Asia, but with poverty and vulnerability to conflict (Cincotta, 2010; Dyson, 2013). Drawing on more realistic population projections, Richard Cincotta warns that:

> by 2030, only Botswana, South Africa, Cape Verde, and Djibouti are expected to have matured significantly beyond this conflict-vulnerable stage of the age-structural transition, leaving sub-Saharan Africa as the remaining epicenter of the 'demographic arc of instability. (Cincotta, 2010)

This leaves us with the question of why so much of the current policy literature is speaking of an impending demographic dividend, when there is considerable evidence that most African countries are not heading in this direction, at least not in the medium term. A lively article called 'The Demographic Future' published in *Foreign Affairs* by Nicholas Eberstadt (2010) casts some light on the situation. Focusing on global demographic trends, Eberstadt raises concerns about shifts in the global distribution of manpower as Western and East Asian societies grapple with rapidly ageing populations and below-replacement birth rates. While the OECD countries and a number of the BRICs are facing mounting pension and health claims on a shrinking pool of workers, sub-Saharan Africa is set to reap the lion's share of growth in the working-age population over the next 20 years. Eberstadt (2010, p. 58) warns that:

> Taken as a whole, these manpower trends point to mounting demographic pressures – and quite possibly, a slowdown in the rate of long-term economic growth. All other factors being equal, these trends also suggest a slowdown in consumer spending, which could perhaps lead to a slowdown in business profits, as well.

... unless countries facing shrinking workforces could tap into the labour and consumer markets of countries with expanding workforces. Under such circumstances, strategies for making more efficient use of global manpower could turn Africa's expanding youth population into a 'demographic dividend'. The question is, for whom? While the evidence does not support claims that African countries are generating a demographic dividend in the classic sense of a youth bulge with falling dependency ratios, what the continent does appear to be generating is a massive army of workers capable of swelling an otherwise shrinking global labour pool. As developed countries manoeuvre to gain access to this valuable resource, the colonial scramble for African territory that took place in the nineteenth century seems set to repeat itself in the twenty-first century as a transnational scramble for African labour. As with earlier scrambles for African resources, it is not clear that Africans will be the beneficiaries.

Informal Labour Markets and Global Linkages

Current policy speculation about the benefits to be reaped by linking Africa's expanding informal economies into global labour demand tends to sidestep a large and growing body of evidence about the worrying effects of formal–informal labour linkages. Nearly a decade of research on the link between globalisation, liberalisation and labour informalisation suggests that global linkages with informal labour markets by way of GVCs have been less an engine of rising employment and incomes than an engine of vulnerable employment (Barrientos, 2000; Carr & Chen, 2008; Lund & Nicholson, 2003; Nadvi, 2004). Similar concerns have been raised about the exploitative effects of new models that deploy NGOs or labour brokers to harness the informal economy for development (Barrientos, 2008; Cross & Street, 2009; Dolan, Johnstone-Louis, & Scott, 2012; Theron, 2005). This existing empirical research offers the possibility of moving beyond enthusiastic speculations about the potential of global formal–informal linkages for addressing African youth unemployment to a consideration of the actual distributional and developmental effects of such linkages.

Research on the dynamics of global value chains between Africa and OECD countries has raised concerns that global linkages tend to expand rather than reduce levels of informality, and lead to processes of 'adverse incorporation' of labour. A number of studies have pointed out that the dynamics of competition in GVCs tends to exacerbate poverty and vulnerability at the bottom of the chain, owing to competitive pressures to shift risks and costs down the chain. Nadvi (2004) and Barrientos (2008) trace the processes through which GVCs create 'poverty nodes' through casualisation, contract labour, and the concentration of low-paid, unprotected work at the bottom of the chain where vulnerable workers, dominated by women, children and migrants, are concentrated. As Nadvi (2004, p. 28) explains:

> ...workers within GVCs, at all points, are increasingly vulnerable to changing employment contracts and the increasing casualisation of work. These developments emerge from the competitive logic of the chain, where suppliers are not only more tightly integrated to their buyers, but also must enhance efficiency, lower costs, raise quality and take on more functions.

Using recent data from Africa and Asia, Nadvi shows that, while integration into GVCs provides more employment, it tends to intensify rather than reduce vulnerable employment. Integration into global horticultural value chains in Kenya created nearly 100,000 new agricultural jobs, but many of them were vulnerable jobs, lacking in job security or basic social protection. Research by Barrientos, Tallontire and Dolan (2003, p. 1514) on horticultural value chains in Zambia, South Africa and Kenya found that women account for 50–75 per cent of total employment, but are concentrated in vulnerable employment relations involving seasonal, casual, risky and insecure work. These concerns are corroborated by the ILO's (2013a, p. 93) observation of a growing gender gap in vulnerable employment in sub-Saharan Africa, which has increased by 14 points between 1991 and 2012, putting women's vulnerable employment at 84.9 per cent, relative to 70.6 per cent for men.

Concerns have also emerged about the distributional effects of labour linkages across the formal–informal divide, even where they have been associated with developmental success stories as in India and China. PCC Huang (2011) uses detailed quantitative and institutional analysis to argue that China's use of 'planned informalisation' is both exploitative and unsustainable. He shows that linking informal labour into global demand creates jobs for the poor, but on terms that shift resources away from labour, whose informal status leaves them ineligible for benefits or decent wages: 'with cheap wages and reliance on the informal economy, the profits from such production devolve mainly to outside investors, not to the Chinese workers or the Chinese economy'. The result has been an expansion rather than a contraction of vulnerable labour, and a growing burden of negative social and environmental externalities that are posing an increasing threat to Chinese growth and stability (Huang, 2011, p. 29).

Similarly, in India, numerous scholars have focused attention on the regressive social and distributional effects of incorporating unorganised labour into formal production systems through a range of subcontracting, putting out, casualisation and labour brokering arrangements (Breman, 1996; Harriss-White & Gooptu, 2001; Marjit & Maiti, 2006; Sinha & Adam, 2006). Nicola Phillips (2011) and Harriss-White and Gooptu (2001) highlight the use of informal institutions of caste, gender and migrant labour systems to create pools of tied labour incorporated into GVCs in garment and other industries. Instead of fostering more solidary labour relations, linkages based on kinship and community are often harnessed by formal sector and global businesses to tie labour into increasingly exploitative and socially binding 'contracts' devoid of legal standing.

Overall, recent research indicates that, rather than helping informal workers onto a global ladder of opportunity, participation of informal labour in GVCs is often associated with 'immiserising growth' and 'social downgrading', especially in sub-Saharan Africa (Barrientos, Gereffi, & Rossi, 2011; Goger, Hull, Barrientos, Gereffi, & Godfrey, 2014; Rossi, 2011). In a study of the horticulture, garment and tourism sectors across eight African countries, Goger et al. (2014, pp. 1–2) contend that:

> this relationship between insertion into GVCs and development is not automatic and the outcomes can be very uneven. In many cases, economic growth has instead been achieved through a low-road development strategy, in which growth on the business side is associated with the erosion of social protections, rights, and wages for workers and declining market access and bargaining power for small businesses.... in the African context, GVC participation in itself is not enough to ensure that small producers and vulnerable workers will be better off.

In addition to intensifying the vulnerability of labour, there is also mounting evidence that linking formal and global firms to sources of informal labour actually expands rather than reduces the share of labour working informally. In the Indian context, Siggel (2010) shows how labour market linkages across the formal–informal divide have contributed to a reallocation of labour from the formal to the informal economy in the textile as well as a range of service industries, where they continue to serve the labour needs of formal sector and global firms by way of a range of subcontracting and outsourcing arrangements. He hints at the dark underbelly of the phenomenon of 'jobless growth' in India, where formal sector firms not only fail to create sufficient formal jobs, but are actively closing down formal sector jobs in order to hire labour on cheaper terms in the informal economy: 'though regular employment in the formal sector shrank, the substitution of casual workers for regular ones through outsourcing may have enlarged the informal sector, but may also have led to a decline in informal workers' real wages' (Siggel, 2010, p. 101; see also; Sinha & Adams, 2006).

A similar process has been documented in a DIAL study of informal labour markets in Kenya (Bocquier, 2005). Using a range of census and household survey data, the author notes that 'most of the employees of the so-called informal sector are actually informally contracted by formal large, medium or small-scale enterprises ... formal enterprises still employ a great majority of the workforce in Nairobi, but more and more on an informal basis' (Bocquier, 2005, p. 17). By 1999, informal workers constituted 28 per cent of wage employees in Nairobi, and 88 per cent of informal employees were actually employed by formal sector firms. He argues that policies directed at encouraging the informal sector have not encouraged the growth of informal enterprises, but have led more formal enterprises to use informal contracts, leading to the 'informalisation' of formal sector employment. Already in the early 1990s, Mazumdar and Mazaheri (2002) note that nearly one-third of the Kenyan manufacturing sector was made up of informal employees, compared to 25 per cent in Zimbabwe, and 10–15 per cent in Zambia, Tanzania and a few West African countries. This process is corroborated by current trends in the expansion of the Kenyan informal economy, which appears to be driven largely by an expansion of informal wage employment rather than informal small-scale enterprise (Heintz & Valodia, 2008; ILO, 2012).

Labour contractors, celebrated by the current development establishment for their potential to facilitate the matching of informal labour supply with global labour demand, have also been associated with the expansion rather than the alleviation of vulnerable informal employment. While labour contractors have played an important role in job creation in South Africa, particularly in the mining and service sectors, they have been widely associated with the creation of more unstable, low-paid and unprotected work through the circumvention of labour legislation (Barrientos, 2011; Theron, 2005). Barrientos and others have highlighted the role of such third-party labour contractors in evading not only state labour regulation, but corporate codes and standards, intensifying rather than alleviating the vulnerability of labour (Barrientos, 2008). Even the 2013 World Development Report concedes that labour contractors, referred to as 'the temporary staffing industry', are associated with increasingly unstable and unprotected work.

> A worker employed in temporary staffing services is less likely to contribute to pension funds or health insurance and is generally seen as more vulnerable. ...Workers in these jobs typically face lower earnings ... They also face a lack of benefits, coverage by labour laws and job security. (World Development Report, 2013, p. 57)

In both South Africa and Namibia, moves have been made to ban these agencies, and there are widespread internal pressures for greater regulation of this sector owing to its negative effects on workers' earnings and access to benefits (All Africa, 2013; van Eck, 2010).

New models for building links between the formal and informal economies through the intermediation of NGOs, social enterprises and other institutional intermediaries have also come under scrutiny. Julia Elyachar (Elyachar, 2005, 2012) raises questions about the increasing deployment of NGOs and other intermediary organisations to help formal sector businesses 'leverage' the institutional resources of the informal economy. Under the guise of being 'honest brokers', NGOs contribute to capturing informal arrangements and institutional resources for the profits of formal sector firms, thereby shifting resources away from the needs of informal operators:

> With community networks conceptualised as social capital, NGOs become a vantage point from which outsiders could gain access to the value that those social networks produce. NGOs can potentially tap the vaunted trust and mutual respect of social networks for capitalist firms. (Elyachar, 2005, p. 188)

Ethnographies of the microinsurance and microcredit systems highlight the aggressive appropriation of social networks and informal institutions to access informal labour and consumer markets, combined with the use of formal contracts, bureaucracies and rules of conduct to limit claims from informal actors on formal sector resources (Bähre, 2012; Hietelahti & Nygren, 2011). The new institutional 'ecosystems' emerging to facilitate formal sector linkages with the informal economy have been described as new mechanisms of 'accumulation by dispossession' (Cross & Street, 2009; Dolan et al., 2012; Elyachar, 2005). Instead of facilitating improved access to resources and opportunities for poor workers, formal–informal linkages are used to hijack the social capital of informal workers in the service of greater formal sector profits.

Overall, the evidence suggests that linking African informal labour markets into the formal and global economies leads to an increase rather than a decrease in the vulnerability of labour, and an expansion rather than a reduction in the size of the informal economy. Far from directing resources into the informal economy to upgrade firms and improve wages and working conditions, labour linkages across the formal–informal divide tend to extract value through the expanding informalisation and exploitation of labour by way of subcontracting, outsourcing, casualisation and brokering arrangements. Expanding demand for labour through sustained participation in GVCs does not appear to alter this dynamic. Research from a range of African countries has shown that economic gains within GVCs tend to benefit formal workers while informal workers continue to suffer from deteriorating working conditions (Barrientos et al., 2011; Goger et al., 2014). As Goger et al. (2014, p. 19) observe in the African apparel sector, 'Even in the best instances of economic upgrading, the terms of employment for informal workers are highly precarious, usually leading to social downgrading.'

In addition to weak regulatory protection, informal labour arrangements tend to weaken coherent labour organisation needed to make effective claims, exacerbating the vulnerability and invisibility of informal workers (Gallin, 2001; Lund & Nicholson, 2003). Under such conditions, the wealthy but ageing populations of the world's wealthier economies seem well placed to reap a dividend from Africa's expanding unemployed and vulnerable labour force, but there is little sign of any imminent demographic dividend for African populations. Global links need to focus on larger firms and formal labour if African workers are to become winners rather than losers. As Gereffi and Luo (2014, p. 19) explain: 'Firms benefit most from participation in GVCs if they are relatively large, technologically advanced, professionally managed, and have diversified export markets. . . . Workers benefit most from GVC participation if their working conditions are relatively formalised.'

Conclusions: Reaping the Whirlwind

A careful look at the evidence suggests that the bulk of African countries, particularly in Central and West Africa, are not even close to generating a demographic dividend. Indeed, the realities of socio-economic and health reversals during the 1980s and 1990s have stalled the demographic transition in many African countries, creating a situation of rapid population growth, catastrophic unemployment, and high dependency ratios despite almost a decade of vigorous economic growth (DIAL, 2007; Ibrahim Forum, 2012, p. 11; Ranis & Gollin, 2013). These pressures have been compounded by the realities of jobless growth in the formal economy, channelling the bulk of Africa's labour force into an expanding informal economy where they face low wages and unstable, unprotected employment.

Under these circumstances, efforts to recast Africa's labour force and expanding informal economy as resources for development seem counter-intuitive. On closer inspection, however, there are obvious benefits to First World investors and policy-makers, even if Africa's expanding workforce stands to gain rather less. Africa's large informal labour markets have become increasingly attractive to international business as a source of cheap labour and new consumer markets in the face of looming labour deficits in the developed world. While tapping African informal labour markets may look like a win–win strategy from the boardrooms of Western businesses and policy think tanks, the prospects of this approach look considerably more problematic from the teeming cities and deprived rural areas south of the Sahara. As the ILO (2013a, p. 93–94) has noted in a recent Global Employment Report, the core problem in Africa is not finding work, but the productivity and conditions of work, and the benefits that people derive from their work. 'Overall, in Sub-Saharan Africa, the youth unemployment problem is more of quality (underemployment, vulnerability and working poverty) than quantity.' The same ILO Report (2013a, p. 104) points out that 'Just focusing on job quantity is associated with higher rates of vulnerable employment in the short run ... results suggest that these increased opportunities often do not come along with wages or decent income.'

Simply linking these vulnerable informal labour markets into GVCs tends to perpetuate rather than to address these problems. A development strategy that expands global demand for African workers without improving the wages and conditions beyond what is already available in the informal economy just replaces jobless growth with 'immiserising growth' (Kaplinsky, 2000). Glossing over these realities may serve the short-term interests of attracting international investors, but they will do little to carry out the kind of economic change necessary to expand access to decent livelihoods for Africa's burgeoning labour force.

In a recent study of violence and youth unemployment, Christopher Cramer (2010) highlights the darker consequences of emphasing the issue of job quantity over job quality. He argues that youth violence is linked as much to demeaning and exploitative employment as to unemployment, and that insecure or disaffected workers are particularly vulnerable to political mobilisation. This suggests that policy approaches that focus on plundering Africa's labour resources may well create more problems than solutions. Unless linkages with the global economy offer Africa's unemployed and informally employed youth something more than an ongoing stream of low-income unstable work, African informal labour is likely to become more of a threat than a resource. Given the continent's sensitive history as a supplier of unfree labour, turning Africa into a vast informal labour reserve for the global economy risks fanning the flames of discontent already erupting in the form of the Arab Spring, Islamic extremism in Somalia, Mali, Nigeria and Kenya, and mass youth uprisings in Burkina Faso. These insurgencies of unemployed and informalized African youth are giving a whole new meaning to the term 'Africa Rising'.

Acknowledgements

I would like to thank Tim Dyson and Thandika Mkandawire and two anonymous reviewers for helpful comments on this paper. Any failings are of course my own.

Disclosure statement

No potential conflict of interest was reported by the author.

Note

1. While recent estimates by the ILO (2013b) and Vanek, Chen, Carré, Heintz, and Hussmanns (2014) put the size of sub-Saharan African informal economy in second place behind South Asia, these estimates reveal an over-representation of

Southern African countries where informal economies are small, and an under-representation of West African countries, which are both more populous and have much larger informal economies (see Mkandawire, 2010).

References

African Development Bank. (2013). *Millennium Development Goals (MDG) report: Assessing progress in Africa toward the Millennium Development Goals*. UN/AU/ADB/UNDP.

African Economic Outlook. (2012). *Promoting Youth Employment:*. AfDB, OECD, UNDP, UNECA.

All Africa. (2013). *Namibia: Labour hire law survives challenge*. Retrieved from http://allafrica.com/stories/201306280755.html

Bacchetta, M., Ernst, E., & Bustamante, J. P. (2009). *Globalisation and informal jobs in developing countries*. Geneva: ILO/WTO.

Bähre, E. (2012). The Janus Face of Insurance in South Africa: From Costs to Risk, from Networks to Bureaucracies. *Africa, 82* (1), 150–167.

Barrientos, S. (2000). Globalization and Ethical Trade: Assessing the Implications for Development. *Journal of International Development, 12*, 559–570. doi:10.1002/(ISSN)1099-1328

Barrientos, S. (2008). Contract Labour: The 'Achilles Heel' of Corporate Codes in Commercial Value Chains. *Development and Change, 39*(6), 977–990. doi:10.1111/j.1467-7660.2008.00524.x

Barrientos, S. (2011). 'Labour chains': Analysing the role of labour contractors in global production networks. *BWPI Working Paper No. 153*. Manchester: Brooks World Poverty Institute.

Barrientos, S., Dolan, C., & Tallontire, A. (2003). A Gendered Value Chain Approach to Codes of Conduct in African Horticulture. *World Development, 31*(9), 1511–1526. doi:10.1016/S0305-750X(03)00110-4

Barrientos, S., Gereffi, G., & Rossi, A. (2011). Economic and social upgrading in global production networks: A new paradigm for a changing world. *International Labour Review, 150*(3–4), 319–340. doi:10.1111/j.1564-913X.2011.00119.x

Birdsall, N., & Sinding, S. W. (2001). How and why population matters: New findings new issues. In N. Birdsall, A. C. Kelly & S. W. Sinding (Eds.), *Population matters: Demographic change, economic growth, and poverty in the developing world*. Oxford: Oxford University Press.

Bocquier, P. (2005). Informal Sector versus Informal Contracts in Nairobi, Kenya. *DIAL Working Paper 10*.

Bongaarts, J. (2008). Fertility Transitions in Developing Countries: Progress or Stagnation?. *Studies in Family Planning, 39*(2), 105–110.

Bongaarts, J., & Casterline, J. (2012). Fertility Transition: Is sub-Saharan Africa Different? *Population and Development Review, 38*(Supplement), 153–168.

Breman, J. (1996). *Footloose Labour: Working in India's Informal Economy*. Cambridge: Cambridge University Press.

Caldwell, J. (1986). Routes to low mortality in poor countries. *Population and Development Review, 12*(2), 171–220.

Carr, M., & Chen, M. (2008). Globalization, social exclusion and gender. *International Labour Review, 143*(1–2), 129–160.

Christiansen, L. J., Parsons, H., & Fairbourne, J. (2006). Building Entrepreneurship in Subsistence Markets: Microfranchising as an Employment Incubator. *Journal of Business Research, 63*(6), 595–601.

Cincotta, R. (2010). *The Future of Sub-Saharan Africa's Tentative Fertility Decline*. New Security Beat: Retrieved from http://www.newsecuritybeat.org/2010/08/the-future-of-sub-saharan-africas-tentative-fertility-decline/.

Cook, S. (2008). The Challenge of Informality: Perspectives on China's Changing Labour Market. *IDS Bulletin, 39*, 48–56. doi:10.1111/j.1759-5436.2008.tb00444.x

Cramer, C. (2010, November). *Unemployment and participation in violence*. World Development Report 2011 Background Paper. Washington, DC: World Bank.

Cross, J., & Street, A. (2009). Anthropology at the Bottom of the Pyramid. *Anthropology Today, 25*(4), 4–9. doi:10.1111/anth.2009.25.issue-4

DIAL. (2007, February). *Youth and labour markets in Africa*. A critical review of literature, Working Paper 49, Département de la Recherche, Agence française de développement.

Dolan, C., Johnstone-Louis, M., & Scott, L. (2012). Shampoo, saris and SIM cards: Seeking entrepreneurial futures at the bottom of the pyramid. *Gender & Development, 20*(1), 33–47. doi:10.1080/13552074.2012.663619

Dolan, C., & Roll, K. (2013). Capital's New Frontier: From 'Unusable' Economies to Bottom-of-the-Pyramid Markets in Africa. *African Studies Review, 56*(3), 123–146. doi:10.1017/asr.2013.82

Dreze, J., & Sen, A. (2002). *India: Development and Participation*. Oxford: Oxford University Press.

Dyson, T. (2013). On democratic and demographic transition. *Population and Development Review, 31*(1), 83–102. doi:10.1111/j.1728-4457.2013.00553.x

Eastwood, R., & Lipton, M. (2011). Demographic transition in sub-Saharan Africa: How big will the economic dividend be? *Population Studies: A Journal of Demography, 65*(1), 9–35. doi:10.1080/00324728.2010.547946

Eberstadt, N. (2010). The demographic future. what population growth – and decline – Means for the global economy. *Foreign Affairs, 89*(6), 54–64.

Elyachar, J. (2005). *Markets of Dispossession: NGOs, Economic Development, and the State in Cairo*. Durham & London: Duke University Press.

Elyachar, J. (2012). Next Practices: Knowledge, Infrastructure, and Public Goods at the Bottom of the Pyramid. *Public Culture, 24*(1 66), 109–129. doi:10.1215/08992363-1443583

Ferguson, J. (2015). *Give a man a fish: reflections on the new politics of distribution*. Durham: Duke University Press.

Gallin, D. (2001). Propositions on trade unions and informal employment in times of globalization. *Antipode*, *33*(3), 531–549. doi:10.1111/1467-8330.00197

Garcia, M., & Fares, J. (Eds.). (2008). *Youth in Africa's Labour Market*. Washington, DC: World Bank Publications.

Gereffi, G. and Luo, X. (2014). *Risks and opportunities of participation in global value chains*. World Bank Policy Research Working Paper No. 6847. Washington, DC : World Bank Group.

Goger, A., Hull, A., Barrientos, S., Gereffi, G., & Godfrey, S. (2014). *Capturing the Gains in Africa: Making the Most of Global Value Chain Participation*. Durham, NC: Duke University Centre on Globalization, Governance and Competitiveness.

Harriss-White, B., & Gooptu, N. (2001). Mapping India's World of Unorganized Labour. *Socialist Register*, *37*, 89–118.

Heintz, J., & Valodia, I. (2008). *Informality in Africa: A review*. Working paper no. 3. Cambridge, MA: WIEGO.

Henriques, M., & Herr, M. (2008). The Informal Economy and Microfranchising. In J. S. Fairbourne, S. W. Gibson, & W. G. Dyer (Eds.), *Microfranchising: Creating Wealth at the Bottom of the Pyramid*. Cheltenham: Edward Elgar.

Hickey, S., & du Toit, A. (2007). Adverse incorporation, social exclusion and chronic poverty. *CPRC Working Paper 81*. Manchester: Chronic Poverty Research Centre, University of Manchester.

Hietelahti, J., & Nygren, A. (2011). Microcredit as a Socio-Political Institution in South Africa: The Complexity of Rules, Logic and Power. In F. Hossain, C. Rees, & T. Knight-Millar (Eds.), *Microcredit and International Development: Contexts, Achievements and Challenges*. Abingdon: Routledge.

Huang, P. C. C. (2011). The Theoretical and Practical Implications of China's Development Experience: The Role of Informal Economic Practices. *Modern China*, *37*(1), 3–43. doi:10.1177/0097700410386434

Ibrahim Forum. (2012). *African Youth: Fulfilling the Potential*. Dakar: Mo Ibrahim Foundation.

ILO. (2012). *Statistical update on employment in the informal economy*. Geneva: Author.

ILO. (2013a). *Global Employment Trends*. Geneva: Author.

ILO. (2013b). *Women and Men in the Informal Economy: A Statistical Picture*. Geneva: Author.

ILO. (2014). *Global employment trends 2014: Risk of a jobless recovery?* Geneva: Author.

International Monetary Fund. (2012). *Sub-Saharan Africa Maintains Growth in an Uncertain World*. IMF Survey Magazine: Countries and Regions. Retrieved from http://www.imf.org/external/pubs/ft/survey/so/2012/CAR101212B.htm

Jütting, J., & de Laiglesia, J. R. (Eds.). (2009). *Is Informal Normal? Towards More and Better Jobs in Developing Countries:*. Paris: OECD.

Jütting, J., Parlevliet, J., & Xenogiani, T. (2008). Informal employment – reloaded. *IDS Bulletin*, *39*, 28–36. doi:10.1111/j.1759-5436.2008.tb00442.x

Kaplan, R. (1994). The coming anarchy. *Atlantic Monthly* 273(2), 44–76.

Kaplinsky, R. (2000). Globalisation and Unequalisation: What Can Be Learned from Value Chain Analysis? *Journal of Development Studies*, *37*(2), 117–146. doi:10.1080/713600071

Kistruck, G. M., Beamish, P. W., Qureshi, I., & Sutter, C. J. (2013). Social Intermediation in Base-of-the-Pyramid Markets. *Journal of Management Studies*, *50*(1), 31–66. doi:10.1111/j.1467-6486.2012.01076.x

Kotze, C. (2011). *Breaking the broker*. Technically speaking: The road ahead: Deloitte. Retrieved from http://www.iasplus.com/en/binary/safrica/1106ts.pdf

London, T., & Hart, S. (Eds.). (2011). *Next Generation Business Strategies for the Base of the Pyramid: New Approaches for Building Mutual Value*. Uper Saddle River, NJ: Financial Times Press.

Lund, F., & Nicholson, J. (2003). *Chains of Production, Ladders of Protection: Social Protection for Workers in the Informal Economy*. Durban, South Africa: School of Development Studies, University of Natal.

Marjit, S., & Maiti, D. S. (2006). Globalization, Economic Reform and Informal Labor. In B. Guha-Khasnobis & R. Kanbur (Eds.), *Informal Labor Markets and Development*. Helsinki: Palgrave-MacMillan.

Marsden, E. (2013). Why has the demographic transition stalled in sub-Saharan Africa? *New Security Beat*. Retrieved from http://www.newsecuritybeat.org/2013/08/demographic-transition-stalled-sub-saharan-africa/

Mazumdar, D. & Mazaheri, A. (2002). *Wages and employment in Africa*. Aldershot: Ashgate Publishing.

Mkandawire, T. (2010). On Tax Efforts and Colonial Heritage in Africa. *Journal of Development Studies*, *46*(10), 1647–1669. doi:10.1080/00220388.2010.500660

Nadvi, K. (2004). Globalisation and poverty: How can global value Chain Research Inform the Policy Debate?. *IDS Bulletin*, *35* (1), 20–30.

National Bureau of Statistics. (2011). *Annual Socio-Economic Report*. Nigeria.

Phillips, N. (2011). Child labour in global production networks: Poverty, vulnerability and 'adverse incorporation in the Delhi garments sector. *Chronic Poverty Research Centre Working Paper No. 177*. Manchester: University of Manchester.

Ranis, G., & Gollin, D. (2013). Macroeconomic perspectives. In H. Hino & G. Ranis (Eds.), *Youth and employment in sub-Saharan Africa: Working but poor*. Abingdon: Routledge.

Rossi, A. (2011). *Economic and social upgrading in global production networks: The case of the garment industry in Morocco* (Doctoral Thesis), University of Sussex.

Schoumaker, B. (2009). Stalls in fertility transition in sub-saharan Africa: Real or spurious?. Working paper no. 30. Département des Sciences de Population et du Développement, Université Catholique de Louvain.

Shapiro, D., & Gebreselassie, T. (2008). Fertility transitions in sub-Saharan Africa: Falling and stalling. *African Population Studies*, *22/23*(1/2), 3–23.

Sheth, S. (2013, 21 January). *BPO for the BoP – defining Impact Sourcing and its potential to boost employment opportunity. Next Billion*: Retrived from http://www.nextbillion.net/blogpost.aspx?blogid=3112.

Siggel, E. (2010). The Indian Informal Sector: The Impact of Globalization and Reform. *International Labour Review, 149*(1), 93–105. doi:10.1111/(ISSN)1564-913X

Sinha, A., & Adam, C. (2006). Reforms and Informalization: What Lies Behind Jobless Growth in India. In B. Guha-Khasnobis & R. Kanbur (Eds.), *Informal Labour Markets and Development*. New York: Palgrave Macmillan.

Sneeringer, S. E. (2009). *Fertility transitions in sub-Saharan Africa: A comparative analysis of cohort trends in 30 countries*. DHS Comparative Report No. 23. Calverton, MD: USAID.

The Economist. (2000). Hopeless Africa. May 13.

The Economist. (2011, December 3). The Hopeful Continent: Africa Rising.

Theron, J. (2005). Employer or intermediary: Labour brokers and the triangular employment relationship. *Industrial Law Journal, 26*, 618–649.

UNDP. (2008). *Creating value for all: Strategies for doing business with the poor*. Geneva: Author.

van Eck, B. P. S. (2010). Temporary Employment Services (Labour Brokers) in South Africa and Namibia. *Potchefstroom Electronic Law Journal, 13*(2), 107–126. doi:10.4314/pelj.v13i2.60256

Van Rensburg, J., Veldsman, A., & Jenkins, M. (2008). From technologists to social enterprise developers: . *Information Technology for Development, 14*(1), 76–89. doi:10.1002/itdj.20088

Vanek, J., Chen, M. A., Carré, F., Heintz, J., & Hussmanns, R. (2014). Statistics on the Informal Economy: Definitions, Regional Estimates and Challeneges. *Working Paper No. 2*. Cambridge MA: WIEGO.

Webb, J. W., Kistruck, G. M., Ireland, R. D., & Ketchen, D. J. (2010). The Entrepreneurship Process in Base of the Pyramid Markets: The Case of Multinational Enterprise/Nongovernment Organization Alliances. *Entrepreneurship: Theory and Practice, 34*(3), 555–581.

World Bank. (2014). *Unemployment, youth total (% of total labor force ages 15–24) (modeled ILO estimate)*. Retrieved from *http://data.worldbank.org/indicator/SL.UEM.1524.ZS.*

World Development Report. (2013). *Jobs*. Washington, DC: World Bank.

‘Integration’ or ‘Selective Incorporation’? The Modes of Governance in Informal Trading Policy in the Inner City of Johannesburg

ANTONIO PEZZANO
Department of Asian, African and Mediterranean Studies, Università degli Studi di Napoli, L’Orientale, Napoli, Italy

ABSTRACT *This article explores the modes of governance in informal trading policy in the inner city of Johannesburg. It highlights the different and contradictory empirical models of informal trading management which result from the interaction of multiple and plural local actors on the ground and the different strategies employed by informal traders in engaging the state. The article argues that Johannesburg municipal authorities exert a contradictory double agenda instead of governing the complexity of informality. The result is asymmetric governance functional to a neoliberalisation of the urban policies which produces a selective incorporation of informal traders from above and from below.*

Introduction

This article explores the ‘real governance’ of informal trading policy in the inner city of Johannesburg, based on an empirical analysis undertaken during three stages of research field-work: a first exploratory stage conducted in November and December 2010, and two following stages of collecting data on the ground (September to November 2011 and March to April 2013).

The purpose of the study is to explore urban governance of informality beyond neoliberal rhetoric. It examines power relations and decision-making processes using a political rather than a normative analysis of the policy-making process and focusing on a relational concept of power. Specifically, the aims of the study are to identify the plural and complex institutional configuration of state authorities (different spheres of government, political and administrative municipal authorities and corporatised municipal-owned entities) that produce policies in order to control territory, and to highlight how they are entangled with multiple social actors (informal traders, stakeholders, trade unions) and practices competing over the institutionalisation of power relations (Hagmann & Péclard, 2010). The study focuses on the voice of informal traders engaging plural state authorities and other non-state actors in multiple sites of urban governance (Lindell, 2008), and on the practices and agencies shaping the different empirical models of informal trading management on the ground.

The argument in this article is that Johannesburg municipal authorities do not govern the complexity of informal trading in the streets of the inner city. In fact, they do not follow an open and coherent strategy, despite the prolific production of policy documents. The result is asymmetric governance, which is functional to a neoliberalisation of the urban policies. On the one hand, intolerant forms of space control, defined in terms of a ‘neocolonial reordering of space’ by Steck et al. (2013, pp. 147, 155–157), reproduce historical patterns of repression and co-optation which limit and fragment the informal traders’ agency; on the other hand, variegated interests and actors emerge and organise autonomously on the ground in new entrepreneurial models of informal trading management, within a 'neoliberal reordering of space' (Steck et al., 2013, pp. 158–162). These new models are driven mainly by the private sector, which partially and exclusively integrates a minority of street traders in the city improvement districts (CIDs), while the majority of them are relegated to unmanaged and congested areas of the inner city where they are excluded from full access to social and economic citizenship.

On Urban Governance of Informality

According to Lindell, informality is

> a complex political field with many collective players who may articulate different visions, rationales and interests. The way these different collective actors relate to each other is an important dimension of this politics – they may ally, compete or work against each other. These highly diverse actors may relate to relevant centres of power in very different ways. These centres include urban authorities and central state institutions, but also 'sovereignties' and loci of power located beyond the administrative reach or the territorial confines of the state. The analysis of contemporary politics of informality thus [...] takes account of [...] the various actors and governing powers that they may engage with and of the various scales of social struggles in which informal actors may participate. (Lindell, 2010a, pp. 25–26)

To capture the complexity, variety and ambiguity of state and social agents' behaviour in Africa, in-depth empirical research and analysis is necessary in order to unpack the multiple dimensions of local dynamics and the plural forms of action and practices that comprise 'real governance', in contrast with the normative approach of international financial institutions, which promote an ideal of 'good governance' (Olivier de Sardan, 2008). As Meagher (2009, p. 9) puts it, a grounded-theory approach, anchored in fieldwork, is essential to an exploration of the complex regulatory and organisational processes 'intertwining cultural institutions, social agency and political authority' that shape the governance of informality in different empirical contexts.

The nature of the politics of informality is multiple, entangled and contingent, and the term 'informal' can be used in many ways. I do not wish to engage here in the 40-year-old theoretical debate on the definition of the term,[1] but I do wish to criticise the ambiguous and contradictory use of the term by the Johannesburg municipal authorities in official public policy. Generally I would also question the dichotomous and all-comprehensive use of the term by most international agencies or state authorities, either from a developmental (ILO, 2002, 2013) or entrepreneurialist perspective (De Soto, 1989, 2000). Going beyond the dichotomy 'informal-formal', particularly in urban contexts, means to reveal interests and strategies competing for resources and spaces in a 'mode of urbanization' (Roy, 2005). In short, it is a question of detecting power relations; whether they create exclusion or inclusion. These relational processes of negotiation do not occur 'outside' but 'with the complicity of the state' (Meagher, 1995). In sub-Saharan Africa, the state has been, historically, and still is defining 'formality' and 'legality' to the benefit of urban-based elites, thus excluding the majority and creating the marginalisation and criminalisation of informal actors (Jenkins, 2004). This power is exerted in the hybrid and interrelated Foucauldian dimensions of 'domination' and 'resistance' so that the state is entangled in governing society (Sharp, Routledge, Philo, & Paddison, 2000). Thus, the key question to answer is: 'Who, really exerts power, how and where?' To answer the question, it could be useful to consider Allen's (2004) notion of various modes of power (from coercion to manipulation) which co-exist and are mediated by a variety of actors and agencies. This view was taken up again by Lindell (2008, pp. 1880–1886) who, with her concept of multiple sites and scales of governance in African cities, outlined a framework consisting of multiple *sites* or loci of power that may involve various *modes of power*, at different *scales* where modes and practices of governance are exercised and contested; a variety of *actors* who shape and contest localised rules of governance; various layers of *relations* and a broad range of *activities* or *practices* of governance aimed at steering economy and society. In this multi-layered and entangled governance, the state is the main, but not the only centre of power. Nonetheless, the state, particularly local government in a context of neoliberal decentralised governance, plays a key role and exercises influence over actors and activities, over and above the design and implementation of policies, in the delivery of services or control of urban development.

The aim of my research is therefore to analyse the relations between the informal actors, the plural state actors and the other governance actors, particularly the private sector and trade unions, instead of a normative analysis of public policy-making and implementation. Thus it focuses on the municipal modes of governance which operate on the ground to institutionalise the informal trading policy according to specific norms (formal and practical) and plural forms of authority (Olivier de Sardan, 2014).

Informal Traders and the State in Africa

Street traders are emblematic examples of informality in African cities, where their presence is not new (Coquery-Vidrovitch, 1991). Since early colonialism the management of street vendors, derogatively called 'hawkers', was perceived by most municipal authorities as an issue related to African urban dwellers' access to citizenship. Street trading has always been a concern for public authorities of colonial and post-colonial cities because its use of central and strategic public spaces frustrates the formal planning of a modernist vision. As they struggled to control and rule the phenomenon, the public authorities developed an attitude intolerant of street traders, who were prevented from accessing public spaces and excluded from the right to the city. Thus public management of street trading was confined to the realm of politics and policies of marginality.

Continuities with the modernist agenda on informal trading are present in the entrepreneurialist practices of contemporary African cities conceived of as 'world-class cities' and aiming to attract international investment. In this concept of the African city, informal activities are to be either formalised or erased from city centres, which are transformed into emblematic spaces for shop-window strategies (Steck et al., 2013, pp. 146–147). Eviction and harassment have marked the history of the relationship between urban street traders and local authorities (Potts, 2008). But the response from traders has varied in the different contexts (Brown, 2006; Hansen & Vaa, 2004; Lindell, 2010a, b). Analysis of the relations between the state and informal actors cannot be universalised; it must include a historical perspective. Depending on historical trajectories or even on particular circumstances, the state represses, co-opts or even creates alliances with informal traders and the agency of informal traders varies from a passive moving away and returning to their selling sites to 'the quiet encroachment of the ordinary' (Bayat, 1997, 2004), to collective action contesting the state. Clearly, 'the relations between informal actors and the state cannot be reduced to either unequivocal antagonism or to hybrid clientelist networks . . . The various – and apparently contradictory – modalities of power used by the state may coexist and be combined' (Lindell, 2010a, pp. 16–17).

The mismanagement and the asymmetric governance evident in the central business district (CBD) of Johannesburg is actually a mix of state interventions shaped around policy and arbitrary practices to hamper the consolidation of collective organisations. This apparently contradictory behaviour of the state results from a plurality of actors and interests operating differently within its structure. While officials follow a strategy of legitimising informal traders through the implementation of policies shaped around 'formalisation', 'incorporation' or 'integration', they can, at the same time, also pursue their own interests through predatory practices which, reshaping the relationship between the state and the informal traders and keeping them in a constant uncertain 'state of exception' between legality and illegality, enables officials to exercise their power in order to exploit the vendors. What is difficult to prove is whether these practices constitute a misuse of state power by the officials who use the legitimacy of the state to act in their own interest, thus taking advantage of power imbalances in urban politics, or whether this asymmetry in governance is a deliberate strategy to keep the informal traders' organisations fragmented and to prevent or limit the political potential of collective actions. It is important, however, according to Lindell (2008,

2010a, b), to observe that the state is not a unified and coherent oppressive power and that new spaces of engagement for the agency of informal traders can be opened up to influence the implementation of policy.

The informal traders' agency in engaging with the state is various and multiple, sometimes also contradictory. They use and take advantage of the plurality of state actors and the different levels of government as well as of the dynamics of urban politics (Bénit-Gbaffou et al., 2013). As Lindell (2010b) argues, the agency of informal actors can be explained in terms of 'voice' in addition to the 'exit' option. Most of the first literature on informal sector activities in the 1980s conceived the agency of social actors in terms of 'exit', whether this took the form of individual or collective trajectories of disengagement from the state (Rothchild & Chazan, 1988). In the last few decades, a growing body of literature has highlighted the complex and wide-ranging forms of collective agency in which informal actors engage with the state, contesting unfavourable policies and regulations and claiming recognition, basic socio-economic rights and participation (Lindell, 2010a). However, we cannot consider these mobilisations as political agency and a voice capable of addressing all the various forms of exclusion. Although manifestations of the 'voice' of informal traders and workers are increasing in Africa, 'informal political voice has not yet replaced the politics of exit' (Meagher, 2010, p. 62). There is, rather, a continuum from individual to collective agency in the multiple scales of engagement and modes of power of urban politics. The questions to pose are firstly, how the different social (individual and collective) agencies and political practices interrelate and to the benefit of whom, and secondly, how and why the social actors shift from 'exit' to 'voice' strategies in specific situations. Moreover, to better understand the politics of informality it is also necessary to look at the various degrees and layers of power relations *within* the internal mechanisms of grassroots organisations and *outside* in the relations with other non-state actors, which may be social actors, such as trade unions and global movements of informal workers, or stakeholders, such as private-sector enterprises which are playing an increasing role in corporatised governance contexts (Lindell, 2010b).

More focused analyses on the collective organisation of informal actors highlight various internal issues, beyond the external influence of political and state authority, that can prevent political agency and hinder their scale-up to a political dimension: the personalisation, lack of accountability and poor representativeness of leadership; scarce resources; only occasional mobilisation on a limited range of operational, pragmatic issues; difficulty in including wider participation; division and stratification along the lines of income, age, gender, origins and identity (ethnicity, race and nationality). I will discuss some of these issues in relation to informal traders' agency in the inner city of Johannesburg later in this article.

Informal Trading Policy in Johannesburg

In terms of the number of employed people and contribution to gross domestic product, South Africa's informal sector is relatively small compared to those of other African countries. However, the sector represents the only opportunity to be employed and to escape poverty for many Africans. Among them, informal traders are a significant component.[2] In the inner city of Johannesburg, official figures estimate approximately 10,000 informal traders but the same municipal authorities estimate that there are many more; the estimated annual turnover of informal trade is around R4.2 billion[3] (City of Johannesburg [JDA], 2009, p. 37).

The history of informal trading in Johannesburg is as long as the history of the city itself and it was characterised by a recurrence of repression and efforts at regularisation by the municipal authorities. But the traders proved resilient and continued trading during and after the apartheid era, becoming a distinctive feature of the urban environment in the last few decades.[4] We can identify some historical continuities in public policy: the double agenda and contradictory behaviour of municipal authorities using a co-optative strategy to incorporate a segment of 'regularised' informal traders while excluding the majority as 'illegal'.

After the explosion in the number of street traders during the transition era, the City of Johannesburg has tried to develop mechanisms to regulate the sector within the regeneration programmes of the inner city. These plans aimed to create a vibrant residential and retail 'world-class' city centre where the presence of unlicensed informal traders in the streets was considered a residual phenomenon of the second economy, which was to be phased out.[5] The City thus demarcated non-trading zones to have a limited number of trading spaces. The consequent scarcity of legal trading spaces created a mass of illegal traders who were subjected to harassment and impoundment by enforcement agents. The repression, criminalisation and marginalisation of these 'informal' activities was necessary for the development of the 'formal' economic system within a modernist vision of the city, inspired by the concepts of order, security and public health – a continuation of colonial and apartheid legislation.

Over the last years, the attitudes and discourses of the city developers, planners and public officers have changed.[6] From being seen as an unwanted sector of disordered and dangerous activities, informal trading is now seen to have potential as a viable means to reduce urban poverty and unemployment in a developmental framework of sustainable and inclusive growth. This change was expressed in the recent *Joburg 2040: Growth and Development Strategy*. The document asserts the essential role of 'a robust informal sector' 'in supporting economic resilience and sustainability' and the need to design 'supportive regulatory approaches for the management of informal trading' (City of Johannesburg, 2011, pp. 25, 98, 34). However, this new proclaimed approach is far from being realised and the existing informal trading policy and bylaws of the City of Johannesburg are still ambivalent and contradictory.

The current informal trading policy (City of Johannesburg, 2009) combines a basic approach on 'formalisation' and 'upgrading', focusing on the development of regulated 'market' and 'linear market' facilities within business improvement districts, with some developmental approaches to local development[7] which consider these 'survivalist' activities as a social protection for poor households affected by the low growth rate in the national economy as a result of the economic crisis.

The definition of informal trading in the policy reveals the reductive and dualistic approach of Mbeki's 'two economies'[8] and the exclusive, incorporating vision of 'African world-class city' elaborated in the previous strategic plans (City of Johannesburg, 2007; GJMC, 2001)[9] and does not contemplate the complexity of the 'informal economy' as a wider heterogeneous continuum, from entrepreneurial to survivalist enterprises and informal workers. In fact, the City of Johannesburg still has difficulty in designing and developing a consistent policy towards informal trading, denoting a gap between statement and agency. The normative approach of policy is based on rhetorical statements of inclusiveness and integration into economic, spatial and social development, predicting a paradigm shift from 'formalisation' to 'integration', but is contradicted by the designed model of management, which puts into effect the 'categorisation' of informal traders as part of an exclusive incorporation in the inner city renovation plan. Private sector 'accepts' a 'normalisation' of informal trading activities, but with restricted access to the 'renovated' zones.[10] The driving dominant model is still the neoliberal 'corporate governance' of local government, which promotes a private-sector-driven development and marginalises the low-income sectors of the urban population (Beall, Crankshaw, & Parnell, 2002; Bond, 2005). In fact, this reconceptualisation of informal trading does not differ too much from the late apartheid deregulation of hawkers, taxis and shebeens which was useful to the government, in need of a labour intensive sector which avoided the costs of welfare for the majority of the African population (Rogerson & Hart, 1989, pp. 32–33). In practice, we are witnessing a redefinition of the neoliberalisation processes of public action which creates partnership between the public and private sectors and 'normalises' or 'institutionalises' the participation of social actors. In this remodelling, neocolonial and modernist repertoires are reactivated to control and order the space, but within a new public management and entrepreneurialist framework.

In this context, in April 1999 the Johannesburg Council established the Metropolitan Trading Company (MTC), a profit-driven company, whose main purpose is to develop and manage informal trading and public transport facilities. In the following years, other municipal-owned entities were established: the Johannesburg Metropolitan Police Department (JMPD) and the Johannesburg

Development Agency (JDA). The former manages the City's crime prevention strategy and bylaws enforcement. The latter has the particular mandate of the inner city renewal, a revaluation of capital assets in the inner city. This vision, which aims at regenerating Johannesburg as an 'African world-class city', characterised the first decade of the millennium. Informal trading has been subjected to it and the 'counter-voice' of informal traders and workers has not always been heard by the municipal authorities. As the municipality pushes forward with its plans to renovate the inner city and attract private investment, traders are removed from the streets and partly placed in markets, even if they disagree. In the implementation of the informal trading policy and bylaws, the City promotes plans such as 'linear markets' and 'smart cards' in order to demarcate restricted areas in the inner city where traders are allowed to operate only with a license or permit issued by the MTC. This strategy largely failed to provide all excluded street traders with alternative opportunities for trading or with formal employment. It ultimately resulted in strict bylaws enforcement by the metropolitan police and often unfair and corrupt management by the municipal officials, while the privatisation of public space proceeded, in the form of city improvement districts (CIDs).

However, the new policy, while ambivalent and wavering between 'formalisation' and 'normalisation', opens new spaces of engagement for the agency of the informal traders. To better understand the articulation between the regulatory processes of public policies and the agency of informal traders and the private sector, it is critical to outline the informal trading management practices and to highlight challenges and conflicts, but also the innovation and potentialities of the different models that emerge on the ground.

Normative and Empirical Models of Informal Trading Management

The gap between normative and empirical models of street-trading management is evident in the CBD and inner city of Johannesburg. The shift from 'formalisation' to 'integration' is happening only in the discourses, as corporate managers and public officials relate in the interviews.[11] But a 'selective incorporation' emerges on the ground: on the one hand, an integrated, but not open and participatory, system regulates the sector for a restricted number of informal traders in the CIDs' linear markets, useful to the corporate interests investing in the revival of the inner city; on the other hand, chaotic mismanagement leaves the majority of informal traders in unmanaged, unserviced and unregulated congested areas of the CBD where they are excluded from full access to social and economic citizenship.

The City of Johannesburg was basically trying to implement a management model which differentiates between informal traders and supports the development of only the structured categories of trading – 'permanent' and 'linear' markets. These deliberately restrictive practices generate a vicious circle of mismanagement that Bénit-Gbaffou (2015, pp. 60–62) has termed the 'public production of scarcity'. Deciding univocally to restrict legal trading spaces to structured markets leads to the 'illegalisation', and therefore criminalisation, of a majority of the traders, who cannot be managed other than through repression or corruption. In this way, the City also creates competition amongst traders that manifests as xenophobia.

If we examine more closely what happens on the ground we may understand better the dynamics of 'real' governance in the management of informal trading and try to answer questions on the kind of 'inclusion': whether 'integrated' or 'incorporated'.

The municipality of Johannesburg presents a complex system of governance of informal trading where multiple actors interact at different scales and in different phases of the policy-making process. Different layers of relations between actors and interests correspond at each different phase of the process – what is of particular interest is the decision-making process and how responsibilities are shared. The responsibilities in implementing the different phases are entrusted to various municipal authorities: the Department of Economic Development demarcates areas for informal trading; MTC, now replaced by JPC (Johannesburg Property Company),[12] allocates spaces and collects rental fees; the metropolitan police (JMPD) enforces bylaws. In all these phases, the municipal authorities were to consult the stakeholders and social actors. But the extent to which they are involved varies. As corporate and/or political interests at stake rise, so the participation and influence of informal traders decreases and the locus of power recedes from the ground.

The process is least transparent and the decision-making process more restrictive and less participatory when it comes to the demarcation of designated areas, although the Businesses Amendment Act of 1993 requires a demonstrated consultation of stakeholders before municipalities demarcate any restricted or prohibited trading areas. It is difficult to find out what criteria, if any, the municipality adopted in deciding on demarcated areas. The interest at stake here is the use of land and it is likely that the main responsibility for decision-making is linked to the more general urban planning process, which the top political municipal authority (the mayor and his cabinet) shares with national and international public and private actors. The responsibility for implementation, however, is given to the Department of Economic Development, which is supposed to consult the informal traders through the 'invited' space (Cornwall, 2008) of the City's Informal Trade Forum (ITF). According to the traders, the ITF is not regularly called and it has been reduced to a forum that responds merely to current operational problems. The words of an informal traders' leader are revealing: 'There is no forum where all stakeholders (including people, informal traders) are engaged to discuss an issue like demarcation which involves a wider discussion about the planning and renewal of the City. Instead the municipality is selling places to the big investors. The big property owners decide to evict people and street vendors!'[13]

In the allocation of spaces where fewer actors and interests compete, informal traders are more engaged and the entanglement of municipal authorities in the processes of governance is more evident. In this phase, after designating a demarcated area, municipal officers and managers collaborate with representatives of informal traders in identifying and registering informal traders to whom they allocate space. It is evident that representation is a crucial issue. In the process of setting and implementing the electronic system of registration based on 'smart cards', MTC created an empirical database from surveys conducted with the assistance of task teams – advisory bodies composed of informal traders appointed, not elected, to the Forum – and block leaders, well-known traders who had been operating for a long time in a particular demarcated area, elected at the block level to represent traders in meetings with the municipal authorities. Both the task teams and block leaders are perceived by traders as an instrument of a divide-and-rule, co-optative strategy in the hands of municipal authorities, although the block leaders are also considered the most grounded popular representatives of traders because of their long-term presence and knowledge of issues on the ground. Despite the fact that informal traders are involved in the process, the degree of participation is uneven. In a situation where there is no reliable record-keeping, relying on remunerated task teams or giving prominence to block leaders who have been on the streets for longer periods could help municipal authorities to manage the designated area but could also contribute to further contention and division among the associations of informal traders and favour informal power holders,[14] increasing corrupt behaviour to the detriment of the poorest and weakest informal street traders. In presenting their platform position, prepared for the Joburg 2040 Growth and Development Strategy (GDS 2040), the Coalition of Johannesburg Street Traders, facilitated by the Congress of Trade Unions (COSATU), asked that corruption in the system be addressed, and demanded participation in the decision-making processes regarding the allocation of space and the attribution of smart cards.

We can argue that opacity, uncertainty and slowness in the key process of allocation could be interpreted as 'dysfunctional' to a market-oriented model of governance, but it is 'functional' to the mode of power through which municipal authorities exert control over traders. That is confirmed by the fact that there are many unmanaged areas, mostly populated by migrants and not organised traders, where the presence of municipal authorities is visible only through the collection of rent and the maintenance of order with harsh bylaw enforcement operated by the police.

In this asymmetric system of governance, the mismanagement of the municipal authorities mirrors the emergence of the entrepreneurialist model in the CIDs, where the linear markets are managed by the private sector in partnership with the public authority.

The central improvement district has become a dominant model in the restructuring of local government in South Africa (Didier, Morange, & Peyroux, 2013; Didier, Peyroux, & Morange, 2012; Peyroux, 2008). Though CID management should be supplementary to the municipal authority, focusing on services such as marketing, security, cleaning and maintenance of public spaces, the municipality of Johannesburg has progressively been disengaging and outsourcing the management of the CBD and the inner city to the powerful private-sector agencies that supported the urban regeneration programmes. Of course, this neoliberalisation trend has also affected street trading. Over the last years, Central Johannesburg Partnership (CJP)[15] has gained ground in law enforcement and the management of informal traders and taxi operators.

Initially the informal traders positioned themselves against the establishment of this model. In particular, the South African National Traders' Retail Alliance (SANTRA) criticised the eviction of street traders from designated prohibited zones in the new Braamfontein CID. Edmund Elias, spokesperson of SANTRA, was concerned about a trend which has actually become the current reality: a restricted number of street traders who can safely operate in CID-managed areas while the majority of informal traders are confined to more and more congested and unmanaged areas in the CBD or in non-lucrative areas on the outskirts of the inner city or in the townships.[16] As the CID model spread over the whole inner city, the informal trading management of CID linear markets, such as the one on Kerk Street in the Retail Improvement District (RID), became the 'best practice' to follow. It is interesting to note that the same informal traders' leaders, who were initially against the formation of CIDs, are now wishing for a city informal trading management model which reflects the RID one in the effective integration of street traders,[17] although that is a model closed to newcomers and not democratically participatory. In fact, the participation of traders is limited to consultation on a few issues that directly concern them, while the decision-making power is in the tight hand of the CID board, ruled by the property owners and big retailers. The construction of consent around this model, desired not only by the private sector but also by the municipal authorities and informal traders, raises the question, in a Foucauldian sense, of the capacity of the system to foster 'technologies of the self' that serve the interests of capital (Steck et al., 2013, p. 159).

Diversified Strategies of Informal Traders Agency Engaging the State

The chaotic mismanagement of the municipal authorities and the emergence of a new entrepreneurialist model of informal trading management is hardly conducive to the agency of traders' organisations and the creation of social movements. Nonetheless, forms of participation, although handed down from above, open spaces for informal traders to bargain for their visibility and legitimacy, and to claim their rights.

In 2011, the newly elected Mayor of Johannesburg, Parks Tau, launched the general city strategy, Joburg 2040: Growth and Development Strategy (GDS 2040), through a process of public outreach which included, beyond discussions with City departments and consultations with experts, a process of engagement with stakeholders and decision-makers across all sectors within the City. The outreach process and the ensuing implementation of the strategy revealed change and continuities in the interaction between municipal authorities and informal traders, as well as the contradictory double agenda of this 'inclusive' municipal strategy. In September 2011[18] informal traders were invited, along with all stakeholders, to voice their concerns and present their case in a 'participatory' process. The municipality approach was not really participative. The Department of Economic Development called for a preparatory meeting where the managers tried to direct the discussion according to a pre-set agenda, stopping issues coming from the ground. But informal traders, with the support of COSATU representatives and researchers from Wits University, asked for and obtained more preliminary meetings in order to discuss and elaborate their platform before participating in the GDS outreach process. The result of these meetings – which were 'created' participation spaces, rather than 'invited' spaces from the authorities – was a position paper in which the informal traders demanded more participation and self-management and improved engagement on the part of the municipality.[19]

While informal traders were invited to share their opinions and present their position in official meetings, the metropolitan police harassed hawkers on the inner city streets and shortly afterwards municipal officers, accompanied by councillors of the opposition party, served eviction notices and chased informal traders away from various neighbourhoods around the inner city.[20]

In the months after the GDS 2040 meetings, several other episodes of harassment occurred. Informal traders demanded a meeting to discuss informal trading bylaws and enforcement. The Department of Economic Development was forced to call this meeting on 11 May 2012. Although the municipality officially claimed to have reached an agreement with informal traders on reviewing bylaws, one of the most vocal associations representing street traders in the inner city, SANTRA, which came to the meeting with legal assistants, was actually forced out (ESSET, 2012; Pongoma, 2012). This episode is interesting because it demonstrates that when the engagement of informal traders with the municipality is confrontational, the participatory process is stopped by the municipal authorities; as shown in other contexts in South Africa, the participation of stakeholders in the invited spaces often results in 'spectator politics' (Williams, 2006).

The municipal authorities' double agenda which, on the one hand, starts processes of inclusion, accommodating many informal traders, and on the other, appears to be more sensitive to formal retailers' interests, sweeping away as many 'illegal' traders as possible, is a continuity, as demonstrated by the events of Operation Clean Sweep in late 2013.[21] The launching of a new policy is always an opportunity for the municipal authorities to reassert their control on space and to enforce 'order and security' (Rogerson, 1990, pp. 125–126). The strategy of the municipality of Johannesburg seems to be a constant selective incorporation of a limited number of informal street traders, necessary to the development of an 'African world-class city', while excluding the majority, who are criminalised and fought as 'illegal' – a strategy which has repeatedly been denounced by the informal traders' representatives.[22]

Despite the municipal double agenda, informal traders are not passive; they exercise their agency to open and reconfigure spaces and to combine different strategies in engaging with different state levels and authorities, as in the cases of the Gauteng Provincial Government Platform in 2012 and 2013 and the appeal to the Constitutional Court against the Operation Clean Sweep forced evictions in December 2013. Although the traders' agency has not yet had the effect of deeply changing the unbalanced power relations in their favour, it has nonetheless driven the metropolitan government to reshape urban governance.

Facing the ambivalent 'stop and go' strategy of the City of Johannesburg after the launch of the GDS 2040 outreach process, some informal traders' leaders then intensified relations with the higher level of provincial government, particularly the Gauteng Economic Development Portfolio Committee and the Gauteng Department of Economic Development.

The Gauteng Provincial Government has followed a developmental approach of inclusive economic growth in its *Gauteng Employment Growth and Development Strategy* (GEGDS), emphasising that the informal economy is 'a means of contributing towards income generation for people who have access to no income' (Gauteng Provincial Government, 2011, p. 25). This approach was substantiated by the Economic Development Portfolio Committee meetings chaired by Nkosipendule Kolisile who then became MEC for the Department of Economic Development. During 2012 and the first half of 2013, first the Committee and then the Department of Economic Development created a platform of engagement with the informal traders.

This platform was used by the participant actors for various reasons but they converged on the common need to bypass government at the City level. The informal traders thus played on political competition between the local and the provincial levels of government to legitimate and consolidate their own position. The combined interplay reveals on the one hand, the political agenda, focused on an inclusive economy and decent work, of MEC Kolisile – who was also trying to enlarge and strengthen his constituency in view of the upcoming 2014 election – while on the other hand, the informal traders were trying to consolidate their position in opposition to a hostile and unfavourable municipal management concerned with being a 'world-class African city'. So, the informal traders legitimated the provincial government position in constructing a platform for a coalition of street traders' organisations rather than the position of the local metropolitan governments, which tended to deepen their fragmentation and division. The provincial government was very critical of municipalities' implementation of informal trading policy, as documented in the various engagement workshops (Matjomane, 2013, pp. 90–108). The municipal approach was considered restrictive and unsupportive of informal trading, more inclined to law-enforcement institutions than developmental measures, as well as a cause of fragmentation and marginalisation of informal traders.

The strategy of the Gauteng Provincial Government was presented in workshops held between November 2012 and June 2013, in which representatives of informal traders were invited to participate. The principal aim was a 'normalisation' of the sector through the provision of a legal framework in line with the national regulatory process,[23] the regularisation of informal traders and the creation of a united platform.

Both the calls for regularisation and unity were favourably accepted by the majority of the representatives of informal traders' associations present at the 22 April workshop. These leaders were rethinking their strategies about 'regularisation' because they could see favourable opportunities in the government programmes supporting the previously marginalised sections of the economic society. This diversified strategy of engagement could be seen as a 'selective incorporation from below' (Meagher & Lindell, 2013, p. 68). But to better understand the selective nature of this incorporation it is necessary to analyse specifically who the actors of engagement are, and where and when this happens.

Although the majority of speakers at the workshop stressed the importance of the unity of informal traders, divisions emerged when the South African Informal Traders Forum (SAITF), one of the pre-eminent traders' organisations, was indicated as leading the process because of its historical practices of engagement with the provincial government. At the end of meeting the Chairman of SAITF called for preparatory meetings in order to map out a united position for presentation at the Informal Traders Summit scheduled in July,[24] but most of the other leaders did not attend these meetings. From the beginning of the process, Matjomane (2013, p. 86) noticed competitiveness and personal and utilitarian use of the platform by some leaders willing to network with the key influential organisation known as the Gauteng Enterprises Propeller (GEP).[25]

This last episode discloses historical features of the informal traders' agency which make them fragile: the fragmentation of street traders' organisations, despite a long and vocal presence; low accountability and representativeness of their leadership and unequal access to decision-making processes. The fragile nature of participation and the weak governance in the informal traders' organisations derives not only from the fluctuating trajectories and opaque behaviours of the associations and their leaders, but also from the complicity of public authorities. Personalisation of leadership and low participation foster relations of patronage and impede a democratic consolidation of informal traders' organisations, and although they can be vocal and accountable in terms of responsiveness, their processes and practices are not transparent. In fact, it is quite impossible to get a statute of the associations or to record regular meetings with all members. Interviews with street traders in the CBD brought out allegations that some leaders' management of associations is based in personal political ambition or economic interest, while others collect money in the guise of subscription fees to allocate secure spaces in markets or on streets and to protect street traders from police harassment.[26] These practices imply connivance between municipal authorities and some association leaders, which hampers collective organisation. On several occasions, municipal officers have manipulated traders' leadership to endorse their plans without consulting traders, thus dividing them (Thulare, 2004, pp. 6–7). Informal traders' leaders who were interviewed reported the municipal authorities' deliberate practice of preventing some organisations from convening regular meetings.[27]

The individualistic personalisation of the leadership is also one of the reasons why the informal traders' associations do not have a historical relationship with the trade union movement. In Johannesburg, COSATU only recently is trying to facilitate a collective organisation of informal traders, as we saw in the case of GDS 2040 meetings.[28] In that case, embryonic, innovative forms of representation emerged from the fragmentation of the informal traders' agency and resisted the capture of the municipal policy structure. COSATU, with much effort, also facilitated a coalition of

Johannesburg street traders and organised their representation at the SALGA workshops for a national Informal/Street Trading Policy Framework, held in March 2012. COSATU's commitment should not be over-emphasised, however: its intervention came from national campaigns and not from local input.[29] Some street traders organisations' leaders are still pessimistic and mistrustful of the role played by COSATU and StreetNet in organising the coalition and they have openly challenged it.[30]

The representative network of informal traders is still fragile and struggles to represent the traders as an interest group and to scale up to political voice and action. The informal traders' organisations are mobilised more on issues affecting their daily business, such as eviction, police harassment and confiscation of goods (sometimes just as a strategy on the part of the leaders to control and take advantage of the allocation process), than on united claims about their class position as exploited 'casual', 'marginalised', 'precarious' workers. Nonetheless, despite fragmented and personalised leadership, traders are able to resist and successfully oppose structural injustices, as in the case of Operation Clean Sweep.

In October 2013, the mayor launched Operation Clean Sweep with brutal removals of thousands of informal traders from the CBD and inner city streets. The campaign, inspired by the member of the mayoral committee (MMC) responsible for development planning, Ross Greeff, aimed at 'restoring' the inner city and 'combating lawlessness' identifying as the main problems illegal trading, dumping and littering, land and building invasions and the illegal water and electricity connections. Although the programme of action was intended to address the various challenges that had contributed to urban decay, supposedly in accordance with the newly launched Inner City Transformation Roadmap, the emphasis was only on the 'short-term' plan of the operation: to remove traders from the streets – without giving them an alternative solution. If we analyse the dynamics and process of this situation, we can again raise issues which constitute the main focus of this article: the contradictory, double agenda of the municipalities conflicting with the persistent agency of the traders.

Operation Clean Sweep did not come about overnight. One year before, in October 2012, two reports were issued from the office of MMC Greeff outlining the Mayoral Clean Sweep initiative within the more general strategy of the City. So, it is not surprising that the City tried to make an agreement with some traders' representatives (blocks' and organisations' leaders) to detect and remove the 'illegal' traders, before starting the operation.[31] In fact, it was only when police officers, far from consulting with leaders, indiscriminately chased out non-authorised and authorised traders, that the traders started to contest the operation (Bénit-Gbaffou, 2014, p. 6). Again, this attests to a contradictory double agenda of the municipal authorities. As the City is about to implement a new 'cohesive and participatory' strategy with discourses of sustainability and resilience, it simultaneously reactivates restrictive and repressive practices and repertoires following a 'neo-colonial reordering of space'. In announcing the reformulation of a more proactive policy, engaging all stakeholders in an inclusive process, they needed a 'clean sweep' to keep out unwanted social actors and incorporate a selected number. But, in this case, the criminalised traders reacted with a confrontational agency that to a certain extent derailed the municipal strategy. After failed negotiations with the municipality for the verification of a re-registration process and a negative judgment by the South Gauteng High Court, two organisations, SAITF and SANTRA, lodged an appeal with the Constitutional Court as a matter of urgency. On 5 December 2013, the Court ruled in favour of the traders, recognising the urgent need to stop the evictions and to allow traders to return to their workplaces. The Court judgment was not simply a victory for all traders, whether it was the result of an efficient shared legal strategy or an immediate response serving the narrow interests of 'legal traders'. The Court, beyond condemning the operation as an act of 'humiliation and degradation' in itself, also unmasked and limited the City's restrictive policy approach, which was considered 'unlawful', 'indiscriminate', 'flawed', and 'in flagrant disregard of the traders' rights'.

In practice, the successful legal action of traders revealed the restrictive and exclusionary implementation practices of the municipality, based on a law-enforcement approach, which were cynically justified in terms of 'convenience' to hide the chronic failure of street-trading management, notwithstanding progressive and developmental national and municipal normative frameworks. Moreover, it compelled the City of Johannesburg to find other, less restrictive – at least temporarily – legal ways to implement its policy and to open up spaces of negotiation. Where this process is leading is yet to be seen. It seems that the two victorious litigant organisations, and consequently all the others, have gained a certain degree of recognition and leverage over state officials, which could re-establish constructive engagement with the City. However, the 'participatory', but sanitised and depoliticised process undertaken by the City, throughout 2014, to define ways forward for the regulation of informal trading spaces in the inner city in line with the Constitutional Court judgment, urges caution. At the same time, engagements on the ground between some traders' organisations and the private sector are creating innovative proposals for street-trading management, such as the pilot project in Park Station, proposed by SANTRA and CJP, in the immediate aftermath of Operation Clean Sweep (Bénit-Gbaffou, 2015, pp. 76–80).

Conclusion

In the last few decades, the neoliberalisation process of the municipal authorities in Johannesburg has firstly considered informal activities as a temporary phenomenon, to be phased out with 'sustainable economic growth'. But because of the resilient informal traders' agency, the City of Johannesburg has elaborated a more 'integrated' discourse of informal trading management, which was not then substantiated in the policy implementation. Clear contradictions emerged between normative and empirical models of management. The result is a deliberate, asymmetric system of governance of informal trading in the CBD and inner city of Johannesburg. In practice, historical continuities of co-optative strategies are evident in public policy: a 'selective incorporation' of a restricted number of informal traders, which is useful to corporate interests investing in the revival of the inner city, but produces the exclusion, criminalisation and marginalisation of the majority of informal traders. The municipal authorities have thus exerted their power and control over traders, putting forth a contradictory double agenda where the rhetoric of participation contrasts with the repressive enforcement of bylaws. Despite the municipal double agenda, informal traders were able to open and reconfigure spaces and to combine various strategies in engaging with different levels and authorities of the state in what we can consider a 'selective incorporation from below'.

In continuing this research, it will then be crucial to understand which groups or individuals among traders are benefiting from this two-way 'selective incorporation' in terms of access to state facilities and to policy decision-making processes and/or in terms of political voice. The ability to engage the state does not always foster collective political action because conditions, modalities and the timing of engagement are more often decided by state or private sector actors, particularly in a context of deliberately fragmented and asymmetric urban governance. The more informal traders have restricted access to the state, the less space there is for negotiation and collective representation that can challenge the state and change policies. However, the informal traders in Johannesburg have been able to shape new, although embryonic, forms of collective voice and engagement and to create strategic alliance with other institutions and organisations in order to claim their rights and to protect their activities, as the Constitutional Court victory after Operation Clean Sweep demonstrates.

Disclosure statement

No potential conflict of interest was reported by the author.

Funding

The last stage of this research was funded by the Italian National Interest Research Project PRIN 2010-2011 'State, Plurality, Change in Africa' [prot. 201048XHTL_003].

Notes

1. For an analysis of the debate see Skinner (2008); Hart (2008); Potts (2008).
2. In 2014, trade still accounted for 43.5 per cent of jobs in the informal sector, although this had declined by 2.5 percentage points since 2008. In Gauteng, over 50 per cent of the persons running an informal business were in the trade industry. For statistical data on the South African informal sector, see Statistics South Africa (2015). For a comparison on employment data with other African countries see ILO (2012).
3. The figure represents around 5 per cent of total turnover of the inner city, compared to the 16 per cent of formal trade sector.
4. For a history of informal traders in Johannesburg see Rogerson (1990); Rogerson and Beavon (1985); Beavon and Rogerson (1980, 1982).
5. For a critique of the post-apartheid urban development of Johannesburg, which produces new spatial dynamics of exclusion, see Murray (2008, 2011).
6. Interviews with Justice Mashele, MTC acting CEO, 22 November 2011; Hans Jooste, CJP general manager, 28 October 2011; Lebo Mashego, AFHCO Urban Development Manager, 18 October 2011. See also *Seminar on The South African Informal City*, Johannesburg, 15 November 2011, http://www.informalcity.co.za/.
7. For the 'developmental' approach to the informal sector in South Africa, see Dewar (2005); Davies and Thurlow (2009).
8. On the debate about Thabo Mbeki's 'two economies' and the 'informal economy' see Bond (2007); Frye (2007); Devey, Lebani, Skinner, and Valodia (2007).
9. For a review of the policy-making, see Hlela (2003).
10. 'In this urban renewal plan, private business *accepts* and wants informal traders, but they should be regulated' (interview with Hans Jooste, 28 October 2011).
11. The general manager of CJP, Hans Jooste, refers to 'the need of integrated systems of management' that includes 'regulated informal traders' among all stakeholders and role players. The last acting CEO of MTC, Justice Mashele, while reasoning about the new model to manage informal traders, raises the question whether to 'regularise' or to 'control' informal traders, which can be translated as 'normalisation' or 'incorporation', because, in the first case, he talks about policies to create employment; in the second, he speaks about the possibility to 'accept no more than 5000 street traders in the inner city development programmes, restricting access and opportunity to newcomers' (interviews with Hans Jooste, 28 October 2011; and with Justice Mashele, 22 November 2011).
12. The change of management from MTC to JPC created confusion among informal traders who considered it as an apparent more than a substantial change. They were concerned about the fact that they would interact with the same MTC managers and officials whom they had criticised, but who were transferred to the JPC (Matjomane, 2013). Although the shift to JPC was justified in terms of efficiency in managing informal traders, we could argue that the main concern of the municipality is to better manage the rental issue. The function of JPC is to maximise the value of the City properties.
13. Interview with Sam Khasibe, 14 October 2011.
14. This was also the situation reported 10 years ago (see Hlela, 2003, p. 2).
15. Central Johannesburg Partnership is the company established in 1992 to revitalise the inner city. One of its prominent tasks is the management of CIDs. But it also manages the Johannesburg Inner City Business Coalition (JICBC), the lobby group of the inner city property owners acknowledged as stakeholders within the Inner City Regeneration Charter. Now CJP works through outsourcing agreements in partnership with(in) Urban Genesis.
16. See Johannesburg inner city summit: A community perspective of urban regeneration, SANTRA, press release, May 2007, pp. 2–3, as well as other SANTRA press releases (as cited in Tissington, 2009, pp. 29, 32–33; 41–44).
17. Edmund Elias, personal communication, 19 March 2013. See also the street trading management pilot plan which SANTRA and CJP are negotiating around Park Station, reported by Bénit-Gbaffou (2015, pp. 76–80).
18. The thematic discussions of the Joburg 2040 GDS were held in nine weeks in August and September 2011. In particular, the 'economic growth' week, which included informal trading, was held from 24 to 30 September. The contributions of all sectors were summarised and developed in the vision document published in October 2011. See City of Johannesburg (2011).
19. See Coalition of Johannesburg Street Traders (facilitated by COSATU) (2011). The slogans titling the proposal points are 'Nothing for us without us!' and 'Work with us not for us!'.
20. For a report of the events see Motshegwa (2011a, b) and see also Democratic Alliance chase the last three Norwood hawkers. SANTRA Press Release, 17 October 2011.
21. For more details see http://joburgtraderesources.wordpress.com/.
22. In the words of Edmund Elias, spokesperson of the SANTRA: 'As the Johannesburg Department of Economic Development continues to *preach development*, repression continues. That department is acting in bad faith and continues to support punitive police action against the very people it is mandated to manage', (SANTRA, press release, 19 February 2012), and more explicitly, denouncing the repressive and selective incorporation during Operation Clean Sweep, 'What fuels confrontation is to allow a small group (linear market) back whilst the rest (street trade) not' (SANTRA, press release, 28 November 2013).
23. The Department of Trade and Industry, in line with the New Growth Path, was looking at the informal economy as a target of intervention and created a unit to develop a National Strategy on Informal Sector. The person responsible for the unit, Vukile Nkabinde, was present at a workshop held on 22 April and started an engagement with some informal traders' leaders, particularly on the burning question about the draft Licensing of Businesses Bill launched on March 2013.

24. The Informal Traders Summit was held on 9 and 10 July, preceded the day before by a visit from MEC Kolisile in Johannesburg CBD. The Summit aimed to initiate a process for the formation of an umbrella body of informal traders and the formulation of an Informal Trading Policy for Gauteng, looking specifically at xenophobia and corruption in the sector, police harassment and victimisation of traders, as well as micro-financing projects. This strategy should have been developed together with local municipalities and law enforcement agencies in an intergovernmental approach, and concluded by July 2014. A few days after the Summit, MEC Kolisile died in a car accident. This sudden death stopped the process.
25. The Gauteng Enterprises Propeller (GEP) is a provincial government agency established in 2005 under the auspices of the Department of Economic Development to co-ordinate stakeholders for the benefit of small-, medium- and micro-entrepreneurs (SMMEs) in Gauteng and to provide non-financial and financial support for them. Kolisile supported more commitment from the agency in assisting and training informal traders and a review of the GEP's funding model to make provision for more accessible loans.
26. Interviews with street traders in Faraday, Park Station, Joubert Street, October–November 2011.
27. 'Xolani disturbs the creation of regular meetings among traders called by SAITF every Wednesday. He calls block and market leaders for other meetings in his office and then he cancels them at the last minute. Or he intimidates people threatening inspection tour and the like' (interview with Sam Khasibe, 14 October 2011). This practice is confirmed by Christinah Kedikiloe (interviewed at Faraday Market, 10 October 2011).
28. The role of COSATU, as expressed by the Campaign Co-ordinator, was 'to give a technical support and develop a methodology to facilitate the organisation from a fragmented reality, but not to organise directly informal traders' (interview with George Mahlangu, COSATU Campaign Co-ordinator, Johannesburg, 7 October 2011).
29. For the integration of street traders in national and international networks, as in *World Class Cities for All* (WCCA) campaign, see Çelik (2010).
30. Explicit criticism was expressed by some leaders during the workshop on 22 April 2013 as well as in other circumstances at ITF, as related by Matjomane (2013, pp. 160–166).
31. It was a complex issue to define who and how many were the 'legal' traders. As Bénit-Gbaffou (2015, p. 61) remarks, 'There are many different traders status between legality and illegality. Being registered in the City or in the Central Johannesburg Partnership databases; having a smart card; having a lease and proof of rental payment; having a demarcated trading site – are different ways of defining 'being legal', that are not always articulated and are certainly difficult to navigate.' See the same report for a discussion of the figures of various estimates related to the traders.

References

Allen, J. (2004). The whereabouts of power: Politics, government and space. *Geografiska Annaler, Series B: Human Geography, 86*, 19–32. doi:10.1111/geob.2004.86.issue-1

Bayat, A. (1997). Un-civil society: The politics of the 'informal people'. *Third World Quarterly, 18*, 53–72. doi:10.1080/01436599715055

Bayat, A. (2004). Globalization and the politics of the informals in the global South. In A. Roy & N. Alsayyad (Eds.), *Urban informality: Transnational perspectives from the Middle East, Latin America, and South Asia* (pp. 79–102). Lanham, MD: Lexington Books.

Beall, J., Crankshaw, O., & Parnell, S. (Eds.). (2002). *Uniting a divided city. Governance and social exclusion in Johannesburg.* London: Earthscan.

Beavon, K. S. O., & Rogerson, C. M. (1980). The persistence of the casual poor in Johannesburg. *Contree: Journal of South African Urban and Regional History, 7*, 15–21.

Beavon, K. S. O., & Rogerson, C. M. (1982). The informal sector of the apartheid city: The pavement people of Johannesburg. In D. M. Smith (Ed.), *Living under apartheid: Aspects of urbanisation and social change in South Africa* (pp. 106–123). London: George Allen and Unwin.

Bénit-Gbaffou, C. (Ed.). (2014). *A political landscape of street trading organizations in inner city Johannesburg, post Operation Clean Sweep.* Johannesburg: CUBES research report, University of the Witwatersrand.

Bénit-Gbaffou, C. (Ed.). (2015). *In quest of sustainable models of street trading management. Lessons for Johannesburg after Operation Clean Sweep.* Johannesburg: CUBES research report, University of the Witwatersrand.

Bénit-Gbaffou, C., Dubresson, A., Fourchard, L., Ginisty, K., Jaglin, S., Olukoju, A., … Vivet, J. (2013). Exploring the role of party politics in the governance of African Cities. In S. Bekker & L. Fourchard (Eds.), *Governing cities in Africa. Politics and policies* (pp. 17–41). Cape Town: HSRC Press.

Bond, P. (2005). *Elite transition: From apartheid to neoliberalism in South Africa.* Pietermaritzburg: University of KwaZulu-Natal Press.

Bond, P. (2007). Introduction: Two economies – Or one system of superexploitation. *Africanus, 37*(2), 1–21.

Brown, A. (Ed.). (2006). *Contested space: Street trading, public space, and livelihoods in developing cities.* Rugby: ITDG Publishing.

Çelik, E. (2010). *Street traders: A bridge between trade unions and social movements in contemporary South Africa.* Baden-Baden: Nomos.

City of Johannesburg. (2007). *Inner city regeneration charter.* Johannesburg: City of Johannesburg Metropolitan Municipality.

City of Johannesburg. (2009). *Informal trading policy for the City of Johannesburg.* Johannesburg: City of Johannesburg Metropolitan Municipality.

City of Johannesburg. (2011). *Joburg 2040: Growth and development strategy.* Johannesburg: City of Johannesburg Metropolitan Municipality.

City of Johannesburg (JDA). (2009). *Inner city BRT station precinct analysis. Market research.* Main report prepared by Demacon, Pretoria.

Coalition of Johannesburg Street Traders (facilitated by COSATU). (2011), Position on street trading (as prepared for the GDS 24–29 Sept 2011, Johannesburg). Document produced at the workshop in preparation for the GDS 2040 outreach process. Original in the possession of the author.

Coquery-Vidrovitch, C. (1991). L'informel dans les villes Africaines: Essai d'analyse historique et sociale [The informal in African cities: Historical and social analysis]. In C. Coquery-Vidrovitch & S. Nedelec (Eds.), *Tiers-mondes: L'informel en question* [Third world: The informal in question] (pp. 170–196). Paris: L'Harmattan.

Cornwall, A. (2008). Unpacking 'participation': Models, meanings and practices. *Community Development Journal, 43*, 269–283. doi:10.1093/cdj/bsn010

Davies, R., & Thurlow, J. (2009). *Formal-informal economy linkages and unemployment in South Africa.* Cape Town: Centre for Poverty Employment and Growth, HSRC.

De Soto, H. (1989). *The other path: The economic answer to terrorism.* New York, NY: Basic Books.

De Soto, H. (2000). *The mystery of capital: Why capitalism triumphs in the West and fails everywhere else.* London: Bantam.

Devey, R., Lebani, L., Skinner, C., & Valodia, I. (2007). The informal economy. In A. Kraak & K. Press (Eds.), *Human resources development review 2008* (pp. 111–133). Cape Town: HSRC Press.

Dewar, D. (2005). A conceptual framework for the formulation of an informal trader policy for South African towns and cities. *Urban Forum, 16*, 1–16. doi:10.1007/s12132-005-0013-0

Didier, S., Morange, M., & Peyroux, E. (2013). The adaptative nature of neoliberalism at the local scale: Fifteen years of city improvement districts in Cape Town and Johannesburg. *Antipode, 45*, 121–139. doi:10.1111/anti.2013.45.issue-1

Didier, S., Peyroux, E., & Morange, M. (2012). The spreading of the city improvement district model in Johannesburg and Cape Town: Urban regeneration and the neoliberal agenda in South Africa. *International Journal of Urban and Regional Research, 36*, 915–935. doi:10.1111/ijur.2012.36.issue-5

ESSET (Ecumenical Service for Socio-Economic Transformation). (2012, May 23). The City of Johannesburg has lied about reaching amicable agreement with informal traders [Statement]. Retrieved from http://esset-esset.blogspot.com/2012_05_01_archive.html

Frye, I. (2007). The 'second economy' as intellectual sleight of hand. *Africanus, 37*(2), 175–190.

Gauteng Provincial Government. (2011). *Gauteng Employment Growth and Development Strategy (GEGDS).* Johannesburg: Gauteng Department of Economic Development.

GJMC (Greater Johannesburg Metropolitan Council). (2001). *Joburg 2030: Johannesburg's economic development strategy.* Johannesburg: Corporate Planning Unit, GJMC.

Hagmann, T., & Péclard, D. (2010). Negotiating statehood: Dynamics of power and domination in Africa. *Development and Change, 41*, 539–562. doi:10.1111/dech.2010.41.issue-4

Hansen, K. T., & Vaa, M. (Eds.). (2004). *Reconsidering informality: Perspectives from urban Africa.* Uppsala: Nordiska Afrikainstitutet.

Hart, K. (2008). *Between bureaucracy and the people: A political history of informality* (DIIS Working Paper No. 2008/27). Copenhagen: Danish Institute for International Studies.

Hlela, K. (2003). *Formal policies and informal power: Johannesburg's street traders* (Policy Brief 26). Johannesburg: Centre for Policy Studies.

ILO (International Labour Office). (2002). *Decent work and the informal economy.* Geneva: ILO Department of Statistics.

ILO. (2012). *Statistical update on employment in the informal economy.* Geneva: ILO Department of Statistics.

ILO. (2013). *The informal economy and decent work: A policy resource guide supporting transitions to formality.* Geneva: ILO Employment Policy Department.

Jenkins, P. (2004). Beyond the formal/informal dichotomy: Access to land in Maputo, Mozambique. In K. T. Hansen & M. Vaa (Eds.), *Reconsidering informality: Perspectives from urban Africa* (pp. 210–226). Uppsala: Nordiska Afrikainstitutet.

Lindell, I. (2008). The multiple sites of urban governance: Insights from an African city. *Urban Studies, 45*, 1879–1901. doi:10.1177/0042098008093382

Lindell, I. (2010a). Introduction: The changing politics of informality – Collective organizing, alliances and scales of engagement. In I. Lindell (Ed.), *Africa's informal workers: Collective agency, alliances and transnational organizing in urban Africa* (pp. 1–30). London and Uppsala: Zed Books and The Nordic Africa Institute.

Lindell, I. (2010b). Between exit and voice: Informality and the spaces of popular agency. *African Studies Quarterly, 11*(2/3), 1–11.

Matjomane, M. D. (2013). *Strategies used by street traders' organisations to influence trading policy and management in the City of Johannesburg* (Unpublished master's thesis). University of the Witwatersrand, Johannesburg.

Meagher, K. (1995). Crisis, informalization and the urban informal sector in sub-Saharan Africa. *Development and Change, 26*, 259–284. doi:10.1111/dech.1995.26.issue-2

Meagher, K. (2009). *Culture, agency and power: Theoretical reflections on informal economic networks and political process* (DIIS Working Paper No. 2009/27). Copenhagen: Danish Institute for International Studies.

Meagher, K. (2010). The politics of vulnerability: Exit, voice and capture in three Nigerian informal manufacturing clusters. In I. Lindell (Ed.), *Africa's informal workers: Collective agency, alliances and transnational organizing in urban Africa* (pp. 46–64). London and Uppsala: Zed Books and The Nordic Africa Institute.

Meagher, K., & Lindell, I. (2013). ASR forum: Engaging with African informal economies: Social inclusion or adverse incorporation? Introduction. *African Studies Review, 56*(3), 57–76. doi:10.1017/asr.2013.79

Motshegwa, L. (2011a, October 4). Norwood street traders given the boot. *North Eastern Tribune.*

Motshegwa, L. (2011b, October 20). National Traders' Alliance fight for street traders. *North Eastern Tribune.*

Murray, M. J. (2008). *Taming the disorderly city: The spatial landscape of Johannesburg after apartheid.* Ithaca, NY: Cornell University Press.

Murray, M. J. (2011). *City of extremes: The spatial politics of Johannesburg.* Johannesburg: Wits University Press.

Olivier de Sardan, J. P. (2008). *Researching the practical norms of real governance in Africa* (Discussion Paper 5). London: Africa Power and Politics Programme.

Olivier de Sardan, J. P. (2014). Abandoning the neo-patrimonialist paradigm: For a pluralist approach to the bureaucratic mode of governance in Africa. In L. Koechlin & T. Förster (Eds.), *The politics of governance: Actors and articulations in Africa and beyond* (pp. 75–92). New York, NY: Routledge.

Peyroux, E. (2008). City improvement districts in Johannesburg: An examination of the local variations of the BID model. In R. Pütz (Ed.). *Business improvement districts: Ein neues Governance-Modell aus Perspektive von Praxis und Stadtforschung* [A new model of governance from the perspective of practice and urban research] (pp. 139–162), (Geographische Handelsforschung, 14). Passau: L.I.S. Verlag.

Pongoma, L. (2012, May 17). Informal traders rubbish 'deal' with Johannesburg. *The New Age Online.* Retrieved from http://www.thenewage.co.za/50962-1009-53-Informal_traders_rubbish_deal_with_Johannesburg

Potts, D. (2008). The urban informal sector in sub-Saharan Africa: From bad to good (and back again?). *Development Southern Africa, 25*, 151–167. doi:10.1080/03768350802090527

Rogerson, C. M. (1990). Informal sector retailing in the South African city: The case of Johannesburg. In A. M. Findlay (Ed.), *Retailing environments in developing countries* (pp. 118–137). London: Routledge.

Rogerson, C. M., & Beavon, K. S. O. (1985). A tradition of repression: The street traders of Johannesburg. In R. Bromley (Ed.), *Planning for small enterprises in third world cities* (pp. 223–245). Oxford: Pergamon Press.

Rogerson, C. M., & Hart, D. M. (1989). The struggle for the streets: Deregulation and hawking in South Africa's major urban areas. *Social Dynamics, 15*(1), 29–45. doi:10.1080/02533958908458459

Rothchild, D., & Chazan, N. (Eds.). (1988). *The precarious balance: State and society in Africa.* Boulder, CO: Westview Press.

Roy, A. (2005). Urban informality: Toward an epistemology of planning. *Journal of the American Planning Association, 71*, 147–158. doi:10.1080/01944360508976689

Sharp, J. P., Routledge, P., Philo, C., & Paddison, R. (2000). *Entanglements of power: Geographies of domination/resistance.* London: Routledge.

Skinner, C. (2008). *Street trade in Africa: A review* (Wiego Working Paper No 5). Manchester: Women in Informal Employment: Globalising and Organising.

Statistics South Africa. (2015). *National and provincial labour market: The informal sector, Q2: 2008–Q2: 2014.* Statistical release P0211.4.3.

Steck, J.-F., Didier, S., Morange, M., & Rubin, M. (2013). Informality, public space and urban governance: An approach through street trading (Abidjan, Cape Town, Johannesburg, Lomé and Nairobi). In S. Bekker & L. Fourchard (Eds.), *Governing Cities in Africa. Politics and Policies* (pp. 145–167). Cape Town: HSRC Press.

Thulare, P. (2004). *Trading democracy? Johannesburg informal traders and citizenship* (Policy: Issues & Actors, vol. 17, no. 1). Johannesburg: Centre for Policy Studies.

Tissington, K. (2009). *The business of survival: Informal trading in Inner City Johannesburg.* Johannesburg: Centre for Applied Legal Studies.

Williams, J. J. (2006). Community participation: Lessons from post-apartheid South Africa. *Policy Studies, 27*, 197–217. doi:10.1080/01442870600885982

Remaking Africa's Informal Economies: Youth, Entrepreneurship and the Promise of Inclusion at the Bottom of the Pyramid

CATHERINE DOLAN* & DINAH RAJAK**

*Anthropology, SOAS, University of London, London, UK, **Anthropology and Development, School of Global Studies, University of Sussex, Brighton, UK

ABSTRACT *In recent years, the quest for 'inclusive markets' that incorporate Africa's youth has become a key focus of national and international development efforts, with so-called bottom of the pyramid (BoP) initiatives increasingly seen as a way to draw the continent's poor into new networks of global capitalism. SSA has become a fertile frontier for such systems, as capital sets its sights on the continents' vast 'under-served' informal economies, harnessing the entrepreneurial mettle of youth to create new markets for a range of products, from solar lanterns and shampoo to cook stoves and sanitary pads. Drawing on ethnographic research with youth entrepreneurs, we trace the processes of individual and collective 'transformation' that the mission of (self-) empowerment through entrepreneurship seeks to bring about. We argue that, while such systems are meant to bring those below the poverty line above it, the 'line' is reified and reinforced through a range of discursive and strategic practices that actively construct and embed distinctions between the past and the future, valuable and valueless, and the idle and productive in Africa's informal economies.*

1. Introduction

In recent years, urban youth have emerged as a major focus in development agendas. At times condemned as a lost generation of deprived, restless agents of lawlessness, at others celebrated as resilient, creative, flexible catalysts of grass-roots capitalism, they are the subject of contradictory moral discourses that paint them as both the obstacle and panacea to development. Prospects of formal employment in Africa's shrinking blue-collar sector have receded, leaving the growing population of urban youth at the margins of formal markets, reliant on the 'second economy', a vast reservoir of energy to be simultaneously contained and converted into appropriate human capital. With hopes of formal jobs fading fast (together with the commitment of governments to provide them), the quest for 'inclusive markets' that incorporate Africa's youth has become a key focus of national and international development efforts, with so-called bottom of the pyramid (BoP) initiatives (Prahalad, 2004) increasingly seen as a way to draw the continent's poor into new networks of global capitalism (Blowfield & Dolan, 2014; Eade & Sayer, 2006; Rajak, 2011). Cast variously as enterprising solutions to poverty, inclusive business or microenterprise, BoP initiatives champion youth (and women) as the untapped frontier of enterprising energy, an army of aspirant entrepreneurs who serve at the vanguard of economic growth and poverty reduction by selling goods and services door-to-door. The BoP win–win promises to conjure individual agency from economic disenfranchisement, offering up entrepreneurship in place of employment. Crucially, it is a moral mission that not only catalyses the transformation of the individual into industrious entrepreneurial citizen, but charges them with the responsibility of bringing about a second order of moral transformation, that is, serving the wider societal project of 'good growth', a double moral injunction for the 'poor to help themselves' in order to help the economy (Elyachar, 2002, p. 500).

This celebration of grass-roots capitalism is not new (see, for example, Blim, 2005), nor is the elevation of the twin targets of microentrepreneurship (with which development has had a very long engagement) and youth as the embodiment of development. What is of particular interest, we suggest, is that while this new paradigm of development places the 'raw entrepreneurial energy of the people' (Chang, 2010, p. 53) at the heart of economic growth, we see a significant shift from earlier framings of African entrepreneurialism in which it was cast as innate (even indigenous), needing only to be unleashed,[1] to an emphasis on training, disciplining and transformation, driven as much from without as from within. A key focus now, is on the *making* of the microentrepreneur as a pivotal economic agent that must be brought into being through the assistance of external agencies. While the entrepreneurial spirit may reside in all, liberating the inner entrepreneur is not a matter of simply removing the constraints on market access and thereby 'democratising the market'. But, rather, what we find here is a great emphasis on training at a practical, psychological and moral level to produce this army of entrepreneurs who are enjoined to relinquish the quest for formal employment and go from 'job-seeker' to 'job-creator'. The entrepreneur emerges as both beneficiary and catalyst, producer and product of this new economy of development.

The result of this focus on 'producing' entrepreneurs (and entrepreneurialism), has been the advent of a range of practical new enterprise initiatives (commonly driven by multinational business) which aim to galvanise a generation of 'precocious entrepreneurs', animating individual aspirations to 'make good on the promises of the free market' (newly re-rendered as the *inclusive* market) (Comaroff & Comaroff, 2000, p. 308). This vision of a personalised economy of development is certainly compelling, shifting the focus from macroeconomic restructuring to a more humanised focus on individual self-actualisation. Autonomy, ingenuity, self-mastery, home-grown innovation and freedom from the dependence of aid and welfare are just some of the moral and social goods that this discourse of new entrepreneurship in development lays claim to as both the driver and product.

It is no surprise then that youth entrepreneurship has gained such traction among a broad constellation of actors. From national governments to international financial institutions, donor agencies and NGOs, from big business to start-ups, diverse actors with varying interests are rallying behind the potential of BoP enterprise to discipline, and at the same time unleash, a new generation of African microentrepreneurs. Out of this constellation, novel partnerships and hybrids are emerging as the vehicles for stimulating and leveraging the productive power of youth entrepreneurship and facilitating access to market opportunities. Through an ethnographic case study of one such hybrid, a social enterprise aimed at youth empowerment in Kenya, this article examines the values, expectations, material practices and outcomes of the entrepreneurial project. Drawing on ethnographic research conducted in 2012–2013 with youth entrepreneurs, we trace the processes and routines of individual and collective 'transformation' that the mission of (self-) empowerment through microenterprise seeks to bring about.[2]

Operating at the borders of hope and despair, we ask to what extent do these schemes deliver meaningful possibilities of inclusion and mobility through market opportunity, or merely the elusive (and highly exclusive) hope of success (James, 2011, p. 334)? We suggest that if we look beyond the allure of entrepreneurial possibility we find a model of economic development that depends almost entirely on consumption – or more specifically retail – as the engine of a jobless growth, offering contingent opportunity in place of secure employment. While the development discourse of BoP entrepreneurship with its heroic self-starter is enticing, the life it conjures and validates can be risk-ridden and precarious, spinning survivalism into resilience, and 'getting by' into resourcefulness, leaving individuals responsible for seeking 'their own *individual* solutions to the *socially* produced troubles' (Bauman, 2004, p. 90, emphasis by author).

We begin, in the first section, by looking at the broader backdrop of mass joblessness, rapid urbanisation, an expanding young population and informal markets, against which BoP enterprise has emerged as a key strategy for turning social crisis into economic opportunity. We then turn to our case study to explore the concrete processes, technologies and rituals of training and socialisation through which the values, skills and opportunities of BoP business are transmitted and embedded, converting 'yesterday's "criminal" into tomorrow's "entrepreneur"' (Heron, 2011, p. 2). We argue that, while such systems are meant to bring those below the poverty line above it, the 'line' is reified and reinforced through a range of discursive and strategic practices that actively construct and embed distinctions between the past and the future, valuable and valueless, idle and productive. In the final section we consider how (and whether) these broader ideals of entrepreneurship are internalised as personal expectations of 'making it' among those who have been recruited to the ranks of young entrepreneurs. Ultimately, we ask, to what extent these aspirations translate into experiences of material success and mobility, or persist as dreams deferred.

2. A Trinity of Despair (and Hope): Urbanisation, Unemployment and Youth Enterprise

Two decades of jobless growth across much of sub-Saharan Africa, but most significantly in those countries feted as the continent's engines of growth (South Africa, Nigeria, Kenya) has left young people with little meaningful hope of formal, let alone, secure employment. As Meagher (this issue) highlights, the reduction in jobs has disproportionately affected young job-seekers, with the rate of youth unemployment across Africa on average twice that of the adult population. In Kenya, young people between the ages of 15 and 34 make up 80 per cent of the 2.3 million unemployed, while 15–29 year olds account for around 30 per cent of those categorised by the OECD as 'poor' (OECD, n.d.). The importance of these statistics, and the crisis they portend, became apparent in the nation's post-2007 election violence, when the 'youth problem' figured prominently in the conflagration that erupted across the country (World Bank, 2007).[3] As Page (2012, p. 5) warns, the social and political ramifications of chronic mass joblessness are manifest:

> Africa is not creating the number of jobs needed to absorb the 10–12 million young people entering its labour markets each year, and as recent events in North Africa have shown, lack of employment opportunities in the face of a rapidly growing, young labour force can undermine social cohesion and political stability.

Indeed the problem of youth unemployment, as both economic and social crisis, is intimately linked with that of rapid unplanned urbanisation, resulting in new exclusionary processes of citizenship that are contiguous with profound spatial inequalities (Robinson, 1997). Over the past 20 years, rural poverty and conflict have driven migrants to urban areas across Africa, and the rate of urbanisation (the highest in the developing world at 3.5%) shows no signs of slowing over the next 20 years (Ncube, 2012). More than 70 per cent of Africa's urban population lives in slums – around 200 million people – the majority of whom are between the ages of 15 and 24 (Palitza, 2013). Kenya is no exception: Nairobi is home to approximately 2.5 million slum dwellers, 60 per cent of the citiy's population, tightly clustered in about 200 informal settlements (APHRC, 2014).[4] Lacking in basic infrastructure and services – sewerage, waste management, workable roads, water and power, as well as clinics, schools and security services – these informal conurbations are both literally and figuratively 'off the grid'. As spaces marked by the absence of formal state presence and development planning, they are viewed commonly in public and political discourse as repositories of lawlessness, crime and squalor, re-engaging a centuries-old 'fear that the accumulation of the 'redundant' inside the cities would reach a critical point of self-combustion' (Bauman, 2004, p. 37). Yet, alongside the commonplace fear of slums as a threat to social and political order, we find a contrary representation of informal settlements as sites of market opportunities, created precisely through their abandonment by formal development processes. The combination of chronic impermanence and lack of jobs is seen to open novel possibilities for the private sector to fill the void, offering consumable products in place of services or infrastructure (for example, solar lamps instead of power lines) and entrepreneurial opportunities in place of jobs for those willing to sell them (Cross, 2013; Dolan & Roll, 2013; Redfield, 2012). Such entrepreneurial opportunities are converting Kenya's growing youth population from a liability to an opportunity (Obonyo, 2013), as new models of empowerment through enterprise bring unemployed youth to the market, and market thinking to young people.

The emphasis on re-siting youth as a reservoir of entrepreneurial talent has neatly aligned with efforts afoot to 'modernise' and 'upgrade' Africa's 'underproductive' informal economies (Tokman, 2007), where as much as 72 per cent of sub-Saharan African workers can be found (Sparks & Barnett, 2010). Departing from earlier depictions of the informal economy as a space of disorder and dysfunction, a haven of tax evaders and illicit enterprises that were a 'drag on growth', informality has been rescripted as a potential palliative to Africa's development ills (Dolan & Roll, 2013; Elyachar, 2005; Meagher, 2013; see also; De Soto, 2000). Aid agencies, regional development banks and national governments seek not to contain Africa's spaces of informality but to free them, seeking ways to unlock and redirect their pool of 'natural' assets – resourcefulness, ingenuity, opportunism and socially embedded webs of economic exchange – into new avenues of job creation and economic renewal. A new model of inclusive business – the bottom of the pyramid – offered one such way, creating new markets for goods and services while simultaneously capturing and capitalising on the individual energy and 'collective social capital' of Africa's burgeoning informal economies.

3. Moving the Line: Entrepreneurship at the BoP

Originally conceived by the late CK Prahalad in his seminal work, *The Fortune at the Bottom of the Pyramid: Eradicating Poverty through Profits* (2004), the BoP proposition contends that multinational corporations facing saturated markets in industrialised nations can offset sclerotic growth rates, earn profits and reduce poverty by marketing goods and services to regions excluded from the reach of global markets. The concept, most often associated with corporate giants such as P&G, SK Johnson and Unilever that market consumer goods through micro, often 'door-to-door', rural distribution systems, has evolved beyond MNCs over the past decade to include organisations of varying sizes, levels of capitalisation and ideological orientation, from global manufacturing giants to small social enterprises and non-profit organisations (see review by Kolk, Rivera-Santos, & Rufin, 2014). Indeed, what was originally a model premised on a 'central, controlling corporate apparatus' (Welker, n.d., p. 7) now operates across multiple registers: schemes coalesce an array of actors, materials, knowledge practices and interests; circulate objects of both moral and commercial value, ranging from portable water filtration systems, nutrition supplements, and cook stoves to cosmetics, shampoo and Coca-Cola (Cross, 2013); and traverse diverse geographies from sprawling urban zones of social abandonment (Biehl, 2005) to rural communities living off the grid of infrastructure and beyond the hand the state.

As a model of development, the BoP is a compelling proposition, promising to enfold the poor into new networks of inclusive capitalism. Yet, while seductive in its promise, the phenomenon has attracted relatively little attention from scholars of development. Most analysis, the bulk of which is located in business and management studies, frames engagement at the BoP in instrumental terms, describing how firms like Hewlett-Packard and SK Johnson have turned to 'frontier' markets to generate a 'pro-poor' corporate revenue stream (London & Hart, 2011; Prahalad & Hart, 2002; Prahalad, 2004; Simanis & Hart, 2008), and how a new breed of hybrid (for profit/non-profit) enterprises are driving forward innovations in health, energy, education and water management. Comprised largely of case studies drawn from a small set of industries and companies (Kolk et al., 2014), this literature emphasises the role of strategic management, finance capital, distribution channels and institutional partnerships in shaping the efficacy of BoP enterprises (Hammond et al, 2007); that is, the capacity to deliver profits under the mantle of social purpose. Our article, building on an emergent literature in anthropology (Cross & Street, 2009; Dolan & Johnstone-Louis, 2011; Dolan & Roll, 2013; Elyachar, 2012; Schwittay, 2011), takes a different tack, shifting the lens from the productivity or otherwise of BoP enterprises, that is the question of 'impact', to the cultural economy of BoP entrepreneurship, specifically the forms, practices and meanings through which BoP's project of market-making is enacted. Recent ethnographic work has explored how and with what effects market-led development is assimilating informal economies into the ambit of global markets as geographies of poverty are recast as loci of unmet consumer needs. Dolan and Roll's (2013) exposition of corporate BoP expansion in Africa, for example, describes how business marshals the cultural and knowledge assets of the poor, drawing the less visible worlds of affect and sociality into the process of entrepreneurial innovation. Similarly, Cross and Street (2009) show us how Unilever's marketing of 'accessible' hygiene products (soap) in India reshapes everyday consumption practices, instilling new ways of conceptualising the body, health and personhood in the process of market development (Street & Cross, 2012). Others describe how BoP social enterprises such as Solar Sisters (Davies, 2014) and JITA (Dolan, Johnstone-Louis, & Scott, 2012), and corporate BoP programmes such as British Petroleum (Kay, 2012), Hewlitt Packard (Schwittay, 2011) and Avon (Dolan & Johnstone-Louis, 2011) produce new opportunities for entrepreneurship that not only remake capitalism but the subjectivities and economic lives of the poor. Taken together, this ethnographic analysis points to how inequality and displacement can run alongside the BoP promise of inclusion, raising questions on the exercise and unfolding of 'ethical' business, and its effects on the possibilities individuals envision and realise for themselves and their families.

This article takes up these questions, focusing on the practices business employs to convert the latent dynamism of Africa's informal economies into a usable resource for economic development, by offering youth opportunities to sell a range of products (healthcare, hygiene, consumer goods, energy, food, financial services) to 'poor' consumers. Premised on Avon Corporation's model of door-to-door sales, such 'last mile distribution systems', from Solar Sisters and Living Goods in Uganda, to Health Keepers in Ghana, Yogurt Mamas in Tanzania and Women First Mozambique, are now common features of Africa's development landscape, where a growing number of institutions (for example,, World Bank, USAID, DfID and so forth), support private sector engagement as a way to repurpose 'informal', 'subsistence' or otherwise 'underproductive' workers (see World Bank, 2001). Here, we focus on the opportunities provided by one such initiative – Catalyst[5] – a social enterprise that provides unemployed youth with entrepreneurial opportunities in Kawangware, one of Africa's biggest slums.

Situated on the outskirts of Nairobi, Kawangware is a landscape of constrained possibilities – a labyrinth of makeshift homes where nearly 300,000 residents live 'off the grid' of running water, basic sanitation and electricity (Plan USA, 2012), crafting livelihoods through hustling, peddling and economic ingenuity. Youth under the age of 35, who comprise the majority of the slum's population, face few prospects for employment, a crisis Catalyst's director described as a 'a major problem all over the world' but one that crystallised in Kenya when idle, 'impressionable' youth were readily co-opted into violence following the contested 2007 election. 'It became clear,' she said, that Kenya's under-utilised youth were not only a 'wasted resource' for national development but were fomenting crime and civil unrest in the country (Roopanarine, 2013). They were, she suggested, eating away at Kenya's future, siphoning value from a national project of economic and political renewal.

3.1. The Catalyst Vision

Catalyst's mission is to repurpose Kawangware's reservoir of idle street youth, leveraging their resourcefulness to sell life-improving products in slum communities. Like other BoP distribution systems, Catalyst seeks to mine the entrepreneurial capital honed in Africa's économie de la débrouillardise', what MacGaffey (1991) terms the self-reliance or DIY economy, where livelihoods are crafted through a mélange of hustling, peddling and economic ingenuity. As the director of Catalyst explained, the creativity and cunning required to operate as a trader, vendor or hawker in Kawangware's 'hand-to-mouth economy' is a font of business potential: not only are there millions of unemployed youth endowed with 'incredible raw sales skills' but they are uniquely equipped to solve a 'distribution problem that exists all over the developing world' by selling life-changing goods to untapped, hard to reach markets (cited by Roopanarine, 2013).

Catalyst offers sales training and the prospect of a job to un- and under-employed youth, primarily single parents and 'street kids' between the ages of 18 and 24 who have an intimate familiarity with the nuances, economic strategies and social relations of the slum. Upon successful completion of a two-week training course and evidence of a guarantor, entrepreneurs are eligible to access $75 (£50) worth of products on credit, an arrangement Catalyst describes as 'teaching people how to fish and ... selling fishing rods at the same time' (cited by Miesen, 2013). The organisation operates a daily consignment model: each morning, youth arrive at the office and select an item(s) from an assortment of 30 or so 'life-changing products' such as solar lamps, clean-burning cook stoves, eco-friendly charcoal briquettes and reusable sanitary products, returning the next day to either exchange or replenish their consignment (Interview, 30 April 2013). Agents earn a commission of between 10 and 20 per cent on revenue of the products they sell and a tiered bonus during their first three months.

Catalyst, however, promotes less an opportunity to sell than an entrepreneurial future, a promise of upward mobility that forms the currency of recruitment and business strategies. As the director of Catalyst explained: 'From the beginning we've wanted our sales agents to actually think of themselves as entrepreneurs ... they don't just wake up and sell a product. Every day they need to be making decisions on what product they can sell and where they can sell it.' Though recruits generally come from 'the base' – an informal territory youth occupy in the slum – they are exhorted to define themselves as self-starting entrepreneurs who will find success as up-and-coming businesspeople. As 21-year-old Susan explained, Catalyst was attractive because it offered training and business skills that she could parlay into starting her own business; she would no longer be 'making do' through survivalist activities, but would be 'moving up', 'crossing the line' as a respectable agent of capitalism (Interview, 20 June 2013).

Though Susan conjures the line as a separation between an idle past and prosperous future, the livelihoods of Kawangware's inhabitants are determined by the very permeability of the line between informal and formal markets, between the second economy and the kind of formal entrepreneurial activity that is recognised in the new lexicon of BoP business. Yet, as we will explore in the next section, the processes by which aspirant entrepreneurs are recruited, trained and brought into the Catalyst fold aim to sharpen these lines, translating them into normative boundaries which aspiring entrepreneurs are enjoined to cross in order to access the much-anticipated fruits of the 'inclusive' market.

4. The Entrepreneurial Conversion

At the centre of this project of economic progress and social improvement is an ideal entrepreneur, one who can respond to the moral exhortation to 'help oneself' by embracing the opportunities provided by business initiatives such as Catalyst, to become, as Gordon (1991, p. 44) puts it, 'an entrepreneur of himself or herself'. But before aspirant youth can seize these opportunities, they must be acculturated into the values and virtues of maximisation necessary to equip them for market enterprise. As the director of Catalyst explained, youth need to be 'rigorously shaped' to serve at the frontline of BoP markets: 'They might not be what traditionally we consider employable but after learning how to wake up on time and show up on time and report to a manager and, you know, talk to customers and present themselves, they are.' Indeed, though informal economies are often celebrated for their natural affinity for entrepreneurship, what the Shell Foundation (2005) terms their 'business DNA', in practice entrepreneurial subjectivities and the attendant virtues of responsibility, competition, and risk-taking are whetted.

This occurs through discursive practices that valorise enterprising qualities and promise self-transformation to those who will 'pull themselves up by their boot straps' (Mayoux, 2002, p. 23), as well as through management technologies that seek to inscribe and hone the requisite traits of industry, market discipline and entrepreneurial distinction to succeed in business. In the following, we explore how these techniques – rituals of readiness (training and role plays); professionalisation (bodily discipline); and performance (monitoring and metrics) – seed new norms, dispositions and habits among 'informal' youth in the slum, creating a cadre of entrepreneurs to drive forward BoP's vision of inclusive capitalism.

4.1. Rituals of Readiness: Training and Role Plays

In order to attain the emancipatory and transformative power of the market, a conversion is required, and social enterprises like Catalyst often devote considerable resources to fostering entrepreneurial readiness, tutoring workers' in the principles, goals and ethics of the market (Dolan & Johnstone-Louis, 2011). At the heart of this endeavour, exclaimed one of Catalyst's lead entrepreneurs is 'Training, training, training!' The didactic promise extended to potential recruits relies not solely (or even chiefly) in the lure of immediate material benefits, but in its derivative values: the intangibles of self-empowerment, infusion of the entrepreneurial spirit, and the tantalising prospect of 'making it'. Like many such youth entrepreneur schemes, Catalyst training combines the more prosaic tools and techniques of frontline selling and fluency in the salesperson's patter (knowing the product, reading the customer), with the loftier goals of self-actualisation. Trainers kick off this process of socialisation, underscoring the importance of self-knowledge as the basis for self-realisation:

> Who are you? Are you a choleric or sanguine or a phlegmatic…? We would like to know who you are…Who knows self? Who knows self? [Silence] I am waiting for you to tell me who knows who they are?… There are four groups of personalities. You have to know where you fall under.

The claim, according to Catalyst trainers and managers, is that recruits do not simply learn how to sell Catalyst products door-to-door; rather, they transform themselves. 'Making the economic habitus', as Bourdieu suggests, is not a process of adaptation but of conversion (Bourdieu, 2000, p. 23), in this case to an entrepreneurial rationality: a spirit of calculation and competition, individual self-maximisation, autonomy from the sticky web of dependence on others, self-discipline and, at the same time, risk-taking and opportunism.

The transformation from jobless youth to young entrepreneur is imagined as an overtly moral transformation: 'the guy came to me and said, we want to change your life, if you are interested in changing your life we can do something with you,' a Catalyst entrepreneur recounted, explaining how he had joined. In turn, entrepreneurs present their own stories as testimonies of former lives of grift and hawking forsaken in favour of the redemption offered by true entrepreneurship. These accounts serve as allegorical parables of self-improvement and salvation for future recruits, delineating what is to be considered 'work', while delegitimising petty trade in the informal economy as unproductive, and even economically subversive. Built on the moral certainty of binaries that juxtapose productivity with informality and twin idleness with vice as the chief obstacle to personal and societal progress, these narratives resonate with a strongly Victorian condemnation of indolence as the source of under-development (Smiles, 2002 [1859]). This is exemplified in Silas's story as he told it:

> People in the community were used to seeing me idling around … these days it is not easy to find me because when I leave the house at 7.30 am … I will go to the field and I will market the products as much as I can … people see you as a different person when they see that you can work. They look at you as someone who is hard working. They look at you as someone who is responsible and independent … I have avoided so many bad things I could do in the village. Let me give an example with today … I left home very early, I came to Catalyst and I will get back home very late in the evening. I will take a bath when I get home and take a rest unlike the previous days when I used to think of so many evil things as a result of being idle, (Interview, 27 June 2013)

Indeed Silas's juxtaposition of industry and idleness and clock time and 'African time' is a key marker of the entrepreneurial transition. Aspirant entrepreneurs are expected to master the mechanics of timekeeping, calibrating schedules, prioritising tasks, adhering to deadlines, and making rational decisions about the temporal flow of their days by, for example, spending money on a *matatu* instead of walking or exercising self-control over how long they choose to linger in conversation. Punctuality is taken as a marker of a keen eye, or strong grip, on the future (Bourdieu, 2000, p. 28), drawing a symbolic and material 'boundary' between an aimless past and an abundant future (Rose, 1999). Drilling on time-management and future planning plays a key role in training sessions, both as markers of professionalism and a broader self-mastery:

> If you are told to come to work at 9 am ... what time should you be here? You should be here by 9 am. When some of you come in at 9.30 am... if we entertain you then we will be entertaining a bad habit ... we are preparing you ... *we are preparing you not to be good for Catalyst but for yourself.* (Training, 21 June 2013, emphasis by author)

Time-keeping is one of the more material attributes of the entrepreneurial habitus – alongside dress, gait, style and speech – that Catalyst agents must adopt and perform as markers of their graduation to the status of entrepreneur. At the same time, alongside the celebrated values of self-mastery and discipline, training sessions stressed the somewhat less romantic virtues of grit, sweat and discipline. Though BoP initiatives truck in the promise of self-transformation, they do not, as Comaroff and Comaroff (2000, p. 313) suggest of millennial capitalism, dangle 'the allure of accruing wealth from nothing'. Trainers reiterated time and again, almost as a mantra, 'you have to be very hardworking and not lazing around', an injunction that reminded entrepreneurs that the fruits of the BoP dream were borne through toil and endurance. As a Catalyst trainer emphasised:

> What you are going to do is be prepared. When you go home at night practise with your partner, practise with your friends and practise with your family ... When you are on a football team you do not just show up and play the game, you practise. Right? So when you go out there practise. Don't just sit there and say 'I am going to be great.' The best people, they work hard in whatever they do to achieve what they want. (Training, 21 June 2013)

At the same time, trainers made clear the responsibility incumbent on trainees to make good on the opportunity Catalyst provides. Should they fail to do so, either because of laziness or incompetence, they have only themselves to blame. The opportunity, trainees were told, was much deeper than merely selling products for Catalyst. Rather, through Catalyst, trainees would learn the essence of self-help itself:

> The opportunity you have and the way you will behave ... will connect you to something else. To another thing that might be better. There are so many ways that will open for you while you are still here at Catalyst ... what you should know is that I am not training you to be a failure ... I am, training you so that you can help yourself. (Training, 21 June 2013)

Entrepreneurs are thus apprenticed in the values and transferable skills to join an emergent cadre of Nairobi's young businesspeople, turned from job-seekers, not merely into employees but into job-creators (albeit within the short timeframe of a 10-day training course): 'even when I get out of Catalyst I will use the experience and the skills that I will have gained to start up and run my own business, Susan, a new recruit, explained. Here we see a doubling of the BoP's value proposition; recruits are exhorted not to see the fast cash rewards of peddling solar lanterns as the apotheosis of their entrepreneurial tenure, but rather as a stepping-stone to the much sought after but highly elusive future as a small business owner. This anticipatory future, transfused into entrepreneurs through trainings, has its own productive effects, focusing attention beyond the turbulences of the everyday and rendering failure in the here and now as constitutive of future possibilities.

Helping oneself is also twinned with the broader ethical vision of improving life in the slum, as it is only through selling life-enhancing products that the entrepreneurial self can be actualised. Catalyst trainers presented the role of the newly transformed entrepreneur as an ambassador/evangelist spreading the virtues and opportunities of small business to the 'community' through their engagement with customers and through the social benefit of the products themselves. Catalyst represents itself as 'a solution for a better life' and its sales agents as brokers of a new BoP trickle down of entrepreneurial values and the promise (if not the reality) of material gain. Using role-play on selling solar chargers, Silas showed how this was to be done:

> Silas: Another thing is that you can use it to charge your phone...
> Woman 1: So I can use it in my rural home to charge my phone? And I can also use it to charge other people's phone there at a fee?
> Silas: Yes ... It can be a business.
> Woman 1: I can open up a small shop out there and start up a phone charging business.
> Silas: As long as you have the sun.

The emphasis on the mutuality of personal and societal transformation that Silas embraces, however, obscures the panoply of technologies and concrete practices through which self-empowerment is to be materialised. Despite earlier invitations for trainees to reflect on what kind of person they are, to pursue a quest for self-actualisation, in the end, trainees are enjoined to focus on 'doing' rather than 'thinking' in order to demonstrate their suitability for Catalyst and their readiness to enter the market. On the final day of a training course, the trainer addressed the room of recruits:

> If you want to work say it ... Who is still searching within yourself if you are ready to go to the field? [One youth rises up his hand.] You are still thinking? If you are still thinking then I think we will tell you that we are very sorry for having wasted all your time ... We are very serious here ... I do not want people who are thinking. I want people who are ready to work. (Training, 21 June 2013)

Catalyst draws on a repertoire of corporate management tools such as team building, role-plays and motivational rituals to ensure that doing rather than thinking is patterned into the structure of the day. In the morning, youth gather for a 'briefing', where they are called upon to recount the successes and failures of the previous day. Those with sales are singled out, invited to share the algorithm of their success, and recognised with applause from the group. Entrepreneurs then stretch, cultivating their corporeal agility for walking long hours under a hot sun, and before departing partake in a ceremonial bonding (reminiscent of sports teams before a game), placing their hands together and at the count of three raising their hands in unison and chanting 'Catalyst!' Each day youth re-enact these rituals that aim to reanimate individual drive, and impart a stake in the collection vision of the group.

Similarly, the rituals of readiness include frequent role plays, where participants perform mock sales in a staged setting to give neophyte entrepreneurs an opportunity to rehearse their sales pitch. Though role plays are meant to develop and hone entrepreneurial skills, they also muddy the distinction between discipline and self-improvement. During trainings each trainee assumes a seat alone in the front of the room and improvises a sale to a fictional customer, played by the trainer. At one training session, a steady stream of fledgling entrepreneurs enacted myriad strategies to persuade reluctant customers of the merits of cookstoves and solar lanterns. Though some managed creditable performances, most stumbled to articulate a compelling storyline, inviting heckling from team members and often unforgiving criticism from trainers, who reminded trainees of the fragility of the BoP opportunity: 'In the afternoon we are going out there to sell. Right now I will be eliminating some of you. If you will not be doing it very well today, I will not compromise with you. I want to be left with few people who will deliver. ... You see we are getting less and less as the end approaches.' Indeed, while BoP's 'democratisation' of opportunity implies universal inclusion, not all are chosen, as training, role plays and performance metrics aim to sift out the potentially savvy from the lacklustre entrepreneur, drawing a line between those who generate value and those who are likely to take it away.

4.2. Professionalism

This process of classification – stratifying the entrepreneurial cohort through what Aganost terms 'value coding' – materialises most visibly in the professionalisation of bodily appearance, dress and speech. Deportment crafts a distinction between entrepreneurialism and 'salesman': the former associated with professionalism, upward mobility and status, the latter with no status, meagre commissions and hawking, as one agent put it: 'some think that working as a house help is way better than walking and working as a sales agent'. During training. youth are told that voices should be loud, projection clear, carriage upright, lest people wonder 'how the security guard' let the entrepreneur in. Slouching is disparaged. Smiling and positivity are encouraged, so that entrepreneurs will radiate the transformational possibilities that inhere in the goods they sell. As a supervisor instructed an entrepreneur during a role play, 'You should look so happy as you are giving them the product, so that when they are getting the product, they will feel like you are giving them a [birthday] present' (Training, 21 June 2013). One of the main ways professionalism is forged is through deportment, and in particular through the donning of branded uniforms, identification cards and bags. As entrepreneur Maggie put it, you can't just 'walk around with your product like a hawker showing it to everyone. You walk like a professional' (Interview, 16 June 2013). Uniforms, especially, are a signature feature of 'moving up', signalling the kind of person a BoP entrepreneur is, and conversely, the kind of person they are not (Dolan & Johnstone-Louis, 2011). As a Catalyst entrepreneur said, 'first impressions matter a lot'. The uniform, she said, gives her clout, makes her look professional, and signals to others that she is trustworthy – not a 'hawker' or 'con man'. 'When people see me in uniform,' she said, 'they think that I have a very good job and earn very good money,', repositioning her as a 'hard-working' member of society, as someone who is on the 'up and up' (Interview, 20 June 2013).

Indeed, among BoP entrepreneurial schemes, 'proper' dress is a synecdoche of market success and is emphasised in organisational communications. As one trainer described, appearance is the most essential 'skill' to doing business: 'When you approach a customer and say this product is Ksh3,000, the customer will look at you to see if you are dressed as someone who can sell a product at Ksh3,000,' indicating how deportment not only conveys the respectability of the entrepreneur but signifies the quality of the brands they sell (Training, 21 June 2013). Dress and carriage are also ways the organisation detects entrepreneurial commitment and winnows the enterprising from the apathetic. For example, at one training session, the trainer scanned participants, assessing their appearance and asking those who met his approval to stand up. His eyes settled on a row of women. 'I have always seen you smartly dressed since you started this training. You, too. You and you, and a few of you behind there. But some of you here, you can never dress well. . . . I will only recruit the youths who are standing. The rest of you will not be qualifying to do the job' (Training, 21 June 2013). Such admonitions reveal the significance of entrepreneurs' bodily capital, not only as a prerequisite for eliciting value through the sale of goods, but as a form of derivative value for the organisation's own reputational capital.

4.3. Performance

Underpinning entrepreneurship is the implicit, and at times explicit, claim that the process of conversion involves a shift in mind-set that is both moral and temporal, rejecting the apathy of here-and-now survival for goal-oriented, future thinking, a personal teleology that embodies the modernist preoccupations of classic developmentalist thinking. In contrast to the improvisational, intermittent and piecemeal livelihood activities youth pursue in the slum, BoP entrepreneurship is highly scripted, routinised and temporally ordered. Future planning structures the flow of the day. Catalyst training emphasises the importance of 'learning to be goal-oriented' as a virtue in itself, regardless of whether the goal is achieved, or even achievable. As Stephen, a Catalyst entrepreneur described, he is compelled to set new goals every month even when he has failed to achieve his previous ones. There is also forensic attention on quantification and tracking results. As social scientists have pointed out, numbers are not disinterested forms of knowledge; they convey authority and expertise (Strathern, 2000) and embody powerful social and material effects. At Catalyst, sales numbers reflect the value of the entrepreneur, that is, their results, but also form the compass that orients entrepreneurs' daily activities. You must, one entrepreneur said, 'be able to see it [the goal], you must be able to measure and you must write it down'. Entrepreneurs commit to personal monthly sales targets, usually between 10,000 and 20,000 Ksh [115 to 230 USD], that are carefully tracked and assessed, as high performers earn accolades as embodiments of efficiency while those with 'disappointing' sales face reproach at the 'one-on-one'.

The one-on-one is a bi-weekly performance appraisal that draws entrepreneurs into the sights of market discipline, on the one hand aiming to spur the productivity of 'enterprising' youth, and on the other pulling wayward entrepreneurs back into the fold. Though framed in idioms of collaboration and participation, it is an ambivalent encounter, sometimes sanguine and affirming, other times tense and punitive. For some entrepreneurs the one-on-one casts a shadow of anxiety and disaffection over the days preceding it. One new entrepreneur, Mary, expressed her frustration with the appraisal, complaining that if you haven't made it half-way to your goal by the one-and-one, 'What do they expect you to do in one week to make sales of 30,000 shillings that you have not been doing in the past three weeks? ... It is pressure' (Interview 28 June 2013). For others, however, the one-on-one was invested with trust and empathy, as concerns were shared, problems resolved and commitment renewed. Reflecting on her most recent one-on-one, Susan said she learned 'you cannot give up. You should keep up the spirit. Have it in mind that even when some disappoint you, not everyone will disappoint you' (Interview 20 June 2013).

Both targets and the one-on-one afford metrological scrutiny of entrepreneurial competence (von Schnitzler, 2008), bringing hitherto disorderly youth into new forms of economic calculation (Callon, 2009, p. 270). This scrutiny extends to the daily progress chart, where the qualification of 'enterprising', 'ambitious' and 'capable' assumes material form as a set of data points on a spreadsheet, hung in pride of place on the wall as you enter the organisation). Though the chart manifests efficiencies and accomplishments (where, what and how much an entrepreneur sells), it also unmoors the 'real world' of selling from the fabric of the urban slum, stripping away the plethora of connections and relations that shape and constrain entrepreneurial success. The capriciousness of consumers, the perils of poor infrastructure, the depleted body, the emotional weight of poverty and the extent of social networks an entrepreneur has to exploit – all of which condition performance – recede from view. Entrepreneurial fitness becomes a technical means–ends calculation, where revenue is commensurate with performance and the entrepreneur a sum of his/her economic transactions.

Of course, the data do not simply represent 'facts', that is, the productivity of labour, but also surveil entrepreneurs in new ways (see Carrier & Miller, 1998). Describing this, one entrepreneur explained:

> The chart is updated every day ... Every morning they must ask who made sales the previous day. And if you do not rise up your hand then you feel like you are being watched. If two days down the line you do not rise up your hand as having made a sale ... then you will definitely feel like you are being watched.

It is not only management that watches however, as the progress chart exposes entrepreneurial performance to public view. It allows everyone to 'see whether you are going up or not', becoming the yardstick by which value is measured and an augur for entrepreneurial promise. Individual achievement and success are publicly applauded in daily ritualised performances geared to catalysing internal competition between entrepreneurs. The inscriptions on the chart and the public recognition mirror what entrepreneurs should think of themselves, but also what others are thinking about them; again, a form of 'value coding' (Anagnost, 2006) that reifies the distinction between the responsible, enterprising and ambitious and those who are not. But the verdict of not being good enough can loom large. It makes you, reflected entrepreneur Silas, 'have a weird feeling ...

when you come to look at this chart and find someone has made a sale and you have not. ... I happen to feel that if I sell more I will be more appreciated' (Interview 27 June 2013). Failure itself, as organisations acknowledge, can be productive (Harford, 2011), motivating lacklustre performers to kick-start their entrepreneurial drive so that 'everyone will clap' and they 'will also be seen from the chart'. But it can also be dispiriting, as the chart not only passes a judgement in the here-and–now, but is endowed with prophetic power, predicting (and establishing a hierarchy) between those who are likely pull themselves up by their bootstraps and enrich themselves and those who will not.

Indeed, the performance chart, like the training sessions and one-on-ones, is intimately bound up with the broader moral question of who remains within and beyond the domain of inclusive business. As the director of Catalyst told us, 'you have superstars and you have kind of the average and then you have the bottom 10 per cent of those that you should be letting go every month'. This 'letting go' and the separations it entails are a constitutive feature of BoP entrepreneurship, as success hinges on bracketing off the 'economically active' from the underproductive poor (Rankin, 2001; Roy, 2010, p. 99). Indeed, as trainers reiterated, training sessions were not simply pedagogical; they were competitive selection processes, aimed at culling 'the best' to the exclusion of 'the rest'. The imperative for trainees to demonstrate worthiness as a true entrepreneur, by embracing this competitive and meritocratic individualism was equally stressed: 'that is why we all go to school, be in the same class and learn the same things but it is one person who will emerge as the number one' (Training, 21 June 2013). Ultimately, the approbation of market competition runs contrary to the language of inclusive markets that promises to draw the marginalised into the embrace of market opportunities rather than creating processes which can further their exclusion; in short, as Mary put it, 'without sales you aren't anybody' (Mary, 28 June 2013). According to this Darwinian logic, failure to sell, or failure to sell in sufficient volume, signifies a deeper failure to make good on the promise of transformation, and the injunction to help oneself, by squandering the opportunities of the market.

5. Dreams Deferred

Catalyst's mix of evangelism and management technologies has, to some extent, seeded 'an entrepreneurial mentality' aligned with an expectation of material transformation (Dolan & Johnstone-Louis, 2011). But to what extent is the promise of transformation internalised and fulfilled? The accounts of a number of Catalyst sellers suggest a rather ambivalent picture, the faith in entrepreneurial transformation was tempered by a worldly acknowledgement of the constraints to realising its rewards. Joshua encapsulates this ambivalence. At the outset, he recounted his biography as a moving testament of salvation and conversion, from street child to businessman, from criminality and idleness to the morality and productivity of the true entrepreneur, brought about by the combined agency of Catalyst training and self-mastery:

> I didn't have a job. I used to idle around the streets, steal from people in the market ... abuse alcohol and drugs ... I would say, what got me encouraged, it is the moral I had when I was coming from the streets. I came out of the streets wanting to change and become a better person ... women perceived me as a bad person especially from the market. They knew me from when I was a small boy. I was never a decent person ... They saw me sell products that can change lives. They saw I was serious to change and that is how they started buying from me ... In my first life I was in the streets. Right now I live in house ... Catalyst has changed my life.

Yet, with a notable change of tone, Joshua undercut this initial expression of faith in the exuberant promise of transformation through the Catalyst way, expressing a more pragmatic valuation of his own 'story' as moral and material currency – –both to recruit new 'youth agents' and to raise external donor money for the initiative:

> She took a few videos of me, she started selling my story ... How I live in the streets and how I want to change and I need help, the story sold out well and they started receiving funds ... Then I was put in charge of leading the morning meeting, taking out the white visitors who came; I would take them out to the slums whenever they came ... My story really sold. (Interview, 26 June 2013)

Joshua's assessment of the marketability of 'his story' was pointed. After all, as he had commented earlier, in this new economy of development 'everything is sales' – whether the products peddled by Catalyst recruits, or their stories mobilised to sustain the myth of broad-based entrepreneurship. This disjuncture between the anticipated rewards and lived experience of entrepreneurship was reinforced as Joshua went on to speak of the need to maintain the myth of deeper transformation through training as inducements for new recruits. When he is recruiting, he said, he puts up posters announcing that youth 'are needed urgently for *TRAINING! TRAINING! TRAINING*!' not sales. Most of the youth, he said, 'hate to do sales. So if you write it is a sales job, then they will not come. So I tell them the training can help you start and run your own business ... I don't tell my fellow youths how it really is down here since they will lose hope' (Interview 21 June 2013). The precariousness of these entrepreneurial promises, and the acknowledgement of trainers themselves that the chances of success may remain elusive to many if not most, alert us to the expediency of a doctrine that emphasises (and even privileges) grit and hard graft over business acumen as a key characteristic of the entrepreneur.

Certainly, for many, the dreams of a future animated by entrepreneurial success continued to reside tantalisingly on the horizon, beyond their grasp. Indeed, several entrepreneurs groused that the chase was hardly worth the effort. James, for example, described how he nursed hopes that Catalyst would enable him to stand on his own two feet but he has found the job wanting.

> I have not been able to do it because the money we receive is very little. You might find you made sales of 76,000 shillings [93 USD] and at the end of the day you will receive 8,000–10,000 [115 USD] ... This cannot take you to the end of the month if you are living by yourself here in Nairobi. You need to eat. You need to pay rent, pay transport and other bills. (Interview 28 June 2013)[6]

Mary, who joined Catalyst to save money to open a salon, echoed Daniel's frustration. Never mind the salon, she sighed, she's not been able to raise enough to pay a month's rent. Like most of the youth we met, both were careful 'to appreciate' what they did earn, but their hopes and aspirations ran much deeper. They weren't in the BoP market to 'make-do'; they were staking a claim to upward mobility. As Joshua described, 'I dreamt of becoming a musician ... I am a good rapper, I do hip hop music, *kapuka* music and ... I thought one day I will be able to raise enough money to record the music.' But, he lamented, that is a dream in waiting. Maybe when you come back next year, he said, things will be better but today it is still 'a life of hustle'.

6. Conclusion

The BoP concept continues to gain prominence on the development agenda, tendering a new strategy to marry economic growth and the social good under the mantle of inclusive business. SSA has become an inviting frontier for such systems, as capital sets its sights on the continents' vast 'underserved' informal economies, harnessing the entrepreneurial mettle of youth to create new markets for a range of products.

BoP entrepreneurialism evokes a compelling proposition, circulating a vision where market engagement and moral imperatives are naturally aligned and the 'efficiency' of the private sector offers a salve for the failures of aid and absent states. In Africa especially, where legions of disenfranchised youth are seen as a flashpoint for instability and unrest, BoP's income-earning opportunities are held up as way to stem a brewing social crisis, by transforming idle street youth into productive citizens.

Even on the streets of Nairobi's slums, where youth navigate the borders of desire and despair, BoP entrepreneurship is a seductive antidote to a seemingly precarious and uncertain future, a gateway to the inclusionary, yet elusive, promise of global capitalism. The allure of possibility BoP schemes conjure is why youth like Silas, who have spent their lives in the hustle, are hedging their bets, curbing pursuit of illicit fast cash for prestige and respectability as a 'legitimate' entrepreneur, seeking the chance to parlay their earnings into a small business of their own, carving out a life where work and consumption walk hand-and-hand.

Certainly, participation in BoP's inclusive market initiatives can bring some entrepreneurs a modest income and social recognition, as well as, in some cases, a sense of autonomy, confidence and self-esteem through the earnings accrued (Dolan & Scott, 2009; Dolan et al., 2012). These benefits and the transformational narratives that accompany them are not easily dismissed in a continent where many experience less an adverse incorporation in the global economy than an exclusion from it (Ferguson, 2005). But though entrepreneurs may emerge, if even tenuously, from the 'shadows' of the slum into recognition as 'legitimate' market actors, their inclusion into BoP circuits of capital hinges on an ex ante conversion, as transforming the self is a prerequisite to the realm of hope and possibility the BoP project evokes. Indeed, though these emergent economies of development replace, as Meagher (this issue) notes, old narratives of marginalisation with the new orthodoxy of inclusion, this inclusion turns not on populism or entitlement but on the capacity of the entrepreneur to embody and exercise values bestowed through management tutelage. For the discourse of entrepreneurship combines the celebration of 'an age of the daring individual' (Prentice, 2009), with the everyday graft of 'selling, selling, selling' in equal measure. Here, we find the figure of the new development entrepreneur, whose moral clout and possibilities for mobility inhere not in a genetic predilection for entrepreneurship ('the entrepreneurial DNA'), but rather in their capacity to master and enact the principles of market discipline. As the article suggests, although the emphasis on 'producing' entrepreneurs is meant to breed success, bringing those below poverty line above it through new skills, attitudes and a "tough love" meritocracy, in practice the line itself is crystalised, as fostering distinctions between the productive and unproductive, the professional and hustler, and the enterprising and lazy poor animate the entrepreneurial project.

While enterprise solutions proffer the possibility of redeeming the failure to find gainful employment, responsibility for which is individualised, they shift attention from the failure (and profound inequities) of the economic structure in which their targets exercise limited economic agency. The paradox, of course, is that the experience of entrepreneurship may deliver precisely the opposite of what inclusive business implies, reinforcing the fissures between Africa's redundant urban proletariat and the new swathe of bootstrap capitalists.

Disclosure statement

No potential conflict of interest was reported by the authors.

Notes

1. See, for example, Tiffin (1976).
2. The research consisted of in-depth interviews with Catalyst's directors (2), office management (2), consumers (4) and field entrepreneurs (15). All interviews were conducted by the author or our Kenyan research assistant in the first language of informants, and were recorded, transcribed and coded for analysis. We also spent several days shadowing the selling process, accompanying entrepreneurs on their sales routes through Nairobi, and observed four days of the entrepreneurship training. Analysis of data was informed by the authors' research projects on BoP distribution systems in Uganda, South Africa and Bangladesh.
3. Following the outbreak of violence in the wake of Kenya's (2007) election, the government sought to subdue tensions by addressing the 'problem of youth unemployment' through *Kazi Kwa Vijana* (Work for Youth), a large-scale public works programme that aimed to employ 'idle' youth in the slums in road building, water harvesting and waste collection (OECD, n. d., p. 1).
4. http://www.kibera.org.uk/Facts.html
5. To protect the anonymity of informants, the name of this scheme and all participants have been changed.
6. The average annual income of entrepreneurs interviewed was approximately 15,000 Ksh (173 USD).

References

African Population and Health Research Center (APHRC). (2014). *Population and health dynamics in Nairobi's informal settlements: report of the Nairobi cross-sectional slums survey.* Nairobi: Author.

Anagnost, A. (2006). Strange circulations: The blood economy in rural China. *Economy and Society, 35*(4), 509–529. doi:10.1080/03085140600960781

Bauman, Z. (2004). *Wasted lives. Modernity and its outcasts.* Cambridge: Polity.

Biehl, J. (2005). *Vita: Life in a zone of social abandonment.* Berkeley, CA: University of California Press.

Blim, M. (2005). The moral significance of petty capitalism. In A. Smart & J. Smart (Eds.), *Petty capitalists and globalization: Flexibility, entrepreneurship and economic development* (pp. 253–270). Albany, NY: SUNY Press.

Blowfield, M., & Dolan, C. (2014). Business as a development agent: Evidence of possibility and improbability. *Third World Quarterly, 35*(1), 22–42. doi:10.1080/01436597.2013.868982

Bourdieu, P. (2000). Making the economic habitus: Algerian workers revisited. *Ethnography, 1*(July), 17–41. doi:10.1177/14661380022230624

Callon, M. (2009). Devices and desires: How useful is the 'new' new economic sociology for understanding market attachment? *Sociology Compass, 3*(2), 267–282. doi:10.1111/j.1751-9020.2009.00195.x

Carrier, J., & Miller, D. (Eds.). (1998). *Virtualism: A new political economy.* Oxford: Berg.

Chang, H. (2010). *Hamlet* without the Prince of Denmark: How development has disappeared from today's 'development discourse. In S. R. Khan & J. Christiansen (Eds.), *Towards new developmentalism: Market as means rather than master* (pp. 47–59). Abingdon: Routledge.

Comaroff, J., & Comaroff, J. (2000). Millennial capitalism: First thoughts on a second coming. *Public Culture, 12*(2), 291–343. doi:10.1215/08992363-12-2-291

Cross, J. (2013). The 100th object: Solar lighting technology and humanitarian goods. *Journal of Material Culture, 18*(4), 367–387. doi:10.1177/1359183513498959

Cross, J., & Street, A. (2009). Anthropology at the bottom of the pyramid. *Anthropology Today, 25*(4), 4–9. doi:10.1111/j.1467-8322.2009.00675.x

Davies, G. (2014). *Rethinking market-based development approaches: Increasing access to domestic-scale sustainable energy goods and services in sub-Saharan Africa* (Unpublished doctoral dissertation thesis). University of Edinburgh, Edinburgh.

De Soto, H. (2000). *The mystery of capital.* New York, NY: Basic Books.

Dolan, C., & Johnstone-Louis, M. (2011). Re-siting corporate responsibility: The making of South Africa's Avon entrepreneurs. *Focaal: European Journal of Global and Historical Anthropology, 60*(Summer), 21–33. doi:10.3167/fcl.2011.600103

Dolan, C., Johnstone-Louis, M., & Scott, L. (2012). Shampoo, saris, and SIM cards: Seeking entrepreneurial futures at the bottom of the pyramid. *Gender & Development, 20*(1), 33–47. doi:10.1080/13552074.2012.663619

Dolan, C., & Roll, K. (2013). Capital's new frontier: From 'unusable' economies to bottom of the pyramid markets in Africa. *African Studies Review, 56*(3), 123–146. doi:10.1017/asr.2013.82

Dolan, C., & Scott, L. (2009). Lipstick evangelism: Avon trading circles and gender empowerment in South Africa. *Gender & Development, 17*(2), 203–218. doi:10.1080/13552070903032504

Eade, D., & Sayer, J. (2006). *Development and the private sector.* Bloomfield, CT: Kumarian Press.

Elyachar, J. (2002). Empowerment money: The World Bank, non-governmental organizations, and the value of culture in Egypt. *Public Culture, 14*(3), 493–513. doi:10.1215/08992363-14-3-493

Elyachar, J. (2005). *Markets of dispossession: NGOs, economic development, and the state in Cairo.* Durham, NC: Duke University Press.

Elyachar, J. (2012). Next practices: Knowledge, infrastructure, and public goods at the bottom of the pyramid. *Public Culture, 24* (1), 109–129. doi:10.1215/08992363-1443583

Ferguson, J. (2005). Seeing like an oil company: Space, security, and global capital in neoliberal Africa. *American Anthropologist, 107*(3), 377–382. doi:10.1525/aa.2005.107.issue-3

Gordon, C. (1991). Government rationality: An introduction. In G. Burchell, G. Gordon, & P. Miller (Eds.), *The Foucault effect: Studies in governmentality* (pp. 1–52). Chicago, IL: Chicago University Press.

Hammond, A. L., Kramer, W. J., Katz, R. S., Tran, J. T., & Walker, C. (2007). *The next four billion: Market size and business strategy at the base of the pyramid.* Washington, DC: World Resources Institute, International Finance Corporation.

Harford, T. (2011). *Adapt: Why success always starts with failure.* New York, NY: Farrar, Straus and Giroux.

Heron, A. P. (2011, April 17–21). *Taming the spider man: From anticolonial hero to neoliberal icon.* Societe Internationale d'Ethnologie et de Folklore (SIEF) 2011 Conference, Lisbon, Portugal.

James, D. (2011). The return of the broker: Consensus, hierarchy and choice in South African land reform. *Journal of the Royal Anthropological Institute, 17*(2), 318–338. doi:10.1111/jrai.2011.17.issue-2

Karnani, A. (2007). The mirage of marketing to the bottom of the pyramid: How the private sector can help alleviate poverty. *California Management Review, 49*(4), 90–111. doi:10.2307/41166407

Kay, E. (2012). *Playing with fire: An MNC's inability to translate its market logic in a culturally complex exchange setting in rural India* (Unpublished doctoral dissertation thesis). University of Oxford, Oxford.

Kolk, A., Rivera-Santos, M., & Rufin, C. (2014). Reviewing a decade of research on the 'base/bottom of the pyramid (BOP) concept. *Business & Society, 53*(3), 338–377. doi:10.1177/0007650312474928

London, T., & Hart, S. (2011). Creating a future with the base of the pyramid. In T. London & S. Hart (Eds.), *Next generation business strategies for the base of the pyramid: New approaches for building mutual value* (pp. 1–18). Upper Saddle River, NJ: Pearson.

MacGaffey, J. (1991). *The real economy of Zaire: The contribution of smuggling and other unofficial activities to national wealth*. London: James Currey.

Mayoux, L. (2002). *Sustainable learning for women's empowerment: Ways forward in micro-finance*. New Delhi: Samskriti.

Meagher, K. (2013, June 29). *The trouble the lurks beneath: Globalization, demography and informal labour markets*. Paper presented at ECAS, Lisbon, Portugal.

Miesen, M. (2013, October 21). Kenya: Life of a salesman - The youth bringing quality products to Nairobi's slums. *Think Africa Press*. Retrieved from http://allafrica.com/stories/201310220130.html?viewall=1

Ncube, M. (2012). Urbanization in Africa, Blog: AFDP: Championing inclusive growth across Africa. Retrieved from http://www.afdb.org/en/blogs/afdb-championing-inclusive-growth-aThe -africa/post/urbanization-in-africa-10143/

Obonyo, R. (2013, October 15). Reducing youth unemployment in Kenya. Retrieved from http://www.worldpolicy.org/blog/2013/10/15/reducing-youth-unemployment-kenya

OECD. (n.d.). Kazi kwa vijana: Youth empowerment in Kenya. Retrieved from www.oecd.org/dac/povertyreduction/48869464.pdf

Page, J. (2012). *Youth, jobs, and structural change: Confronting Africa's 'employment problem'* (Working Paper Series N° 155). Tunis, Tunisia: African Development Bank.

Palitza, K. (2013). News analysis: Africa's rapid urbanisation sets a time bomb. Retrieved from http://www.bdlive.co.za/africa/africannews/2013/08/27/news-analysis-africas-rapid-urbanisation-sets-a-time-bomb

Plan USA. (2012). Kenya: Hopes, dreams, love, and life in Nairobi's Kawangware slum. Retrieved from http://www.planusa.org/contentmgr/showdetails.php/id/2840579

Prahalad, C. K. (2004). *The fortune at the bottom of the pyramid: Eradicating poverty through profits*. Upper Saddle River, NJ: Pearson.

Prahalad, C. K., & Hart, S. (2002). The fortune at the bottom of the pyramid. *Strategy + Business Review, 26*, 54–67.

Prentice, R. (2009). 'Thiefing a chance': Moral meanings of theft in a Trinidadian garment factory. In K. Browne & L. Milgram (Eds.), *Economics and morality* (pp. 123–142). Lanham, MD: Altamira Press.

Rajak, D. (2011). *In good company. An anatomy of corporate social responsibility*. Palo Alto, CA: Stanford University Press.

Rankin, K. (2001). Governing development: Neoliberalism, microcredit, and rational economic woman. *Economy and Society, 30*(1), 18–37. doi:10.1080/03085140020019070

Redfield, P. (2012). Bioexpectations: Life technologies as humanitarian goods. *Public Culture*, *24*(1), 157–184. doi:10.1215/08992363-1443592

Robinson, J. (1997). The geopolitics of South African Cities: States, citizens, territory. *Political Geography, 16*(5), 365–386.

Roopanarine, L. (2013, July 11). Africa's rising population and youth unemployment challenge. *Guardian Professional*. Retrieved from http://www.theguardian.com/global-development-professionals-network/2013/jul/11/africa-kenya-population-youth-unemployment

Rose, N. (1999). *Powers of freedom: Reframing political thought*. Cambridge: Cambridge University Press.

Roy, A. (2010). *Poverty capital: Microfinance and the making of development*. London: Taylor & Francis.

Schwittay, A. (2011). The marketization of poverty. *Current Anthropology, 52*, S71–S82. doi:10.1086/656472

Shell Foundation. (2005). *Enterprise solutions to poverty*. London: Shell Foundation. Retrieved from http://www.shellfoundation.org/download/pdfs/Shell_Foundation_Enterprise_Solutions_to_poverty.pdf

Simanis, E., & Hart, S. (2008). *The base of the pyramid protocol: Toward next generation BoP strategy* (2nd ed.). Ithaca, NY: Center for Sustainable Global Enterprise, Johnson School of Management, Cornell University.

Smiles, S. (2002 [1859]). *Self help*. Oxford: OUP.

Sparks, D., & Barnett, S. (2010). The informal sector in sub-saharan Africa: Out of the shadows to foster sustainable employment and equity? *International Business & Economics Research Journal*, *9*(5), 1–12.

Strathern, M. (2000). *Audit cultures: Anthropological studies in accountability, ethics and the academy*. London: Routledge.

Street, A., & Cross, J. (2012). *Notes from the field: Selling nutraceuticals in highlands Orissa*. Retrieved from http://edinburghmedicalanthropology.wordpress.com

Tiffin, M. (1976). *The enterprising peasant: Economic development in Gombe Emirate, North Eastern State, Nigeria 1900–1968* (Overseas Research Publication No. 21). London: Ministry of Overseas Development.

Tokman, V. (2007). *Modernizing the Informal Sector*.' (DESA Working Paper No. 42 ST/ESA/2007/DWP/42). Retrieved from http://www.un.org/esa/desa/papers/2007/wp42_2007.pdf

von Schnitzler, A. (2008). Citizenship prepaid: Water, calculability and techno-politics in South Africa. *Journal of Southern African Studies*, *34*(4), 899–917. doi:10.1080/03057070802456821

Welker, M. (n.d.). Notes on the difficulty of studying the corporation. Retrieved from http://www.law.seattleu.edu/Documents/berle-center/Welker.pdf

World Bank. (2001). *World development report 2000/2001: Attacking poverty*. Oxford: World Bank and OUP.

World Bank. (2007). *Country social analysis, Kenya*. Washington, DC: Author.

The Domestic Turn: Business Process Outsourcing and the Growing Automation of Kenyan Organisations

LAURA MANN* & MARK GRAHAM**
*African Studies Centre, Leiden, Netherlands, **Oxford Internet Institute and School of Geography and the Environment, University of Oxford, Oxford, United Kingdom

ABSTRACT *After observing the growth of the Indian and Filipino Business Process Outsourcing (BPO) sectors, Kenyan policy-makers and managers made substantial investments in international internet infrastructure and BPO marketing campaigns. While observers continue to discuss the sector in terms of its international work opportunities, in recent years the sector has increasingly focused on contracts sourced from Kenyan and other East African clients. The government has also refocused efforts on attracting international BPO companies. This domestic turn signals both the difficulties of gaining access to overseas work due to the power of incumbents and the increasing use of the internet and ICT-enabled automation within Kenyan organisations. In effect, better connectivity has enabled a two-way globalisation of services: Kenyan BPO companies can access international work opportunities but connectivity has also contributed to the inflow of international business practices into Kenya. The conclusion examines what these shifts might entail for the sector and its workers in future.*

I. Introduction

Business Process Outsourcing (BPO) can loosely be described as service work contracted out to a third party. The term encompasses a range of activities that include customer service work, data entry, transcription, digitisation, financial accounting, auditing and other higher value-knowledge processing such as content development, animation, legal services, engineering design and data analytics. The BPO sector first emerged in Northern economies in response to deregulation and competitive pressures inducing organisations to restructure, increase efficiencies and maximise shareholder value (Batt & Moynihan, 2002; Davis, 2009). Work tasks that once took place within firms came to be standardised and outsourced to outside organisations, often using information and communication technologies (ICTs). Work was first moved to lower wage areas within national economies (Taylor & Bain, 2008) but by the early 2000s, changing communication capacities had allowed such work to be offshored to countries such as India, the Philippines and China, effectively creating a 'global'[1] marketplace for services (Dicken, 2003; Bryson, 2007; Malecki & Moriset, 2008). The increasing geographical spread of BPO has resulted both from pressures to reduce costs and from desires by multinational companies (MNCs) to spread risk across markets (Kleibert, 2014).

BPO has been seen to represent very different facets of economic globalisations. On the one hand, it has been described as offering potential developmental benefits, allowing developing countries to leapfrog industrialisation, acquire new skills and capital, and participate in a flatter and more frictionless global economy (Dossani & Kenney, 2007; Friedman, 2006). Fernandez-Stark, Bamber, and

Gereffi (2011, p. 1) thus write, 'the industry provides a clear illustration of how globalisation has provided opportunities for both employment and business formation in developing countries'. However, others have voiced more cautious assessments, stressing that benefits are 'uncertain and contingent' (Levy, 2005, p. 691) and that the globalisation of services is likely to benefit more highly skilled groups while weakening the security, economic prospects and bargaining power of less skilled workers (Held, 1999). Anxieties about BPO are particularly pronounced in relation to developed economies where fears of job losses dominate discussions.

Since 2004, Kenyan policy-makers and businesspeople have wanted a share of the market. Many hoped the 2009 arrival of fibre optic internet cables into East Africa would allow these economies to break their dependence on primary commodity exports and use the affordances of better internet connectivity to transition into tertiary and quaternary service sector exports (Graham & Mann, 2013). The original vision for the BPO sector in Kenya was therefore export oriented, Kenyan owned and oriented towards the creation of jobs (Graham, Andersen, & Mann, 2015). Estimates released by the Government of Kenya (2007a, b) predicted the sector would create 20,000 direct BPO jobs and contribute 10 billion Kenyan shillings to GDP (approximately 114 million USD).

Few connected the deeper penetration of high speed internet nor the development of an export-oriented BPO sector with the potential for greater domestic outsourcing within Kenya itself (that is Kenyan BPO companies conducting work for other Kenyan companies). Despite a trend of increasing subcontracting already taking place (Mazumdar & Mazaheri, 2002; Bocquier, 2005), policy-makers and businesspeople conceptualised BPO through the early experiences of India[2] and the current experience of the Philippines, and not through the experiences of Northern countries, where discussions of BPO have been linked to more negative forms of domestic labour market restructuring.

Drawing on in-depth interviews with 49 BPO managers and policy-makers, this paper examines the development of the Kenyan BPO sector in close detail. We describe some of the difficulties that Kenyan BPO managers have faced in trying to access international work such as lack of managerial experience, lack of personal connections and physical distance from markets. In response, Kenyan based companies have increasingly turned towards Kenyan and East African clients. The Kenyan government has now shifted to promoting higher value IT enabled services (ITES) such as software development and to attracting prominent multinational BPO competitors into Kenya. Policy-makers hope these efforts will position Kenya as a regional ICT and software development hub. While observers continue to discuss the sector in relation to its potential for export-oriented work and international opportunities (Dihel, Fernandes, Gicho, Kashangaki, & Strychacz, 2012; Hope, 2012; Iraki, 2013; Manning, 2013; Wausi, Mgendi, & Ngwenyi, 2013), [3] these shifts suggest that we need to rethink how we approach the Kenyan BPO sector. The domestic turn signals both the difficulties of gaining access to digital work overseas due to the power of existing incumbents and to the increasing availability and use of the internet within Kenya. In the conclusion, we discuss what these shifts might mean for the future of the sector and its workers.

The paper draws on the results of a research project carried out by the University of Oxford, the University of Nairobi and the National University of Rwanda over the course of 2012 and 2013.[4] 41 managers of Kenyan BPO and ITES companies were interviewed in open-ended extended interviews (1–4 hours in length). [5] A BPO/ITES company was defined as any company that performs or has the potential to perform business processes for clients. The range of participants included aspiring and small-scale BPO/ITES entrepreneurs (self-employed), more established Kenyan companies in the East African Small and Medium Enterprises segment, international companies with Kenyan offices, Kenyan companies working as representatives of international companies, and Kenyan and Indian BPOs operating in the East African and international market. Additional interviews were conducted with the Kenyan ICT Board, the Permanent Secretary of ICT, an advisor to the National Communications Secretariat, the Head of the Communication Workers Union and representatives from kLab, mLab and 88mph (three tech hubs and business accelerator programmes in Nairobi). All 49 interviews were transcribed and coded using a qualitative data analysis software tool.

This analysis was further supplemented by the use of secondary sources like newspaper articles and social media reports, and through on-going communication with research participants. A focus group was held in May 2013, in which research participants were asked to reflect on preliminary findings and to offer their own ideas. With the exception of public statements that have already been made public, the identities of respondents have been anonymised so as to ensure confidentiality. Fieldwork sought to uncover whether or not the arrival of fibre optic internet in 2009 had allowed managers of Kenyan BPO and ITES companies the opportunity to more effectively compete for international BPO contracts and work opportunities. During fieldwork, we discovered that many of the companies included in our sample had refocused towards the domestic market. This paper aims to explain that refocusing and explore its implications.

We first describe the initial hopes for the sector voiced by business people and policy-makers prior to the arrival of fibre optic cables. We then proceed to a discussion of what transpired between 2004 and 2014. Despite substantial investments in infrastructure and marketing, Kenyan BPO firms have struggled to reach into international markets and have increasingly concentrated on local and regional markets.

Sections three to five look at this re-orientation in closer detail. We use the concept of 'sense-making' to understand how Kenyan actors responded to these difficulties. The concept of organisational 'sense-making' (Weick, 1995) refers to the processes through which individuals attempt to understand uncertain and ambiguous circumstances and make sense of their realities. Sociologists and anthropologists have used the concept to understand how virtual or technologically-mediated communities have built common understandings and practices through geographical proximity and shared cultures (Beunza & Stark, 2003; Corbridge & Thrift, 1994; Cramton, 2001; French & Leyshon, 2004; Kumar, Van Fenema, & Von Glinow, 2009; Marazzi & Mecchia, 2007; Spence & Carter, 2011; Stark, 2009; Steinmueller, 2002). In the case of Kenyan BPO, we show how domestic outsourcing came to be seen as a way of bringing 'global practices' into proximate arenas within which Kenyans could make sense of them. The 'domestic turn' should thus be understood as an opportunity for Kenyan companies to better position themselves in international BPO networks while capitalising on the deepening of internet penetration and ICT-enabled automation taking place in local markets. While BPO has been touted as a job creator and export earner, the Kenyan sector is now gearing up towards changing local business models and work practices.

In the conclusion, we suggest that this re-orientation should involve a more pragmatic discussion within the country. Specifically, we discuss whether increased domestic outsourcing is likely to increase forward and backward linkages between multinational BPO networks and Kenya's own national economy, whether these linkages are likely to increase the potentials of disinvestment and relocation or instead increase the potential for economic upgrading within the Kenyan economy and whether or not the sector is likely to provide stable employment prospects for its workers. We draw on the experiences of India and the Philippines to understand these shifts.

II. Visions of the Service Sector in Kenya

In the early 2000s Kenyans began to get interested in BPO. The country needed to create jobs for its growing pool of university graduates, to diminish its dependence on primary commodities and to create export earnings to address its external debt. It was hoped that the BPO sector would help meet all of these objectives by re-orientating the economy away from agriculture and manufacturing and re-positioning Kenya within the global service economy.

On the ground, much small-scale BPO was already taking place. Internet cafés moonlighted as BPO operations afterhours, taking on piecemeal work obtained from online outsourcing platforms like *guru.com, odesk.com* and *elance.*[6] One such operation was E-Business,[7] a two-person operation founded in 2002 that did online research jobs for foreign clients (Singer, 2006). By 2006 the company had changed its name to Preciss International and had grown its staff to 17, doing a wider range of online tasks. Stories about such companies circulated through the conversations and imaginations of Kenyan businesspeople and policy-makers and provided some justification for optimism about a changing relationship between Kenya and the outside world. A number of more established businesspeople began to make substantial investments.

One such person was Nik Nesbitt, a Kenyan businessman working overseas who had planned to return to Kenya to start a business. BPO seemed perfect; it was aligned with the country's wider ICT aspirations, it appealed to government and was understood to be a job creator and export earner. Nesbitt founded Kencall in 2005, setting the stage for other professionally orientated BPOs to enter the market. Technobrain, Horizon, Direct Channel, and Adept (among others) all had large workforces, employing 100–500 workers and initially focused on international work. Of the companies listed above, almost all reported close to 100 per cent international[8] clients before 2009. As the sector began to grow, a Kenyan BPO and Contact Centre Society formed in 2007 and membership soon grew above 30 firms. This association was modelled on India's NASSCOM and the Philippines' BPAP, and was intended to bring players together to improve skills, training, government policy and marketing activities.

In 2007 the government named BPO as one of the six pillars of economic growth in its Vision 2030, a national development plan that sought to establish Kenya as a middle-income country by 2030 (Government of Kenya, 2007a, b). Envisioning Kenya to become the top offshoring destination in Africa, it called for the establishment of a 7500 seat BPO park at the Athi-River Export Processing Zone (EPZ), an aggressive marketing campaign, the development of targeted training programmes, the development of a BPO incentive framework and the formulation of BPO and Contact Centre (CC) policy. BPO was estimated to create at least 20,000 direct BPO jobs and contribute 10 billion Kenyan shillings to GDP. The government also established the semi-autonomous Kenya ICT Board to help promote the sector. In 2008, this board launched 'the Kenyan BPO Value Proposition' and embarked on an ambitious marketing tour of BPO conferences and trade shows around the world.

In 2009, the government commissioned the consulting company McKinsey to compile a report on Kenya's niche within the global market for BPO/ITES (Kariuki, 2010). It confirmed that Kenya could become competitive in call centre and customer service work, stressing Kenyans' neutral English accents and the high number of university graduates in the country.[9] As Kleibert (2014, p. 247) has demonstrated in the Philippines, 'research reveals that location choice factors for BPO companies tend to be primarily shaped by the availability of skilled labour force or "talent"'. The Kenyan ICT Board made visits to countries such as India and the Philippines to sharpen Kenya's value proposition vis-à-vis other destinations in the world. An interviewee who had also worked as an advisor to Indian and Chinese BPO destinations, surmised Kenya's advantage as such:

> The good thing about call centre [work] is the [Kenyan] accents are very, very good and neutral. Number two is there are some amount of saturation levels reaching India and Philippines, and number three is attrition levels in these countries and companies operating in these companies are crazy high ... So I think the customers are ... saying 'I need ... a new source'. (Interview, Nairobi, 22 November 2012)

Kenya sought to position itself as this new source of export-oriented customer service skills. In 2008 Kencall won the Best-Non European Call Centre Award at the Call Centre Focus Conference, the biggest trade show in the industry. This accolade effectively put Kenya on the BPO map. The only thing that held the country back, it seemed, was its expensive and unreliable satellite internet connections.

Before 2009, East Africa was the last region of the world not connected to the global fibre optic grid, and so while Indian and Filipino BPOs were paying $250 per unit for their monthly bandwidth, a similar connection was costing Kenyan companies as much as $1,700 (Mark, 2008).[10] The decision-making process involved in the BPO sector often begins with a discussion of 'seat price': the cost of a workstation per day. With its unusually high internet costs, Kenya was relatively expensive despite its favourable accents and skills (Waema, 2009). As such, the gate to the international economy had yet to open.

But plans were being made to bring a series of undersea fibre optic cables to the port of Mombasa and thus to theoretically transform East Africa's connectivity. This connectivity was publically linked to the BPO sector, with Kenyan politicians and businessmen repeatedly stressing that the cables would connect East Africa to the global service economy (Graham & Mann, 2013). The cable projects included: (1) SeaCom, a privately owned cable, dominated by investment from South Africa,[11] (2) EASSy, a public-private partnership between predominantly South African private investors[12] and development financial institutions[13] and (3) TEAMs (The East African Marine System), a Kenyan government led initiative in partnership with Kenyan internet service providers (ISPs) and the UAE based company, Etisalat. While the government and Kenyan BPO operators stressed that the cables would facilitate the growth of an export-oriented BPO sector, and thus strengthen Kenya's links to the outside world, it is likely that internet service providers envisioned the cables deepening links within East Africa and thus facilitating the distribution of new services to Kenyan and other East African consumers. Seacom came online in 2009, followed by TEAMs and then EASSy in 2010. In April 2012, a fourth cable, Lion-2 also came online.

The manager of one of the largest BPOs in Kenya described the arrival of the cables as the linchpin:

> We thought it would be a marketing tool and we thought it would make all the difference because … we had all the raw ingredients from the supply side … the people, the policies, the willingness to support the industry from the government['s] standpoint, it's a favourable climate with many of our international clients … So we thought we had a lot of those things and now we've got fibre. What else is missing? (Interview, Nairobi, 29 November 2012)

Construction began on the cables in 2007 and the Kenyan government decided to use 78 million Kenyan shillings (about $920,000) from the World Bank Transparency Communication and Infrastructure Programme (TCIP)[14] to subsidise the cost of bandwidth for BPO companies while the country waited for the cables to arrive. It is illustrative that the government used funding earmarked for e-government to promote BPO, thereby revealing the importance of the industry from the government's perspective. The deputy CEO of the ICT Board, Victor Kyalo described how '[t]he purpose of offering subsidy to the BPO sector is to make them competitive in the global market' (qtd. in Mark, 2008). While the subsidy was designed to support existing BPOs struggling with costs, it also had the effect of increasing excitement about the sector and therefore encouraging new firms to enter.

The stage had been set for the BPO sector to thrive. Managers had invested large amounts of their own private money into the sector, building facilities in Nairobi and taking on large workforces in anticipation of international contracts. The government had also made substantial investments, financing fibre optic infrastructure, subsidising bandwidth and introducing training programmes. The sector had ultimately been framed as an export-oriented sector – with the development of EPZs, the use of research to identify a national comparative advantage vis-à-vis other foreign destinations and the launching of an aggressive international marketing campaign. It was intended that Kenyan owned companies would drive the expansion of the sector.

At this point, it was not clear that smaller, or less experienced companies might damage the reputation of larger players by weakening the image of Kenya as a whole. Rather, there was a general push towards generating unbridled excitement about the sector within the country. In this way, policy-makers and private sector spokespeople utilised technocratic ideas about a 'flat' and 'disintermediated'[15] global marketplace in order to encourage investment and public support of BPO.

However, despite initial enthusiasm, business strategies had begun to shift, even by the end of 2008. Companies like Global Connection and Continental had closed their operations, with journalists claiming that even bigger firms were facing closure (Kundu, 2008). After the arrival of the cables, internet prices had not dropped as hoped and firms found themselves struggling to meet costs. The global recession had not helped firms attract international clients (Omondi, 2012).

In both his 2008 and 2012 election campaigns, US President Obama singled out the offshoring of jobs as a key rallying point for his party. In 2008 he repeatedly declared that the United States needed to 'stop giving tax breaks to companies that ship jobs overseas' (Thibodeau, 2012). In 2012 he labelled his challenger, Mitt Romney, a 'pioneer in outsourcing' (Dwyer, 2012). While the true impact of the recession on outsourcing is mixed (on the one hand, recession encourages firms to cut costs, but on the other hand, it pressures politicians to erect protectionist policies),[16] many Kenyan managers cited Obama's speeches as having seriously harmed their businesses. One reason that this discourse might have particularly hurt Kenya, as compared to other destinations like India and the Philippines, was the fact that Kenya needed vocal publicity in order to put itself on the map. By making it difficult for clients to openly endorse a new destination like Kenya, the global recession may have dried up opportunities for new places while maintaining a steady (but less visible) flow to already established countries.

Many Kenyan BPOs went out of business. Others turned to 'impact sourcing',[17] attempting to position Kenya as a site of corporate social responsibility. The impact sourcing BPO, Digital Divide Data opened an office in Kenya. Similarly the impact sourcing intermediary, Samasource entered Kenya to find partners with whom it could pass on work from its US offices. Some of the most established companies came to depend on Samasource for overseas work, creating minority/disadvantaged segments of their workforce in order to be eligible for these contracts.

Most importantly, by 2013, most Kenyan companies had re-oriented themselves towards the domestic market (that is attracting Kenyan clients). All BPO companies within our sample had taken on local or regional outsourcing work and the majority now had more Kenyan clients than foreign clients (the exceptions were the new impact sourcing companies). Those managers that had had close to 100 per cent international clients in 2009, now estimated that international clients only accounted for 20 per cent to 40 per cent of their clients.

One rural BPO project is particularly indicative of these changes. The Rockerfeller Foundation and Enablis (a foundation that promotes entrepreneurship in low-income countries) had teamed up to launch a rural BPO project in the city of Kisumu. The project was initially designed to encourage a large number of individual 'entrepreneurs'[18] to start their own small BPO outfits geared towards international work opportunities. Later these 'entrepreneurs' were instead encouraged to join together as worker-partners in a single company when the challenge of gaining work became more apparent and the organisations realised that they could not operate at scale. The two parent organisations then began to focus on getting the company local work, stressing the project's role in increasing efficiency within local government.

This turn towards the domestic economy was reflected in the statements of key government officials in the ICT Board and the Ministry of Information who now declared local outsourcing a way of making the economy more competitive. In September 2013, *Ratio Magazine* quoted Bitange Ndemo (the former Permanent Secretary in the Kenyan Ministry of Information and Communications) explaining the government's shift:

> Mid-stream we changed policy and indeed communicated that we had shifted from marketing Kenya abroad to local outsourcing. ... It was pointless to continue marketing Kenya abroad when we had sufficient work locally. ... Once we became proficient and realised internal efficiencies, then we could now move to the outside world. We still have the opportunity to use this strategy. (qtd. in Ratio Magazine, 2013)

In our interviews with representatives with the Kenya ICT Board, we were likewise told that the government was now focusing on both stimulating local demand for BPO and attracting large international financial, IT and BPO companies into the country in order to jump-start the sector. As we will explain below, this idea was generally supported by private sector actors. It might seem puzzling why Kenyan operators would want multinational competitors to enter the country – but as the next section demonstrates, these managers had come to appreciate the fact that rather than operating in a flat or disintermediated economy, they operated in an extremely personal, socially connected economy. As Graham et al. (2015) demonstrates, ideas of 'disintermediation' have featured prominently in transnational discourses around the promises of changing connectivity for low-income countries. Despite the fact that they contradict many actual business practices, these discourses continue to be reproduced internationally and within East Africa, even now that the region has fibre-optic connectivity. Nevertheless, within the sector, Kenyan managers had developed more nuanced understandings. They now saw their international competitors as collaborators in improving the image of Kenya in the eyes of foreign clients. BPO came to be spoken about in a new way. Discourse shifted towards promoting BPO as a way to 'modernise', 'digitise' and 'increase the efficiency of' Kenyan organisations.

The next section discusses this shift in more detail, identifying three stages: (1) early mistakes of judgement, (2) realisation of Kenya's bargaining position within the international marketplace, and (3) pragmatic response. We show how the renewed focus on domestic outsourcing resulted from both pragmatic realisations about the role of powerful interests in international BPO networks and from the increasing penetration of the internet into Kenya itself.

III. Early Mistakes of Judgement

While the hype around the arrival of the cables succeeded in generating excitement and investment from domestic investors, some of this hype encouraged inexperienced and small-scale operators to enter the sector. Larger firms like Kencall and Horizon had drawn on Indian, Filipino and American consultants and employees to help structure their operations and train their workforces. Impact sourcing BPOs were likewise supported by international backers that helped them to access foreign expertise. The CEO of the impact sourcing company, Daproim travelled to the headquarters of Digital Divide Data in Cambodia to receive training while workers from impact sourcing Africa, the rural BPO project in Kisumu, travelled to India to receive training from their Indian partner, Ruralshores (Sheth, 2013). Smaller outfits without this international support found themselves in less than profitable circumstances. In particular, less experienced Kenyan managers found it difficult to make sense of the variable costs and values of different forms of work and thereby judge their own capacities to meet deadlines and make profits.

'Joseph', an interviewee who trained BPO managers and employees, used a spreadsheet to explain the complicated matrix he used to determine profitability. He had designed his own formulas and showed the careful calibrations he used to determine different work scenarios, asking questions such as *if x number of workers are missing, how many calls does each individual worker have to complete in an hour in order to meet the client's deadline of y number of sales, given a conversion ratio of z (the number of calls converted to sales)?*[19] Such calculations are complicated for an inexperienced Kenyan manager, who has neither experience nor a clear understanding of the relative costs and challenges of tasks before she takes on a new contract. Because smaller Kenyan companies struggled to make sense of the sector, many made mistakes of judgement.

One manager whose company was considering bankruptcy, explained how he and his colleagues had invested in a smaller sized operation of 15–20 people, hoping to get higher-value engineering work. However, they were encouraged by an Indian company to instead take on lower-value customer service work. It is unclear whether this company was helping or exploiting them, given the kind of low-value, outcome-based work[20] they sourced. It is clear they wanted a Kenyan partner to whom they could pass on work. As the partnership proceeded, the Kenyan managers discovered that they could not make profits within the terms of the contracts. The interviewee described his dilemma as such:

> [W]e approached a few people from Horizon and Techno Brain and they told us that we have 100 people at daytime and 100 people at night. Here we are trying eight people in daytime and four at night . . . We don't have the scale . . . the lady who set this up, she went to India . . . and she saw thousands. It was like warehouses full of thousands . . . I thought: how are you going to compete? If you've got 20 seats and someone's got 2,000 seats, no matter what it is you're doing, he's going to do it much cheaper than you per seat . . . We knew how much it would cost, how much would the Voice Over Internet Protocol cost in America, were we going to go through America or

going to go through India. We did that sort of research. And we knew what we needed to do to make it work. We couldn't reach the threshold. (Interview, Nairobi, 10 December 2012)

Many of the smaller Kenyan BPO operators faced similar problems of scale. In order to compete and get the kinds of clients they needed, they required bigger workforces. But in order to get the bigger workforces, they needed more consistent and profitable streams of work. They therefore found themselves in a catch-22 situation, compounded by their inexperienced management teams and the tendency for young BPO workers to move on to other jobs during slow periods. In turn, prospective clients looked at scalability and long-term capability.

An interviewee who had acted as an advisor to Indian and Chinese BPO destinations described:

If I'm a client outsourcing I'll have first ask how scalable it is. You know, because tomorrow if you as my vendor will not make profits, then I am at risk as a buyer, because that means if you don't make profits, eventually you'll shut down, okay the quality will go down. You'll not be able to pay salaries. (Interview, Nairobi, 14 January 2013)

The small scale of many Kenyan BPOs held them back. They could not access international work because of their small sizes but they could never grow bigger without larger contracts. Their closures damaged the reputation of the country as a whole and damaged the reputation of even the larger companies (Keeler, 2009). For example, one interviewee who had worked in three different Kenyan BPO companies complained:

Some companies started a bit early, that were very influential and they had some very, very big clients. Now those clients left for various reasons, and when you have such kinds of huge clients leaving the country, to be quite honest, since 2008 when one of the biggest clients left Kenya, we have never seen anything bigger until today. (Interview, Nairobi, 28 January 2013)

This problem was magnified by the government's World Bank funded subsidy, which encouraged inexperienced firms to enter the market. In 2009 responding to criticisms about the subsidy, the new CEO of the ICT Board, Paul Kukubo explained in an interview with Kenya's *Ratio Magazine*:

A lot of the people who came in to ask for the bandwidth subsidy were new businesses ... Their problem wasn't bandwidth costs, but a basic lack of capacity and understanding of the industry itself. Many small and inexperienced firms have cropped up in response to government incentives, which established BPO companies say is dragging down the industry's reputation. (Ratio Magazine, 2009)

Viewed through a national lens, the closure of some firms made the whole sector seem too immature and risky. This problem was made plainly clear in the focus group, when participants suggested that Kenya should adopt an accreditation scheme to certify new BPO players. The proposal was suggested both as a way of giving advice and support to new players and of preventing inexperienced and unprofessional players from damaging the country's image. Rather than Kenyan companies interacting remotely through a 'global' or 'flat' marketplace, each individual owner came to see how they operated within an international context, in which companies were judged in part by their national attachments. The good faith that had been extended in 2008 and 2009, when the Kenyan marketing campaign was in full swing, had faded by 2012 and 2013 and larger Kenyan BPOs found themselves on the back foot. This brings us to the second phase: realisation of Kenya's bargaining position within the international market.

IV. Understanding One's Bargaining Position

While the BPO sector is global in scope, and many of its processes are standardised, the sector is still characterised by hierarchies of expertise bound up in particular geographical locations and socio-economic hierarchies (Dicken, 2003; Malecki & Moriset, 2008). In such a context, 'sense-making' (Weick, 1995) requires the close collaboration of partners situated in other areas. To better understand how this geography affects Kenyan companies, Author 1 asked focus group participants to draw representations of their companies' value chains. We include a sample of these representations.

Figure 1 depicts the reliance of Kenyan companies on intermediaries in order to access work contracts. This particular participant interpreted this reliance as preventing his company from providing secure employment to workers. Figure 2 demonstrates the importance of having 'presence in client countr[ies]' while Figure 3 shows the high costs of hiring direct employees in Western economies and the distrust that participant had of existing agents who 'are not that beneficial'. Together, these drawings depict the struggles Kenyan managers face in establishing contact and trust with clients across distance.

As others have noted, the difficulties in calculating the intangible values and immaterial labour of BPO work makes negotiating new contracts challenging (Marazzi & Mecchia, 2007; Spence & Carter, 2011; Steinmueller, 2002). Hawkins, Mansell, and Steinmueller's (1999) show that while ICT infrastructures may theoretically allow for a disintermediation of work, such disintermediation 'challenges the business of many existing companies' (p. 383), who may not so easily hand over access to existing chains of value. For the client, there are costs associated with new suppliers and so clients 'place value on cultivating *stable* communities' (p. 387). While these stable communities serve to stabilise the flow of commodified work across distance and allow for participants to make sense of their environments, they are made up of incumbent firms and consultants motivated by their own interests. The globalisation of such work therefore requires social negotiation and alignment of corporate strategies across firms.

Impact (or social enterprise) intermediaries like Samasource have offices in the United States and trusted agents who assure clients face-to-face that projects will be completed in a timely and professional manner. Larger Indian and US BPO companies also have such presence, maintaining offices in several different regions and shifting work between workforces within their networks. These companies have built brand names, reserves of customer loyalty and tacit knowledge of the processes and the wider market. Once their representatives have secured a contract from a client, they typically break that contract into smaller packages to divide among smaller units and associates. While smaller companies receive lower margins from subcontracting in this way, they value having a steady flow of work, as it allows them to maintain their workforces.

While managers of impact sourcing companies may be motivated by altruistic wishes to help (and by social enterprise business models that generate value from the framing of their intermediation as altruistic[21]), most larger companies are motivated by straightforward profit calculations. They may pass on work packages that are either unprofitable or that other workforces might be able to complete

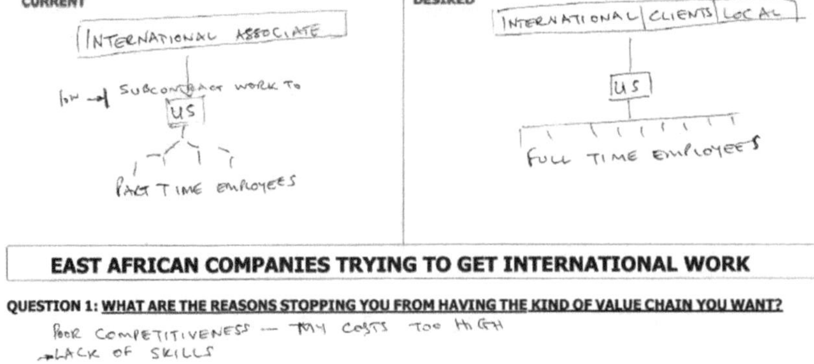

Figure 1. Intermediation within International BPO flows.

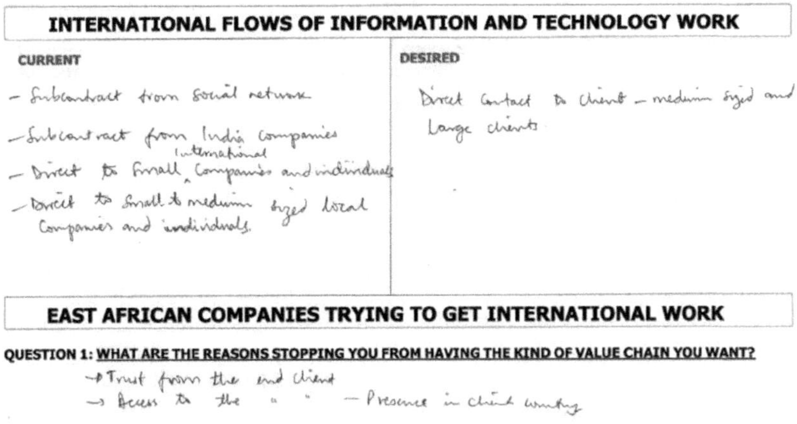

Figure 2. Importance of 'presence'.

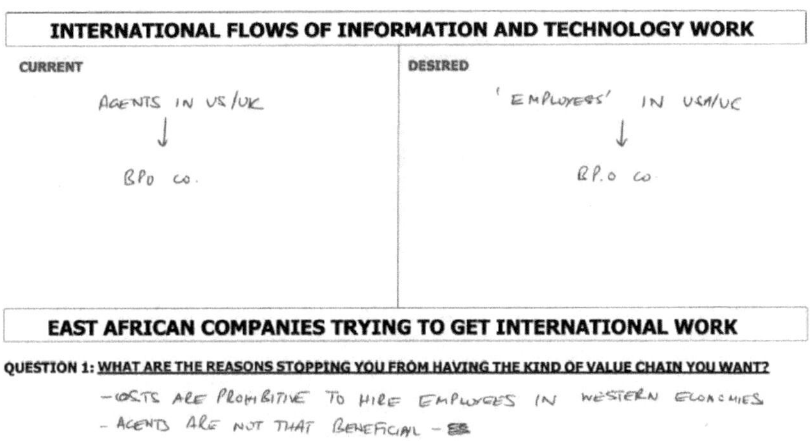

Figure 3. Importance of agents in client economies.

more effectively. Some Kenyan managers believed that foreign associates passed on work that Kenyan workers were better positioned to complete (due to their more neutral English accents), but others suspected their collaborators were only passing on low-value work, while retaining higher-value contracts. Lastly, and perhaps most importantly, established incumbents may be interested in a new destination like Kenya, not just as a source of new workforces, but as potential markets for their own service centres. Multinational companies may therefore wish to develop relationships with local Kenyan companies as a way of gaining access to new opportunities within the country. This last point is especially relevant for Kenya, as Nairobi and Mombasa are transportation and financial hubs for the rest of East Africa.

Like any new firm or country wishing to join this global trade, Kenyan policy-makers and business-people must therefore contend with these incumbent networks and determine the strength of their own bargaining positions. Managers are conscious of the fact that they are not the only country in the world trying to engage. As a manager of one of the largest Kenyan BPO firm described:

> Something like 70 countries have written 'BPO' on their own Vision 2030, 40, 50, so they're all competing for it, and so they would all love to have the Indians come into their country, all the

> Americans and Europeans, which means that those companies are in a buyers' market. So if I'm going to go into Togo or Kenya, Uganda or Botswana: 'What are you going to pay me as a business?' and under the table, 'But what are you going to pay me to come in here?' 'And if you're going to pay me want I want' – oftentimes it's about £10,000 per person – 'then I will comply with your rules, but if you're going to tell me, 'Come in and build your own place and all that stuff, and then pay more for your staff' I'll go to Uganda, I'll go to Botswana.' So there's that competition. (Interview, Nairobi, 22 November 2012)

This competition to attract foreign investment makes the BPO sector particularly vulnerable to exploitation by intermediaries and incumbent firms.[22] Mytelka has thus referred to it as a 'locational tournament' (1999). Kenyan actors are particularly vulnerable due to the late stage in which they are trying to enter.

China and India's early development of BPO in the 1980s and 1990s took place in the context of the dot-com bubble and a drop in international internet costs that made the globalisation of services first possible. Thus their BPO industries benefitted from a first-mover advantage (Athreye, 2003; Carmel, 2003; Krishna, Ojha, & Barrett, 2000). Jana Kleibert has shown how the later entrance of the Philippines meant that it developed a very different model. While local businesses drove the growth of India's BPO sector and such firms have since grown into multinationals in their own right, the Filipino sector is dominated by large multinationals that have almost entirely bought out local companies. Foreign equity in the Philippines' service sector is 93.3 per cent (Yi, 2012, p. 137). While Indian firms were greatly strengthened by strong diaspora links with the United States due to the migration of Indian professionals seeking educational opportunities, the Philippines did not have these same networks. The country lacked relationships with US businesses and had not developed specialised skills like software development. Further, because the Philippines entered the sector when voice-based work was becoming more affordable, it has become dominant in call centre work and has now displaced India as the biggest customer service destination in the world (Kleibert, in press).

Kenya's experience thereby reflects the moment in which the country entered the international market. It was difficult for the country to compete with destinations like India and the Philippines in areas such as voice-based service work, due to the tendency of clients and multinational BPOs to cluster in areas with a proven track record (Kleibert, 2014, in press; Milberg & Winkler, 2013). However, in other areas like mobile phone app development and social media based work, the field might be more nascent and open. Kenya is also privileged in terms of its strategic position within East Africa.

The Kenyan market therefore offers certain opportunities to international service providers; the question is whether it can exploit this position and retain work opportunities within the country. In the next section, we argue that domestic outsourcing has come to be understood as a way for Kenyan managers to both make sense of incumbent networks and as a way to capitalise on the growing penetration of internet into Kenya's (and other East African countries') organisations.

V. Pragmatic Response

After the arrival of the submarine fibre-optic cables, many Kenyan BPO companies had come to appreciate the difficulties of accessing foreign work and dealing with intermediaries. But, in the background, other changes were taking place. The arrival of the cables not only made international connections more affordable, but also made connections within the country more affordable and common.

The deeper penetration of internet and mobile connectivity changed the broader environment for ICT-led economic development. The government thus started to shift its funding and policy-making attention to software developers and other high-value producers, most visibly in the celebration of cases like Safaricom's mobile money platform, M-Pesa and the disaster response crowd-sourcing tool, Ushahidi. The government also began to realise the potential of ICT automation for centralising control over government budgets and reducing corruption and waste. In the summer of 2013, the Kenya Revenue Authority announced that it would become mandatory for all medium and large taxpayers to file and pay taxes electronically (Mutai, 2013). Similarly, it was announced that it would start digitally tracking M-Pesa and bank transfers to identify non-tax paying traders in the informal economy (Omondi & Juma, 2013).[23]

This drive towards efficiency and automation is further taking place in an environment of growing subcontracting within the labour market. As a 2005 study by Philippe Bocquier has found, 88 per cent of Kenyan informal employees were actually employed on flexible contracts by formal firms (Bocquier, 2005). While Kenya is particularly marked in this growing flexibility/informalisation of the labour force, this state of affairs is becoming so conspicuous throughout Africa that the ILO has re-classified the 'informal sector' as the 'informal economy' to account for informal workers working for formal sector firms, facilitated by outsourcing or labour contracting arrangements (International Labor Organizations [ILO], 2009). The introduction of software and ICT automation has the potential to extend sub-contracting employment relations to more middle class or professional workers, with the attendant risk of informalisation in future. In this environment, BPO has come to be conceived as part of a broader transformation of the national economy, as developers in ICT hubs are being encouraged to digitise information systems and 'digitally enable' value chains within Kenya's local economies through software and mobile applications.

By 2012, the Kenya ICT Board had changed its mandate from promoting BPO to promoting ITES. Similarly, a planned 7500-seat BPO park was renamed as the technopolis of Konza City. It was noticeable that BPO was only mentioned in passing at the Konza City opening ceremony. Instead there was much talk about attracting big multinational companies to the industrial park.[24]

Within this broader transformation, managers of Kenyan BPO companies found their place. Domestic outsourcing came to be understood as a way for Kenyan managers to make sense of the industry and manage the wider restructuring of the local economy to their benefit. It would allow Kenyan managers to retain their workers, build up competencies and expand their portfolio of clients. It would also allow foreign actors to evaluate Kenyan capacities. Many foreign clients began to ask, 'What have you done locally?' as a way to gauge competence.

An interviewee who had worked for two BPO companies before becoming an impact sourcing advisor commented:

> [W]e would like to get more work from the government, we want to get more local content into the hands of this people that can be done and there's a lot of work e-governance and just generally hospitals ... So we have had an immense targeting banks and hospitals and the government just to talk about how outsourcing can get into that. ... The Kenyatta national hospital for example, I'm told has data that dates back to 40 years ago and they did, they started digitising just a small section of it, I think about 40 million records or some big number like that ... So when you look at all the faculties in the hospital it means that we haven't even scratched the surface. So there's a lot to be done. (Interview, Nairobi, 29 January 2013)

The manager whose company had struggled to get international clients commented:

> Banks, insurance companies. Manufacturers, for example, we tried to talk to manufacturers about outsourcing their distribution and stocking and knowing which depots need what and all that sort of thing, but they want to hold it in, I think it's trade secrets they're worried about. Alternatively, the Kenya government could promote outsourcing in the domestic market in particular with the government and the companies in which it has shares. So Safaricom has 1500 people and they want to hire another 500, Kenya government owns a large part of Safaricom, if they were to say, 'Safaricom, you need to reserve 300, 400 seats for Kenyan outsourcing business', that would do a world of good to any one of the one, two or three guys that participated in that, it could change their fortunes overnight, they could afford to do A, B, C, D. (Interview, Nairobi, 10 December 2012)

The domestic turn was not *just* a matter of turning to domestic clients in the absence of international clients, but rather it was also an attempt to make the most out of the country's deepening internet penetration and to use the domestic BPO market as a way to build local understandings of the sector and improve the country's global recognition. For this reason, almost all our interviewees claimed that they wanted Indian and other multinational BPO competitors to enter the country. A manager of a large, well established Kenyan BPO asserted that:

> the government could help these companies to get business through a secondary effect such as promoting Indians and others to come to Kenya, therefore it looks like Kenya's attractive, therefore people who don't want those guys may now pick the Kenyans and the Kenyans get more business. (Interview, Nairobi, 29 November 2012)

Another interviewee reinforced this belief, asserting that Indian companies would bring work to Kenya from existing clients:

> The good thing about Spancos and Tech Mahindras [Indian BPO companies] of the world is they have the financial muscle, but more than that they have the global leverage. So they have, the only service various customers from India, from China ... For example ... when they ... say 'now we have a centre in Kenya as well' so ... a big, large company, ... fortune 100, fortune 500, might come and say, 'Fine I'd like to try it out in Kenya'. (Interview, Nairobi, 22 November 2012)

The entrance of such companies was seen by BPO managers to provide a 'demonstration effect'[25] and thus normalise Kenya's reputation as a mainstream destination in the eyes of global clients. One manager even suggested that the government should lure one large multinational BPO company into the country through a lucrative opportunity in a parastatal or other large Kenyan company that would make it affordable for it to enter. Once established, the manager hoped that the multinational company would then expand its operations, attracting contracts with prominent international clients and providing workers and managers with experience and understanding of the systems and processes required.

It was no longer a case of individual Kenyan companies seeking to engage remotely (and some might say, without being identified as Kenyan), but rather making the Kenyan brand something unique. If they could transform the image of the Kenyan economy into an 'ICT hub' through the celebration of software development and automation, then they could create a regional cluster that multinational competitors would want to join. The technocratic discourse that pervaded the speeches of politicians and the media reports on BPO prior to 2009 was thus replaced by a pragmatic realism that even in the digitally-enabled information economy, information flows through people and places. The fibre optic cables have thereby enabled a two-way globalisation of services: the cables have made it possible for Kenyan BPO companies to physically access international work opportunities, but they have also facilitated the entrance of international businesses and work practices, deepening existing tendencies of digitisation and casualisation of labour.

VI. Conclusions

The nature and value of work in the service economy is particularly hard to quantify and communicate to others (Spence & Carter, 2011). As Marazzi and Mecchia (2007) have argued, the production and expropriation of such value from information requires both technological ICT infrastructure and 'socio-cultural machineries' and 'cognitive capital'. The tendency with ICT investments has been to see them as technocratic solutions and as 'win win' scenarios for all participants, but as countries like Kenya gear up to restructure the local economy and engage in flows of international service work, they must bear in mind that powerful incumbent networks exist with their own sets of interests. One does not simply 'tap in' or 'log on' to global opportunities. While high internet and labour costs still hamper Kenya's international competitiveness, perhaps the most formidable barrier has been social distance from clients and knowledge flows. Quite simply, globalisation of services has been structured by power relations (Cooper, 2001). As Massini and Miozzo (2012, p. 19) describes, the relative power of American and European interests vis-à-vis other destinations like India and the Philippines means that higher value activities still remain in advanced economies.

After 10 years of experience, Kenyan managers and owners have gained a keen awareness of how the digital economy actually works: economic opportunities flow not only through fibre optic wires, but through people with their own private interests at heart. Seen in this light, joining the digital economy ultimately means negotiating opportunity with these interested parties and making shrewd decisions about how best to gain strategically from wider restructuring patterns happening within companies both across the globe and within Kenya itself.

The targeting of local clients by BPO companies and the encouragement by government officials to spur ICT innovation (and thus increasing data flows within Kenyan economies and organisations) contains both opportunities and vulnerabilities, unevenly spread between groups. On the positive side, the synergy between the BPO sector and local software developers could allow Kenya to develop a longer-term potential for higher-value BPO. Jyoti Saraswati (2012) has demonstrated the important role played by India's software industry in building relationships with American companies and thus allowing Indian BPO companies to transition from low-value customer service work into higher value services (see also Athreye, 2004). Kenya's current strategy to position the country as an African ICT hub might provide opportunities for Kenyan actors to mimic this experience.

The domestic turn can also serve to more deeply embed the BPO sector into the local economy, potentially creating frontward and backward linkages with Kenyan firms in other sectors. This tendency might cushion the country from external shocks and thus prevent it from developing into a branch-plant economy dependent on fleet-footed multinational companies (Phelps, 2008; MacKinnon, 2012; Kleibert, 2015). These frontward and backward linkages decrease the likelihood that foreign investment will move elsewhere when costs change. If Kenyan clients are involved in negotiations and decision-making between multinationals and Kenyan government officials, then it is possible that multinationals may keep managerial and client-relationship activities within Kenya. These considerations further demonstrate the need for nuanced understandings of BPO and ITES.

On the negative side, however, the Kenyan government's desire to attract multinationals may mean that Kenya follows the trajectory of the Philippines, where domestically owned BPO companies have mostly disappeared. Foreign buy-outs could potentially remove decision-making within such organisations overseas, leading to weaker skill upgrading and social mobility within firms. This loss of control could also mean that foreign companies and governments will have better access to Kenyan government and corporate data flows, which may pose security and ethical implications in future.[26]

Lastly, we must consider the impact on labour relations within Kenya. One might charge that domestic outsourcing is merely a more elaborate way of saying that ICTs are contributing to an informalisation of employment for middle class workers. The re-casting of outsourcing arrangements in the more positive language of BPO shields us from scrutinising the way that deeper ICT penetration might be changing relative bargaining positions. For example, Hope (2012) cites the growing share of services in Kenya's GDP as a sign that the BPO sector is growing successfully, without mentioning that BPO currently accounts for a small share of the much larger and generally informal service sector. Trade in services is dominated by tourism and travel, not BPO (Dihel et al., 2012). Yet commentators still highlight BPO as central when talking about Kenya's service sector. Similarly, while interviewees described how Kenya should mimic the experience of South Africa in building up its service sector, there is evidence to suggest that the structural transformation of the South African economy has been overestimated and that the impressive growth of services might simply be a statistical illusion driven by the outsourcing of 'relatively low-skilled, low-technology activities with limited scope for cumulative productivity increases and negligible potential for generating foreign exchange' (Tregenna, 2010, p. 21).

As many of the managers who established Kenyan BPO operations framed their investments as ways to tackle joblessness, it is important to ask what BPO will do to the Kenyan economy in the future: *Will it create jobs? And will it create the kinds of jobs that both young Kenyans and economic planners want?* Benson Okwaro, the head of the Kenyan Communication Workers Union (CWU) expressed concern that the outsourcing of work within the communication and technology sector could follow the experience of outsourcing within the security services, where private contractors have made it difficult for traditional unions to organise and collectively bargain. The specific characteristics of the BPO sector pose particular challenges. The informality of the sector and its high turnover rates make it hard for unions to maintain contact with members and forge common identities and interests over the long-term (Noronha & D'Cruz, 2006). These challenges are compounded by the commodification and re-distribution of service work across organisational boundaries, which further impede traditional union strategies. Such concerns have been raised by Alex Free (2015) in a recent paper on worker experiences within the Kenyan call centre sector, who found that when companies experienced financial difficulty, workers struggled to receive their wages and found it difficult to seek redress. They felt that their positions were insecure and that they could 'be readily dismissed as easily replaced cheap labour, especially ... [as] those working in BPO are subject not only to their own company's authority, but also that of clients' (2015, p. 60). Finally, there is a danger that domestic outsourcing could lead to a leaking of work to other countries and thus a reduction of jobs, something that some interviewees suggest is already happening.

In sum, this paper has examined Kenya's experience of BPO from 2004 to 2014. We have outlined some of the central barriers that Kenyan BPO managers have faced in trying to access international service work, showing how lack of managerial experience, lack of personal connections and physical distance from markets have all made it difficult for Kenya to emerge as an international BPO destination. In response, Kenyan based companies have increasingly turned towards Kenyan clients, with the Kenyan government now focused both on promoting higher value ITES activities such as software development and on attracting prominent multinational BPO competitors into Kenya. What Kenya now needs is both a more tailored policy to better tackle the changed geographic focus of the sector, and more research into understanding the long-term social and institutional changes that are likely to result. Will changing digital infrastructures allow Kenyan producers and workers to upgrade their skills and assets, and thus increase the country's national competitiveness, or will the closer integration of Kenyan economic activities into international service companies make the country more vulnerable to global shifts? It is too early to predict the full impacts at this early stage but we end by suggesting a more prudent reckoning of both the potentials and vulnerabilities of the changes afoot within Kenya.

Acknowledgements

The authors would like to thank their collaborators, Timothy Waema and Charles Katua for support and helpful input during fieldwork in Kenya. In addition the authors wish to extends thanks to Kate Meagher, Linnet Taylor, Marie Berry, Jana Kleibert, Henrike Florusbosch and Nicolas Friederici for comments on earlier drafts and to the other participants of the panel, *Moving Jobs, Moving Workers* at the European Conference on African Studies, where the paper was first presented. Lastly, we wish to thank the anonymous reviewers who gave excellent suggestions on how to improve the paper. The research project at the core of this report is based on an initial pilot research project funded by the British Academy in 2010. The larger project was funded by a multi-year ESRC-DFID grant (RES-167-25-0701 | ES/I033777/1). For a more detailed description of methodology employed in the project and for a fuller presentation of the data used, please visit: http://www.esrc.ac.uk/my-esrc/grants/RES-167-25-0701/read

Disclosure statement

No potential conflict of interest was reported by the authors.

Notes

1. In this paper we employ the word 'global' to refer to not just non-local processes and practices, but also processes/practices that are genuinely trans-national and trans-continental in their scope (see also Massey, 2005 for the fuller discussion of the term).
2. Later assessments of the Indian BPO sector reveal that it too is moving towards increased outsourcing within the national economy as well (Jana Kleibert, personal communication).
3. It should be noted that many analyses of the Kenyan BPO sector rely on secondary materials (Bryce, Hartley, Kassam, Saloojee, & Williams, 2011; Iraki, 2013; Wausi et al., 2013).
4. The project looked at the impact of fibre optic internet connectivity on three sectors of Kenya and Rwanda's economies: tea, tourism and BPO. This paper focuses on the Kenyan BPO/ITES sector.
5. Author 1, Author 2 and Professor Timothy Waema carried out the interviews with BPO managers and Kenyan policy-makers (49, 10, and 2 respectively).
6. These informal operations were described by several interviewees. Some informal work is still taking place. While these platforms are designed to allow individual users to bid for work, in Kenya, some companies ask employees to use these platforms to source work for the whole workforce, using individual profiles in order to do so.
7. It is unclear whether the firm is still in operation.
8. In order to explicitly address the non-local geographic reach of firms, this article uses the term 'international' to refer to all work and clients outside of Sub-Saharan Africa. Although other East African and South African work is undoubtedly *international*, managers themselves distinguish between international work outside of Africa and regional work within Africa.
9. This segment was also envisioned as complementing other sectors of the economy, like tourism, where customer service and natural accents are also valued.
10. It is worth noting that submarine fibre-optic cables are used for all sorts of digitally mediated connectivity. However, this paper focuses exclusively on internet connectivity.
11. Seacom was formed by the coming together of Industrial Promotion Services (a branch of the Agha Khan foundation in Egypt which owns a 26.25% stake), VenFin Limited (now merged with Remgro Ltd. – both also South African – which owns 25%) Convergence Partners (also South African and owning a 12.5% stake) and Shanduka (also South African and also holding 12.5%). The remaining 23.75 per cent was held by Herakles Telecom LLC (an American company).
12. Telkom/Vodacom, MTN and Neotel.
13. These include the World Bank/International Finance Corporation (IFC), European Investment Bank (EIB), African Development Bank (AfDB), Agence Française de Développement (AFD), and KfW (Kreditanstalt für Wiederaufbau).
14. This was a World Bank programme designed to support e-government and ICT outreach projects.
15. For a discussion of the notion that ICTs and internet connectivity 'disintermediate' financial and service value chains, please see French and Leyshon (2004).
16. See James and Vira (2012) for a description of the impact of the financial crisis on Indian outsourcing.
17. Impact sourcing promises clients to provide their work to members of marginal communities.
18. The quotation marks denote the neoliberal framing of the project. Participants were initially framed as being self-sufficient 'entrepreneurs' in line with Enablis general policy. For a broader discussion of the influence of neoliberal ideologies on African economic development, see Harrison (2010).
19. Question paraphrased from interview discussion (Author 1 fieldnotes).
20. Outcome based work is work whose profits are based on favourable outcomes. For example, a company will only be paid for calls that result in a successful sale, as opposed to the total number of calls made. Such work is generally considered to be challenging and unprofitable, especially for inexperienced companies.
21. For a broader discussion of this conversion process within ethical capitalism, see Catherine Dolan's work in this special issue and in Dolan and Roll (2013, p. 129).
22. In focus groups, participants felt that exploitation primarily occurs when there are disparities of knowledge and awareness.
23. It is unclear what legal and ethical protection governs this activity but according to Safaricom's own terms of service, customers give the company the right 'to disclose any Transaction data or information pertaining to your M-PESA Account to any law enforcement, investigative or regulatory authority including without limitation the Kenya Police, Central Bank of Kenya, Kenya Anti-Corruption Commission, Kenya Revenue Authority or any competent Anti-Money Laundering authority for the purposes of any genuine enquiry and investigation …' This is clearly a controversial activity, and given the contentious nature of debate surrounding Kenya's new data protection law, we are likely to see growing public scrutiny of such behaviour in future. For an indication of the response to such activities from the Kenyan (media-savvy) public, see the blogpost: http://www.thinkersroom.com/blog/2013/07/kra-safaricom-you/
24. Author 1 fieldnotes.
25. For a discussion of the 'demonstration effect' in the Indian BPO sector, please see: Athreye (2003).
26. For a discussion of the privacy and ethical issues of 'big data' in relation to Africa, please see Taylor and Schroeder (2015) and Linnet Taylor's more recent blog entries.

References

Athreye, S. (2003). Multinationals and the evolution of the Indian software industry. East-West Centre *Working Papers Series*, 51. Retrieved from http://scholarspace.manoa.hawaii.edu/bitstream/handle/10125/3664/ECONwp051.pdf?sequence=1

Athreye, S. (2004). Role of transnational corporations in the evolution of a high-tech industry: The case of India's software industry"—a comment. *World Development*, *32*, 555–560. doi:10.1016/j.worlddev.2003.08.011

Batt, R., & Moynihan, L. (2002). The viability of alternative call centre production models. *Human Resource Management Journal*, *12*(4), 14–34. doi:10.1111/hrmj.2002.12.issue-4

Beunza, D., & Stark, D. (2003). The organization of responsiveness: Innovation and recovery in the trading rooms of lower Manhattan. *Socio-Economic Review*, *1*(2), 135–164. doi:10.1093/soceco/1.2.135

Bocquier, P. (2005). Informal sector versus informal contracts in Nairobi, Kenya. Document De Travail, DT/2005-10.

Bryce, J., Hartley, S., Kassam, Z., Saloojee, N., & Williams, B. 2011. Kenya's off-shoring advantage: An emerging BPO cluster in East Africa (Unpublished Microeconomics of Competitiveness Paper). Harvard Business School

Bryson, J. (2007). The second global shift: The offshoring or global sourcing of corporate services and the rise of distanciated emotional labour. *Geografiska Annaler, Series B: Human Geography*, *89*, 31–43. doi:10.1111/geob.2007.89.issue-s1

Carmel, E. (2003). Taxonomy of new software exporting nations. *Electronic Journal of Information Systems in Developing Countries*, *13*(2), 1–6.

Cooper, F. (2001). What is the concept of globalization good for? An African historian's perspective. *African Affairs*, *100*(399), 189–213. doi:10.1093/afraf/100.399.189

Corbridge, S., & Thrift, N. (1994). *Money, power and space*. London: Blackwell.

Cramton, C. D. (2001). The mutual knowledge problem and its consequences for dispersed collaboration. *Organization Science*, *12*(3), 346–371. doi:10.1287/orsc.12.3.346.10098

Davis, G. F. (2009). *Managed by the markets: How finance reshaped America*. Oxford: Oxford University Press.

Dicken, P. (2003). *Global shift*. London: Sage.

Dihel, N., Fernandes, A. M., Gicho, R., Kashangaki, J., & Strychacz, N. (2012). Becoming a global exporter of business services? The case of Kenya. In A. G. Goswami, A. Mattoo, & S. Saez (Eds.), *Exporting services: A Developing country perspective* (pp. 237–267). Washington, DC: World Bank. Retrieved from https://openknowledge.worldbank.org/bitstream/handle/10986/2379/658370EPI188160Box365736B0Exporting.pdf?sequence=1

Dolan, C., & Roll, K. (2013). ASR forum: Engaging with African informal economies. *African Studies Review*, *56*(3), 123–146. doi:10.1017/asr.2013.82

Dossani, R., & Kenney, M. (2007). The next wave of globalization: Relocating service provision to India. *World Development*, *35*, 772–791. doi:10.1016/j.worlddev.2006.09.014

Dwyer, D. (2012, June 25). Obama hammers Romney on outsourcing vs. 'offshoring' explainer. *ABC News*. Retrieved from http://abcnews.go.com/blogs/politics/2012/06/obama-hammers-romney-on-outsourcing-vs-offshoring-explainer/

Fernandez-Stark, K., Bamber, P., & Gereffi, G. (2011). The offshore services global value chain. Duke Centre of Globalization, Governance and Competitiveness. Retrieved from http://www.cggc.duke.edu/pdfs/2011-11-11_CGGC_Offshore-Services-Global-Value-Chain.pdf

Free, A. (2015). 'Development', profiles and prospects: Labour in Kenya's outsourced call centres. *Critical African Studies*, *7*(1), 47–65. doi:10.1080/21681392.2014.901877

French, S., & Leyshon, A. (2004). The new, new financial system? Towards a conceptualization of financial reintermediation. *Review of International Political Economy*, *11*(2), 263–288. doi:10.1080/0969229042000I672804

Friedman, T. L. (2006). *The world is flat: The globalized world in the twenty-first century*. London: Penguin.

Graham, M., Andersen, C., & Mann, L. (2015). Geographical imagination and technological connectivity in East Africa. *Transactions of the Institute of British Geographers*. doi:10.1111/tran.12076

Graham, M., & Mann, L. (2013). Imagining a silicon valley: Technological and conceptual connectivity in Kenya's BPO and software development sectors. *The Electronic Journal of Information Systems in Developing Countries*, *56*(2).

Harrison, G. (2010). *Neoliberal Africa: The impact of global social engineering*. London: Zed Books.

Hawkins, R., Mansell, R., & Steinmueller, W. E. (1999). Towards digital intermediation in the information society. *Journal of Economic Issues*, *33*(2), 383–391.

Held, D. (1999). *Global transformations: Politics, economics and culture*. Stanford, CA: Stanford University Press.

Hope, K. R. (2012). *The political economy of development in Kenya*. London: Bloomsbury.

International Labor Organizations. (2009). The informal economy in Africa: Promoting transition to formality: Challenges and strategies. *ILO Report* Retrieved July 30, 2013, from http://www.ilo.org/wcmsp5/groups/public/@ed_emp/@emp_policy/documents/publication/wcms_127814.pdf

Iraki, X. N. (2013). Outsourcing and vision 2030: An analysis into Kenya's new economic frontier. *African Journal of Business Management*, *7*, 1218–1223.

James, A., & Vira, B. (2012). Labour geographies of India's new service economy. *Journal of Economic Geography*, *12*(4), 841–875.

Kariuki, E. (2010). *Progress report implementation of the Mckinsey report BPO/ITES study recommendations*. Kenya ICT Board. Retrieved from http://www.horizoncontactcenters.com/ke/userfiles/Mckinsey_Report.pdf

Keeler, R. (2009, June 9). Outsourcing to East Africa: Growth industry or misguided ambition? *Ratio Magazine*. Retrieved from http://www.ratio-magazine.com/20090609681/EAC-Regional/Outsourcing-to-East-Africa-Growth-Industry-or-Misguided-Ambition.html

Kleibert, J. (2014). Strategic coupling in 'next wave cities': Local institutional actors and the offshore service sector in the Philippines. *Singapore Journal of Tropical Geography, 35*, 245–260. doi:10.1111/sjtg.2014.35.issue-2

Kleibert, J. M. (2015). Global production networks, offshore services and the branch-plant syndrome. *Regional Studies*, Advance online publication. doi:10.1080/00343404.2015.1034671

Kleibert, JM. (in press). Services-led economic development: domparing the emergence of the offshore service sector in India and the Philippines. In N. Beerepoot, R. Kloosterman, & B. Lambregts (Eds.), *The local impact of globalization in South and Southeast Asia: Offshore business processes in services industries*. London: Routledge.

Krishna, S., Ojha, A.K. and Barrett, M. (2000). Competitive advantage in the software industry: An analysis of the Indian experience. In C. Avgerous & G. Walsham (Eds.), *Information technology in context* (pp. 182–197). Ashgate: Aldershot.

Kumar, K., Van Fenema, P., & Von Glinow, M. (2009). Offshoring and the global distribution of work: Implications for task interdependence theory and practice. *Journal of International Business Studies, 40*(4), 642–667. doi:10.1057/jibs.2008.77

Kundu, S. (2008, June 27). Kenyan BPO dream collides with reality. *IT Examiner*. Retrieved from http://www.itexaminer.com/kenyan-bpo-dream-collides-with-reality.aspx

Levy, D. (2005). Offshoring in the new global political economy. *Journal of Management Studies, 42*, 685–693. doi:10.1111/joms.2005.42.issue-3

MacKinnon, D. (2012). Beyond strategic coupling: Reassessing the firm-region nexus in global production networks. *Journal of Economic Geography, 12*, 227–245. doi:10.1093/jeg/lbr009

Malecki, E., & Moriset, B. (2008). *The digital economy*. Oxford: Routledge.

Manning, S. (2013). *Tech support en Francais S'il Vous Plait!? The challenges of becoming a new global outsourcing hub* (Organizations and Social Change Research Group Report). University Massachusetts. Retrieved from http://ssrn.com/abstract=2258722

Marazzi, C., & Mecchia, G. (2007). Rules for the incommensurable. *SubStance, 36*(1), 11–36. (G. Macchia, Trans.). doi:10.1353/sub.2007.0014

Mark, O. (2008, February 11). World Bank frees funds to support call centres. *Balancing Act*. Retrieved from http://www.balancingact-africa.com/news/en/issue-no-392/telecoms/world-bank-frees-fun/en

Massey, D. (2005). *For Space*. London: Sage.

Massini, S., & Miozzo, M. (2012). Outsourcing and offshoring of business services: Challenges to theory, management and geography of innovation. *Regional Studies, 46*, 1219–1242. doi:10.1080/00343404.2010.509128

Mazumdar, D., & Mazaheri, A. (2002). *Wages and employment in Africa*. Hampshire: Ashgate.

Milberg, W., & Winkler, D. (2013). *Outsourcing economics. Global value chains in capitalist development*. Cambridge: Cambridge University Press.

Mutai, E. (2013, July 14). KRA set to make online filing of taxes mandatory. *Business Daily*. Retrieved from http://www.businessdailyafrica.com/KRA-set-to-make-online-filing-of-taxes-mandatory/-/539546/1914998/-/6bamu0/-/index.html

Mytelka, L. (1999). Locational tournaments for FDI: Inward investment into Europe in a global world. In N. Hood & S. Young (Eds.), *The globalization of multinational enterprise activity and economic development* (pp. 278–302). London: Palgrave Macmillan.

Noronha, E. & D'Cruz, P. (2006). Organizing call centre agents: Emerging issues. *Economic and Political Weekly, 41*(21), 2115–2121.

Omondi, G. (2012, February 5). Kenya: BPO firms suffer from worsening job losses in the west. *Business Daily* Retrieved from http://allafrica.com/stories/201202160548.html

Omondi, G., & Juma, V. (2013, July 17). KRA targets small businesses in bid to raise Sh974 billion. *Business Daily*. Retrieved from http://www.businessdailyafrica.com/KRA-targets-small-businesses-in-bid-to-raise-Sh974-billion/-/539546/1918230/-/iwuo25/-/index.html

Phelps, N. A. (2008). Cluster or capture? Manufacturing foreign direct investment, external economies and agglomeration. *Regional Studies, 42*(4), 457–473. doi:10.1080/00343400701543256

Ratio Magazine. (2009, June 12). Kenya: Bandwidth Subsidy for BPO Did Not Hit the Spot. Retrieved from http://www.ratio-magazine.com/20090612691/Kenya/Kenya-Bandwidth-Subsidy-for-BPO-Did-Not-Hit-the-Spot.html

Ratio Magazine. (2013, September 2). News Analysis: A Boost for the BPO/Outsourcing Industry? Retrieved from http://www.ratio-magazine.com/201309024261/News-Analysis/News-Analysis-A-Boost-for-the-BPO/Outsourcing-Industry.html

Republic of Kenya. (2007a). *Vision 2030: A Globally competitive and prosperous Kenya*. Nairobi: Government of Kenya.

Republic of Kenya. (2007b). *Vision 2030: The popular version*. Nairobi: Government of Kenya.

Saraswati, J. (2012). *Dot.compradors: Power and policy in the development of the Indian software industry*. London: Pluto Press.

Sheth, S. (2013, January 21). BPO for the BoP – defining impact sourcing and its potential to boost employment opportunity. *Next Billion*. Retrieved from http://www.nextbillion.net/blogpost.aspx?blogid=3112.

Singer, B. (2006, February 28). Kenya: Start-up views for outsourcing pie. *Daily Nation*. Retrieved from http://www.plex86.org/computer_2/StartUp-Vies-for-Outsourcing-Pie-3039.html

Spence, C., & Carter, D. (2011). Accounting for the general intellect: Immaterial labour and the social factory. *Critical Perspectives on Accounting, 22*(3), 304–315. doi:10.1016/j.cpa.2010.12.007

Stark, D. (2009). *The sense of dissonance: Accounts of worth in economic life*. Princeton: Princeton University Press.

Steinmueller, W. E. (2002). Knowledge-based economies and information and communication technologies. *International Social Science Journal, 54*(171), 141–153. doi:10.1111/issj.2002.54.issue-171

Taylor, L., & Schroeder, R. (2015). Is bigger better? The emergence of big data as a tool for international development policy. *GeoJournal*, *80*(4), 503–518.

Taylor, P., & Bain, P. (2008). United by a common language? Trade union responses in the UK and India to call centre offshoring. *Antipode*, *40*(1), 131–154. doi:10.1111/anti.2008.40.issue-1

Thibodeau, P. (2012). Amid US outsourcing fears, India's IT firms thrive. *Yale Global*. Retrieved from http://yaleglobal.yale.edu/content/amid-us-outsourcing-fears-indias-it-firms-thrive

Tregenna, F. (2010). How significant is intersectoral outsourcing of employment in South Africa? *Industrial and Corporate Change*, *19*, 1427–1457. doi:10.1093/icc/dtq001

Waema, T. (2009, July). Development of a business process outsourcing industry in Kenya: Critical success factors (IDRC Final Technical Report). Retrieved from http://idl-bnc.idrc.ca/dspace/bitstream/10625/41277/1/129133.pdf

Wausi, A., Mgendi, R., & Ngwenyi, R. (2013, August). Labour market analysis and business process outsourcing in Kenya: Poverty reduction through information and digital employment and digital employment initiative (Research Report 2013) 3. Retrieved from http://sds.ukzn.ac.za/files/ITEM1-researchpaper_KENYA_Aug_FINAL.pdf

Weick, K. E. (1995). *Sensemaking in organizations*. London: Sage.

Yi, S. (2012). Reaching the world through private sector initiative: Service exports from the Philippines. In A. G. Goswami, A. Mattoo, & S. Saez (Eds.), *Exporting services: A developing country perspective* (pp. 121–159). Washington, DC: World Bank. Retrieved from https://openknowledge.worldbank.org/bitstream/handle/10986/2379/658370EPI188160Box365736B0Exporting.pdf?sequence=1

Do Transnational Links Matter after Return? Labour Market Participation among Ghanaian Return Migrants

MARY BOATEMAA SETRANA* & STEVE TONAH**

*Centre for Migration Studies, University of Ghana, Accra, Ghana, **Department of Sociology, University of Ghana, Accra, Ghana

ABSTRACT *Do transnational links matter after return? The study presents the conditions under which migrants participate in the labour market of their home countries. Though transnationalism describes return migration as a circular movement, there is still evidence of permanent return prompting the question of how returnees utilise their transnational links after return. This paper presents an analysis of pre- and post-return experiences of Ghanaian international migrants, focusing on their strategies, assets and labour market participation. The study finds that return migrants keep ties with host countries for the sake of businesses and other benefits which may not be readily available in the home country. The paper suggests that in order to promote national development and enhance national competitiveness in a globalising world, Ghana needs to encourage collaboration amongst its residents abroad and encourage opportunities for the sharing of knowledge and expertise.*

Introduction

Transnational activities of immigrants in western countries have received more attention than migrants' post-return activities in their home countries. This is not surprising because, until recently, return migration had been under-researched in the migration literature. The increasing significance of the return movement led to the first European conference on international return migration held in Rome in 1981 (Kubat, 1981). Following this, Wyman (2005, p. 16), citing some return migration statistics, noted that at least one-third of the 52 million Europeans who left Europe between 1824 and 1924 returned permanently to their homelands. Similarly, the return rate was even greater in the United States in 1931 due to the economic recession: 89,000 persons left the United States compared to only 43,000 immigrants who arrived. It is most likely some of these immigrants found their way into Latin America and the African continent. Despite a lack of adequate data, migration from West African countries is also known to be essentially temporal (Adepoju, 2005; Ba, 2006) due to restrictive immigration policies that have led to a greater emphasis on (forced or voluntary) return as a policy tool or aim (Black & Gent, 2004; Blitz, Sales, & Marzano, 2005).

Such restrictive policies in host countries have deepened the transnational lives of migrants, and for that matter, Ghanaian migrants abroad in the sense that their ties and obligations occur in both their host and their countries of residence (Orozco, 2005). Migrants' attachment to the homeland is overly manifested through transnational practices such as remittances, phone calls and visits, among others (Nuro, 1999). Ghana's Central Bank reported $1.6 billion in remittance inflows in 2009. Between 2009 and 2011, inflows to Ghana were reported to have increased by 23 per cent and by 2011, remittances were said to have accounted for 0.4 per cent of the country's Gross Domestic Product (World Bank, 2014). These remittances are usually used for physical projects particularly businesses, housing, as well as household consumption (Anarfi, Kwankye, & Ahiadeke, 2005; Smith, 2007). Focusing on the activities of migrants abroad has hardly provided a bilateral perspective on the concept of transnationalism. This is striking because the lives of migrants in the countries of origin are also likely to become 'transnationalised' and it would be unrealistic to assume that migrants would readily abandon their transnational activities and links after return.

In this article, our aim is to contribute to the ongoing debate on transnationalism by studying the benefits of transnational links to Ghanaian return migrants. First, the paper provides an overview of the transnational businesses of Ghanaian migrants abroad. This is followed by a theoretical perspective on the transnational approach to return migration. Then, there is a presentation of the methods used in the study and a description and an analysis of labour market participation among return migrants. Finally, the paper ends with conclusions and recommendations.

The Context: Transnational Influence on Migrant Businesses in Ghana

Many of the small businesses in Ghana today have visible links with foreign places, sometimes in their names, but more often, in the products they sell and the services they offer. These businesses range from second-hand goods (slightly used items imported from Europe and North America) such as cars, fridges and clothes to new Italian floor tiles, fashion items and internet services (Smith, 2007). Besides businesses with clearly visible links abroad, there are many others initiated or supported by migrants. It is generally acknowledged that much of the flow of remittances by migrants to the country of origin, whether channelled through formal or informal avenues, is meant for businesses (De Haas, 2003; Grant, 2009; Hamann, 2000). Mazzucato (2005) has indicated with respect to Ghanaian migrants in Amsterdam that 28 per cent of all their remittances were invested in businesses in Ghana, mainly in Accra and Kumasi. According to Asiedu (2005), Diko and Tipple (1992), unskilled Ghanaians migrate abroad primarily to save capital in order to invest in houses and businesses in Ghana, since opportunities to accumulate such funds in Ghana are limited. Asiedu (2005) goes on to claim that a direct relationship exists between the duration of a migrants' stay abroad and their ability to accumulate enough savings for housing and business projects in Ghana. The contribution of remittances to the local economy through business investments is increasingly recognised and welcomed, as these remittances are regarded as being 'production' oriented.

According to Grant (2009), about a third of all returnees operated as 'transnational entrepreneurs' with business associates abroad whom they frequently visited. Most of these business contacts were with their former host countries and typically involved dealing in import-export trade or for client referrals and service sector activities. Others were consultancy works in Ghana that depended on having offices abroad to secure contract work. Besides Grant's (2009) study, which examined in some detail how returnees use their extended family, social and other networks to manage their businesses upon return to Ghana, most studies on return migration do not clearly indicate how migrants sustain their businesses upon return.

Currently, there are two debates on migrants and their roles in business related activities in the economy of developing countries such as Ghana. The first debate looks at the migration-development nexus. It analyses migrants' 'productive' use of their savings through investments in businesses rather than in consumption activities like the purchase of cars, the building of mansions, or funding lavish ceremonies such as funerals (Black, King, & Tiemoko, 2003). The second debate concerns the sustainability of migrants' business investments and their contribution to the national economy. In this debate, it is argued that larger businesses, rather than smaller sole proprietor businesses, can help expand Ghana's economy. These two debates interrelate in examining the contribution of migrants' investments to Ghana's economy and how they alleviate rural and urban poverty and boost other sectors of the economy. Central to both debates is the view that current investments of migrants in businesses are insufficiently innovative. This, it is argued, relates to the unwillingness of migrants to place their hard-earned savings in investments believed to carry risks. These risks might arise if migrants were to pursue new, uncharted niches in the economy, or if they were to partner others in business ventures, pooling capital to establish more capital-intensive businesses. The unwillingness of migrants to take such steps is because they see few other possibilities to make a living in Ghana (Ammassari, 2004; Black, King, & Tiemoko, 2003). Meanwhile, another way by which migrants could avoid these risks is to manage their own business upon return and also give it a transnational face.

While these two debates do raise relevant points, this paper argues that they give insufficient acknowledgement to the efforts migrants make in their bid to sustain their businesses in the national economy.

Transnational Approach on Return Migration

Until recently, migration was understood in terms of two opposing outcomes: permanent settlement abroad or permanent return home. Return migration especially was thought of as the final outcome of the migration process. This relatively static bipolar model is a simplistic and unilinear depiction of migration and return migration that is not consistent with the realities of population movements in an increasingly transnational and interconnected world. Transnationalism refers to the multiple ties and interactions that link people and their institutions across the borders of nation-states (Vertovec, 2009). It emphasises the increased possibilities for migrants and their families to live and/or move between two or more countries and adopt transnational identities. This has become possible because technology has made it easier for migrants to maintain links between their societies of origin and their adopted homes through the use of the telephone, television or internet and be able to remit funds through globalised formal and informal banking systems. Migrants are able to travel back and forth to relate to people and to work and do business in two societies simultaneously (Kyei, 2013; Mazzucato, 2005; Vertovec, 2009). These transnational ties could span over several decades, thereby becoming trans-generational (De Haas, 2003). It is widely acknowledged that these kinds of transnational ties are built on reciprocity and trust amongst family members, friends and business associates.

The transnational emphasis in migration studies is based upon the recognition that modern migration and settlement patterns are increasingly taking place within bipolar and multi-polar structures. This behaviour, which was probably not part of early forms of migration, characterises modern patterns of movements. Some authors argue that migrants may not return definitely to their countries of origin or their parents' birthplaces; they may still maintain various forms of linkages with these countries that could develop into eventual return for permanent settlement (Thomas-Hope, 1999). On the other hand, it could further be argued that even when migrants have returned permanently to their parents' birthplaces, they may still maintain various forms of linkages with the host country.

The transnational approach is thus an attempt to go beyond traditional migration theory and the structural approaches which are informed by and developed in the service of the nation-state and treated migrants as individuals who either departed (emigrants) or arrived (immigrants) (Levitt & Nyberg-Sørensen, 2004). Furthermore, De Haas (2010) argues that the transnationalisation of migrants' lives challenged assimilationist's models of migrant integration as well as the modernist's political construct of 'origin' or 'destination' and that categories such as 'permanent', 'temporary' and 'return migration' are increasingly difficult to sustain in a world in which the lives of migrants are characterised by circulation and simultaneous commitment to two or more societies or communities.

The transnational approach also criticises the notion of space that assumes that physical, social and political spaces perfectly coincide with a geographical space that is radicalised within the boundaries of a nation-state (Jackson, Crang, & Dwyer, 2004). Within this line of thought, the social fields approach proposed by Levitt and Glick Schiller (2004, p. 2) explains that individuals belonging to transnational social fields 'are through their everyday activities and relationships, influenced by multiple sets of laws and institutions. These sets of regulations could make it difficult for return migrants to easily give up their transnational activities and practices even after permanent return. Their daily rhythms and activities respond not only to more than one state simultaneously, but also to social institutions such as religious groups that exist within many states and across their borders.' Therefore, through the transnational approach, we are able to understand that migrants live between the home and the host countries influence and are in turn influenced by what goes on in these two places. In this regard, return migrants may have strong ties with the host country and may exercise their double-citizenship rights to maintain contacts with the host country (Levitt & Nyberg-Sørensen, 2004).

Research Methods and Profile of Study Population

Like most African countries, Ghana has no universal registration of returnees on which to base a random sample and returnees are extremely hard to track (compare Grant, 2009). Anarfi, Kwankye, Ababio and Tiemoko (2003) in their study of the Ghanaian case found that returnees largely mirrored national demographics overall. Cohen (2005) also argues that most returnees relocate to the most globally connected urban centres. Our sample was therefore purposively selected from four major urban centres in Ghana known for the concentration of return migrants. These include the two largest cities in Ghana (Accra and Kumasi metropolitan areas) and the Dormaa/Berekum and New Juabeng municipal areas. The international migration literature (Anarfi, Awusabo-Asare, & Nsowah-Nuamah, 2000; Taylor, 2009) cites these locations as the established return migration flow regions in Ghana.

The study used the snowball technique in selecting its respondents. In order to have as many diverse responses as possible, key informants with in-depth knowledge of the survey areas were recruited to assist the researchers to identify returnees. During the preliminary field trip to the selected sites, 14 returnees were selected. Through chain referrals by the 14 respondents and personal contacts, the researchers finally achieved the required sample size. A total of 138 return migrants from western countries were invited to participate through personal contacts and telephone calls. However, the difficulty and sensitivity of the research only made it possible for 120 respondents to actually participate.

The first section of the survey asked questions relating to migrants' socio-economic circumstances before and after return. The survey instrument was pre-tested to help establish stability, consistency and content validity. It was self-administered and the advantage was that all questions which were relevant to respondents were answered. At the end of the structured questionnaires, respondents were asked to give their consent by providing their contact details for further in-depth interviews. 25 such respondents were selected based on their sex, age and mode of return. The qualitative information focused primarily on post-return experiences and was a follow-up on the structured questionnaires.

The majority of respondents (78%) were between the ages of 30 and 54, including some younger and older returnees. 37 per cent of the respondents were females while males dominated with 63 per cent. A representative ethnic mix was a more difficult task to attain because of the diverse groups as well as the absence of records on ethnicity of emigrants or returnees. Most of the respondents were within their productive ages (with an average age of 42 years). Their educational levels were generally high with 61 per cent having either a university degree or a diploma. Out of the total of 120 respondents, 54 per cent either furthered their education or acquired some kind of training or skills abroad. Respondents were found in all sectors of the Ghanaian labour market with the majority (23%) of skilled returnees in the educational sector as lecturers, researchers or high school teachers. Other skilled returnees worked in the banking, administration, sales/marketing or health sectors. This is attributed to the fact that recent recruitment of skilled personnel appears limited to the teaching and telecommunication sectors as well as some non-governmental organisations (compare Anarfi & Jagare, 2005). Most of the low or unskilled returnees were engaged in trading/businesses (29%) including mechanics, drivers, traders, masons, hairdressers and tailors. 8 per cent were farmers while 5 per cent had no income earning activity. More than half (69%) of the respondents were married, while the rest were either single (22%), separated or divorced (8%) or widowed (1%). About 89 per cent returned voluntarily, while 11 per cent were involuntary[1] return migrants.

The return migrants had stayed in different countries in Europe and North America with the majority coming from the United Kingdom (41%). The average time spent abroad was about nine years with a minimum of one year and a maximum of 44 years. The majority of return migrants came back home because they either felt homesick (32%), had completed their training or ended their contract abroad (21%), wanted to start their own businesses or projects (15%), or had lost their jobs in the host country (8%).

Generally, in our sample selection, we considered many of the important variables that influence the activities of return migrants: location of residence, age, sex, class, level of education and the type of business undertaken by the returnees. Most returnees to Ghana live in Accra and the major urban centres, hence our choice of the capital, Accra, and three of the most urbanised settlements in Ghana. The age of the returnee often determines the type of jobs and businesses that they undertake. Elderly returnees are most likely to be self-employed or work as consultants if they have specialised qualifications. Women with low education are most likely to work in the informal sector which is highly feminised in Ghana (compare Esson, 2013), while middle-aged persons with high education and training will likely seek employment in the public or private formal sector. The income level, or rather the amount of capital available to the returnee determines the kind and level of investments made (see Grant, 2009).

Finally, we must also mention the stellar performance of the national economy during the period of the research and data collection (2009–2010) as this influences the potential success rate of returnees' enterprises. In 2008, Ghana attained the status of a middle-income country and per capital income reached US $1500 in 2009. In addition to income earned from the production of gold, cocoa, tourism, exports of non-traditional goods and remittances from Ghanaians abroad, Ghana started the commercial production of oil in December 2010. These developments resulted in considerable confidence in the economy by foreign and local investors. Furthermore, macro-economic conditions relevant to the performance of any business venture were quite favourable. Economic growth reached a peak of 14.4 per cent in 2011. The rate of inflation and interest rates were falling and the exchange rate was relatively stable (Oxford Business Group, 2011). Thus, the general economic conditions for doing business in Ghana were quite favourable during the period of research.

Labour Market Participation among Return Migrants

In terms of accessing the job market in Ghana, return migrants could be categorised into two. The first category consists of return migrants in wage employment with mostly higher education and/or professional qualifications working in the public or private formal sectors. These include doctors, nurses, lecturers, teachers, engineers and bankers. A little more than half (50.8%) of the return migrants interviewed were found in this sector. The second consists of self-employed return migrants who came to Ghana with capital but only had secondary education; they were either in the private formal or informal sector. About 44 per cent of the respondents were in this area of employment. These enterprises include schools, farms, beauty salons, and building materials and groceries stores. Only six respondents (5%) had no income earning activity as at the time of the survey (see Table 1).

Despite all the preparations made towards their return, most respondents indicated that it took some time to enter the Ghanaian labour market. The majority (78%) of respondents had their jobs within three months of return, while approximately 22 per cent had jobs after three months and beyond. Most

Table 1. Employment of returnees

Nature of Employment	Number	Percentage
a. Wage employment	61	50.8
b. Self-employed	53	44.2
c. Unemployed	6	5.0
Total	120	100

of the respondents who took more than three months in finding jobs were usually those searching for wage employment. In cases where the job search took more than a year, respondents relied on their savings while others depended on extended families, both home and abroad, to make ends meet.

Family members and relatives play a crucial role in the economic behaviours and business ventures of return migrants (Black, King, & Litchfield, 2003; Tiemoko, 2004). Having been away for a number of years, the study revealed that kinship and social networks did not only become the main source of information for return migrants but were also used to establish the needed acquaintances required to secure employment in the formal sector. These networks comprised of those who had the capacity to influence their recruitments as well as those who served only as informants. About 62 per cent of the respondents secured or started their jobs with the help of friends, relatives, schoolmates, church members and associations while 29 per cent either responded to an advert or sent an application and nine per cent returned to their former jobs. Presented below is the experience of one of the respondents re-entering the employment market:

> Emma, a Master's degree holder, secured his first job with an insurance company in 2007, two years after he returned to Ghana. He obtained this job with the assistance of his uncle who had distributed copies of Emma's curriculum vitae to several institutions prior to his return to Ghana. In order to overcome the stigma attached to being 'unemployed', he accepted a job opening based on his Bachelor's degree while he continued to search for a better paid job. In 2008, he was employed by a college as an Assistant Registrar. He stated: 'I will forever be grateful to my uncle and my friend who helped me to secure this job in Ghana'. (Emma, interview in Kumasi, 14 December 2011)

Another respondent shared the following as her experiences with friends and family:

> I saw it as a responsibility because some friends had helped me before and were definitely going to continue assisting me on my return, so I needed to appreciate them. My mother was always asking me to buy gifts for this and that person; she never ceased reminding me of the assistance I received from friends and family. Maintaining contact with friends and family through the internet and telephone increased the bond between us. I remember upon my return, my former Director whom I used to call on phone while abroad, helped me re-enter the job market. (Akua, interview in Accra, 22 January 2012)

Kin and friendship networks are often maintained by returnees through transnational practices while abroad. They enable returnees to secure jobs that would have been difficult to acquire because they had to compete with non-migrants for the limited available vacancies. Therefore, social networks which were maintained while abroad are relevant not only to those who want to start their own businesses but also to those looking for formal jobs in the private and public sectors.

Another significant observation was the willingness of some respondents to work in areas below their educational qualification or in professions they were less enthusiastic about. For some respondents, accepting such offers irrespective of the education and skills they had acquired abroad were the only options available because of the challenges in the labour market.

Some migrants were faced with language problems on their return. For example, in depth interviews with some doctors trained in Russia showed that, on their return home, language was a barrier because they could not translate the names of some hospital equipment from Russian into English. This delayed service delivery at the hospital wards. However, with time they learnt these from friends and other colleagues who had similar experiences (compare Cassarino, 2004).

The other category is self-employed returnees who utilised their networks at home and accumulated resources to set up their private enterprises. Self-employed returnees expressed different reasons for starting their own businesses. These include the need to create employment opportunities, the love for the work they did while abroad and the need to be independent and build a fortune for their children. Indeed, the reasons outlined by returnees hardly support the view that migrants are often entrepreneurial by default rather than choice. In other words, return migrants started their own businesses based on their personal aspirations and attitudes and not because they saw fewer other possibilities to make a living in Ghana (Ammassari, 2004; Black, King, & Tiemoko, 2003).

Most of the self-employed returnees hired stores in the city centre where commercial activities are vibrant. Some respondents came along with capital goods such as electronic machines, corn mills, building materials, computers and cars that aided their businesses. Nana, for example, sold his corn mill in order to start his mattress selling business. She explained further:

> I decided to start my shop in Accra but the rent was so expensive. I came back to Kumasi, surveyed the town very well and I began a mattress shop. Before starting the shop, I sold one of the corn mills and used the capital to start my own business. I was able to buy a lot of mattresses to start the shop. It was moving on very well which made people venture into that business too. (Nana, interview in Kumasi, 28 December 2011)

However, not all returnees had positive experiences with family members and friends. A few returnees complained of the excessive financial demands made on them by their relations and friends and the pressure to meet the high societal expectations from returnees. Some returnees reported being cheated by family members and friends. The most frequent case involved the mishandling of funds meant for investment in housing and businesses (compare Grant, 2009; Kyei, 2013). Nevertheless, the significance of family, friends and social networks in establishing successful businesses and transnational ties cannot be overemphasised. Generally, our findings support recent studies by proponents of the livelihood and the new economy of labour migration approaches that stresses the significance of family and kin ties and network in (return) migration (see De Haas, 2010).

Benefits of Transnational Links on Employment after Return

Although the rise of academic and policy concern with transnationalism might imply that permanent return is becoming less relevant as a process, not just in relation to Africa, transnationalism itself can arguably be conceptualised as a form of return just as it can be seen as a form of integration in host societies (Kivisto, 2001). Thus, contrary to the perspective of northern governments where any return that involves re-emigration is seen as indicating a failure of the sustainability of return (International Organization for Migration, 2003, 2009), an alternative view suggests that in order for return to be sustainable, returnees often need to retain continued access to the wider international, professional and social world in which they have worked and lived. This is reflected in the way in which these respondents continue to value their contacts made abroad after their return. The experience of Junior is related below:

> Junior was trained as a nurse in Ghana. After some years of practising nursing, Junior earned a government scholarship to study abroad and subsequently diverted from nursing and pursued further education as a medical doctor in the UK. After his studies he had the opportunity to specialise and also work with one of the renowned hospitals in the UK. In 2005, Junior returned to Ghana and was employed in one of the Teaching Hospitals in the country. His former employers in the UK sometimes call him to help out in the hospital, especially during the summer breaks. He confirmed that the intermittent call for support gives him the opportunity to earn more income as well as learn new skills in his area of specialisation. He is a member of the Medical Association in both Ghana and the UK. (Junior, interview in Accra, 3 December 2011)

42 per cent (that is, 50 out of 120 respondents) of the returnees said they had professional contacts abroad. In all of these cases, the relationships were built by the individuals themselves. Some returnees, like Junior, maintained contacts and exchanges with their foreign partners through the internet, video link, telecommunication and other social media. Their professional contacts are so

crucial to them that these contacts have become part of their everyday lives in the home country. Many professionals such as doctors, lecturers and engineers who have maintained their foreign networks typically spend their sabbatical in hospitals and schools abroad. Such visits help them to keep abreast with new trends and modern technologies in their jobs while at the same time boosting their incomes back home. It further enhances the ability of return migrants to compete with non-migrants for the opportunities available in the Ghanaian labour market because of the general belief that people who are trained abroad have good work ethics and are smarter.

About half (51%) of self-employed returnees have business contacts abroad. Although some admitted that these business contacts were not too close, they still used them whenever the need arises. Besides their own businesses, some sold imported goods and used items such as television sets, cooking utensils, teacups and mattresses. Some of the respondents attested to the fact that their businesses were booming because many Ghanaians believe that goods from overseas are durable even when they are slightly used. Returnees usually obtain their goods on credit basis from their partners abroad. They then sell the items and pay their debtors thereafter or share any profits made with their business partners depending on the nature of the contract. Businesses were contracted informally on two main levels: in the first case, the return migrant pays for the goods before they are sent to Ghana; and secondly, the partner abroad initially sends the goods and the return migrant pays after sales. These informal arrangements may change overtime. For example, Kweku has a business partner who supplies him with computers from the Netherlands. He explained their relationship thus:

> ... my former colleague in the Netherlands has been supplying me with these computers. I go to the harbour almost every three months to retrieve the goods for the shop. The deal is that, he brings them so that I pay for them after sales. The initial plan was to just sell computers but gradually I had to also include servicing because people kept bringing their broken computers for repairs. As we speak now all these guys are my apprentice [pointing to some four guys who were busy working on some of the computers]. I have trained them for that. (Kweku, interview in Kumasi, 6 January 2012)

Many return migrants who had business partners abroad explained that in order to sustain their position in the transnational arena; they needed to engage partners who were most likely to help them sustain their businesses or association. For this reason, returnees identified trust as a key factor in maintaining these links. Smith (2007) in studying transnational businesses among Ghanaians in the urban sector also identified trust as an important factor. Indeed, among return migrants, there were hardly any formalised agreements in their transnational arrangements. Return migrants engaged in these activities also relied on information collected through family and friends in the selection of their business partners abroad. However, most return migrants also claimed that they were aware of the risks involved in these kinds of transnational arrangements; for example, the other party may not fulfil his part of the arrangement. One of our interviewees who trades in second-hand refrigerators shared his experiences:

> Business is business, it has ups and downs, but so far, my partner and I have been faithful to each other. Since I have been diligent in my sales and sharing of the profit, I don't foresee any breach of contract. We both benefit from the business so why would one cheat on the other. (Mr. Amofa, interview in Koforidua, 25 October 2011)

In this regard, Lyon (2000, pp. 664–665) argues that trust operates when there is confidence in other agents, despite the uncertainties, risks and the possibility for them to act opportunistically. Most of our respondents said they hardly foresee such risks because they have confidence in their partners so long as they (the return migrants) fulfilled their part of the arrangement. This means also that the multiple ties and interactions that link people across the borders of nation states (Vertovec, 2009) can only be successful if it is built on trust and reciprocity.

Other return migrants received financial support from relatives at home and abroad to keep their businesses running. Derrick, for instance, had no capital to start a business upon return. Actually, he returned to Ghana because he had lost his job in Italy. Derrick only had a secondary school certificate, which could not find him a well-paid job in Ghana. In order to make a living, his eldest sister who also lives abroad with her family assisted him to start an electrical shop. Derrick's experiences as well as those of our respondents emphasise the importance of family ties and intergenerational support in establishing and maintaining businesses in Ghana (compare De Haas, 2010).

Apart from professional and business contacts, about 22 per cent of the respondents also had some investments abroad. These include mortgages, bank savings, shops and pension, among others. Some respondents said that they deliberately kept those investments to support them financially since they perceived the Ghanaian economy to have several challenges. Therefore, to sail through these challenges they maintained some links abroad that could assist them financially until they had established themselves back home. Paul shares his story about receiving his pension from the UK thus:

> You know, I was on pension before I returned to Ghana to start this school. So my wife has been remitting my pension pay to me every month. In fact this school is doing well because of my pension pay. Sometimes parents don't pay school fees and meanwhile teachers need to be paid. In Ghana you can hardly go to the banks for loans because their interest rates are too high. (Paul, interview in Kumasi, 23 January 2012)

One of the returnees also said:

> I have a house in Spain which I gave out for rent before coming to live in Ghana. Every month the occupants deposit the rent in my account. At least, if for nothing at all, these monthly incomes keep me going in my transport business and also to fulfil other family obligations. You see, I am fulfilled, when I think of the fact that I have a house in Spain that fetches me money every month. (Adom, interview in Dormaa, 29 September 2011)

To sum up, this paper has identified three major groups of return migrants who developed and nurtured transnational ties in order to establish and grow their enterprises. The first consists of professionals who maintained ties with former colleagues and institutions abroad. Through exchange programmes and short stays abroad they were able to learn new skills and technology and earn some additional income. Generally, both the returnees and their partners and colleagues abroad benefited from such transnational ties despite the associated risks. Our findings tie in with those of Grant's (2009) who illustrated the benefits of transnational links with the case of high-profile Ghanaians such as Patrict Awuah who after a 20 years sojourn in the United States returned to Ghana to establish the Ashesi University, a private, Western-styled, African Ivy League university with the assistance of advisors and former colleagues from US universities.

The second group consists of returnees who established and nurtured their businesses with the assistance of some partners abroad. These foreign partners either provided them with goods on credit basis or some form of financial support. The relationship between the returnees and their business associates were also reciprocal as both partners benefited from the cooperation. Indeed in such cooperation, it was the foreign partners who provided goods on credit or secured loans for their partners in Ghana who took on the risks involved in going into such partnerships.

The third form of transnational ties was those established by returnees with some form of investments abroad. These included those who had savings, mortgages, shops and pensions abroad. Such persons usually utilised the services of a reliable partner abroad, usually a family member or a close confidant who can be trusted with funds and business secrets. The risks involved in such partnerships are very high for the returnees, so such engagements only took place with persons whom they trusted, usually family members or persons they have lived with or have had business dealings with over a long period.

Conclusions and Recommendations

This paper underlines the importance of return migrants to the economy of Ghana. It shows that return migrants utilise the transnational links that they have developed while abroad in accessing new skills and technology, sustaining their businesses, as well as obtaining financial support (mainly credit) from their business partners, family members and former colleagues abroad. These kinds of transnational links provide return migrants the opportunity to access resources which might not be readily available in the home country and also enhance their ability to compete with other businesses in Ghana. Furthermore, through the provision of specialised services in health, education and other sectors, returnees contribute to the improvement in the quality of life in Ghana. Some authors (for example, Ammassari, 2004; Black, King, & Tiemoko, 2003) have argued that migrant businesses are more often on a small scale and lack innovation because they are for the purposes of sustaining migrants' lives at home. On the contrary, our findings revealed that although some of the businesses were small and for sustenance purposes, they provided employment to many residents in Ghana.

However, available literature indicates that some returnees are engaged in businesses that are controversial and not necessarily beneficial to the populace. Grant and Oteng-Ababio (2012), for example, highlight the role of returnees in facilitating the importation of electronic waste into Ghana. Despite its lucrative nature, this business has negative health and environmental impacts on the population. Other authors have pointed out that the effects of returnees building posh houses, establishing successful companies, living a 'good life', travelling frequently abroad and displaying their wealth and so forth are that there will be more migration, inequality, dependency and the brain drain but this remains a debatable assertion. Successful companies established by returnees do provide employment, encourage investment and may result in more people staying in Ghana (see De Haas, 2010).

The paper also shows that return migrants maintain their existence in the transnational space by gaining the trust of their partners and family members. The basis of this trust is familial and the long-term association with their partners abroad. Although there are huge risks involved particularly in the business ties that they enter into with their overseas partners, most returnees we interacted with hardly perceived such risks, so long as they fulfilled their part of the agreement. Furthermore, the business and professional contacts between the returnees and their partners were mutually beneficial. Both parties benefited financially from the arrangements. To the returnees, income generated from their businesses and the expertise and skills they acquired while abroad enabled them to expand their businesses and improve upon service delivery in Ghana. Their partners abroad also earned additional income as a result of the collaboration with the returnees.

Generally, the findings support the argument on transnational network formation that suggests that the multi-stranded relationships and interactions proposed by transnationalism are often sustained through trust that is established through informal arrangements and relationships.

Finally, in spite of the above findings, we would like to reiterate the fact that our research was based on a small sample of 120 respondents obtained through the use of the snowball sampling method. This was largely due to the absence of reliable data on return migrants to Ghana and the difficulty in estimating the population of returnees. The extent to which our findings are representative of the situation of return migrants throughout the country can therefore be justifiably raised. Furthermore, it is worthwhile noting that the political and economic situations in Ghana during the period of the research were particularly good. A stable democratic political system that promoted free enterprise and a growing economy with bright prospects following the discovery of oil in 2007 contributed to the general euphoria and the high business confidence in the country during the period of the research. These conditions encouraged many Ghanaians abroad to return home and set up businesses. However, given the fragility of Ghana's economy, it is unclear whether the favourable investment climate in the country can be maintained in the long term. This will influence the willingness of return migrants to stay and invest in the country in the future.

Following from our findings, we make the following suggestions. First, in order to promote national development and enhance national competitiveness in a globalising world, Ghana needs to strengthen both its educational and business sectors. With this goal in mind, Ghana needs to encourage collaboration between its citizens and foreign countries and encourage opportunities for the sharing of knowledge and expertise (Asiedu, 2010; Hart, 2006; Lynn & Salzman, 2006). For example, the government should remove barriers and limitations placed on return migrants' and expatriates' travels and also provide subsidies and other forms of assistance to return migrants so that they can work more effectively with their overseas counterparts towards the promotion of national development. In order to enhance such engagements, a database of third-country nationals who left host countries (for example, North America and Europe) at the expiration of their temporary residence or work permit should be created so there could be a provision for long-term, multi-entry visas for such return migrants. Alternatively, there could be an understanding that former migrants would be given priority for obtaining tourist or business visas under simplified procedures.

These endeavours call for the strengthening of institutions responsible for the collection and assembling of data on migration such as the Ghana Immigration Service, the Customs Excise and Preventive Service, and the Ministry of Foreign Affairs so that they can provide regular, timely and comprehensive data to help formulate effective and comprehensive migration policies for the nation. There should also be more effective collaboration with global efforts by the International Monetary Fund (IMF), the World Bank, the Organisation for Economic Co-operation and Development (OECD) and other United Nations' (UN) bodies and institutions to sort out existing inadequacies and discrepancies in migration data sets. Furthermore, the impact of investment of return migrants within specific sectors of the Ghanaian economy needs to be evaluated.

Disclosure statement

No potential conflict of interest was reported by the authors.

Notes

1. The situation of involuntary returnees was not discussed in the paper because their number is too small for any statistical analysis.

References

Adepoju, A. (2005). *Migration in West Africa.* Paper prepared for the Policy Analysis and Research Programme of the Global Commission on International Migration, Global Commission on International Migration.

Ammassari, S. (2004). From nation-building to entrepreneurship: The impact of élite Return migrants in Côte d'Ivoire and Ghana. *Population, Space and Place, 10*(2), 133–154. doi:10.1002/(ISSN)1544-8452

Anarfi, J., Kwankye, S., Ababio, O. M., & Tiemoko, R. (2003). *Migration from and to Ghana: A background paper* (Working Paper No. C4). Brighton: University of Sussex, Development Research Centre on Migration, Globalisation and Poverty.

Anarfi, J. K., Awusabo-Asare, K., & Nsowah-Nuamah, N. (2000). *Push and pull factors of international migration: Country report Ghana.* Luxembourg: Eurostat.

Anarfi, J. K., & Jagare, S. (2005, December). *Towards the sustainable return of West African. Transnational migrants: What are the options?* Paper presented at a conference on New Frontiers of Social Policy, Arusha.

Anarfi, J. K., Kwankye, S., & Ahiadeke, C. (2005). Migration, return and impact in Ghana. A comparative study of skilled and unskilled transnational mirants. In T. Manuh (Ed.), *At home in the world? International migration and development in contemporary Ghana and West Africa* (pp. 204–226). Accra: Sub-Saharan Publishers.

Asiedu, B. A. (2005). Some benefits of migrants' return visits to Ghana. *Population, Space and Place, 11*, 1–11. doi:10.1002/(ISSN)1544-8452

Asiedu, B.A. (2010). Some perspectives on the migration of skilled professionals from Ghana. *African Studies Review, 53*(1), 61–78. doi:10.1353/arw.0.0324

Ba, H. (2006). *Les statistiques des travailleurs migrants en Afrique de l''Ouest* [Statistics of migrant workers in West Africa], Cahier des Migrations Internationales. Genève: Bureau International du Travail.

Black, R., & Gent, S. (2004). *Defining, measuring and influencing sustainable return: The case of the Balkans* (Working paper T7, Research.7). Sussex: University of Sussex: Development Research Centre on Migration, Globalisation and Poverty.

Black, R., King, R., & Litchfield, J. (2003). *Transnational Migration, Return and development in West Africa* (Final Research Report to DFID). Sussex: University of Sussex, Sussex Centre for Migration Research.

Black, R., King, R., & Tiemoko, R. (2003). *Migration, return and small enterprise development in West Africa: A route away from poverty?* Sussex: University of Sussex, Sussex Centre for Migration Research.

Blitz, B., Sales, R., & Marzano, L. (2005). Non-voluntary return? The politics of return to Afghanistan. *Political Studies*, *53*(1), 182–200. doi:10.1111/post.2005.53.issue-1

Cassarino, J.-P. (2004). Theorising return migration: A revisited conceptual approach to return migrants. *International Journal on Multicultural Societies*, *6*(2), 253–279.

Cohen, J. (2005). Remittance outcomes and migration: Theoretical contests, real opportunities. *Studies in Comparative International Development*, *40*, 88–112. doi:10.1007/BF02686290

De Haas, H. (2003). *Migration and development in southern Morocco: The disparate socioeconomic impacts of out-migration to the Todgha Oasis Valley* (Unpublished PhD thesis). Radboud University, Nijmegen.

De Haas, H. (2010). Migration and development: A theoretical perspective. *International Migration Review*, *44*(1), 227–264. doi:10.1111/imre.2010.44.issue-1

Diko, J., & Tipple, A. G. (1992). Migrants build at home: Long distance housing development by Ghanaians in London. *Cities*, *9*(4), 288–294. doi:10.1016/0264-2751(92)90029-5

Esson, J. (2013). A body and a dream at a vital conjuncture: Ghanaian youth, uncertainty and the allure of football. *Geoforum*, *47*, 84–92. doi:10.1016/j.geoforum.2013.03.011

Grant, R. (2009). *Globalizing city. The urban and economic transformation of Accra, Ghana*. Syracuse, NY: Syracuse University Press.

Grant, R., & Oteng-Ababio, M. (2012). Mapping the invisible and real "African" economy: Urban e-waste circuitry. *Urban Geography*, *33*(1), 1–21. doi:10.2747/0272-3638.33.1.1

Hamann, V. (2000, November). *Migration and development: The investment of migrants in the high emigration area of Zacatcas, Mexico*. Paper presented at the ISA Conference: International Migration in Latin America Enters a New Millennium, Buenos Aires.

Hart, D. M. (2006). From brain drain to mutual gain: Sharing the benefits of high-skilled migration. *Issues in Science and Technology* (fall). Retrieved from www.issues.org

International Organization for Migration. (2003). *World migration 2003: Challenges and responses for people on the move*. Geneva: International Organization for Migration.

International Organisation for Migrants. (2009). *Migration in Ghana: A country profile*. Geneva: International Organization for Migration.

Jackson, P., Crang, P., & Dwyer, C. (2004). Introduction: The spaces of transnationality. In P. Jackson, P. Crang, & C. Dwyer (Eds.), *Transnational spaces: Introduction: The spaces of transnationality* (pp. 1–23). London: Routledge.

Kivisto, P. (2001). Theorizing transnational immigration: A critical review of current efforts. *Ethnic and Racial Studies*, *24*(4), 549–577. doi:10.1080/01419870120049789

Kubat, D. (1981). *The politics of return: International return migration in Europe*. New York, NY: Center for Migration Studies.

Kyei, O. M. B. (2013). *Return and reintegration of Ghanaian migrants. A study of the migration experience and reintegration of Ghanaian returnees* (Unpublished PhD Thesis). Centre for Migration Studies, University of Ghana, Legon.

Levitt, P., & Glick Schiller, N. (2004). Conceptualizing simultaneity: A transnational social field perspective on society. *International Migration Review*, *38*(3), 1002–1039. doi:10.1111/j.1747-7379.2004.tb00227.x

Levitt, P., & Nyberg-Sørensen, N. (2004). The Transnational turn in migration studies. *Global Migration Perspectives*, *6*, 2–13.

Lynn, L., & Salzman, H. (2006). Collaborative advantage. *Issues in Science and Technology*, *4*, 74–82.

Lyon, F. (2000). Trust, networks and norms: The creation of social capital in agricultural economies in Ghana. *World Development*, *28*(4), 663–681. doi:10.1016/S0305-750X(99)00146-1

Mazzucato, V. (2005). *Ghanaian migrants' double engagement: A transnational view of development and integration policies* (Report No. 48). Geneva: Global Commission on International Migration, Global Migration Perspective.

Nuro, E. A. (1999). *Brain drain from Ghana: Case of university lecturers* (Unpublished MPhil Thesis). Department of Geography and Tourism, University of Cape Coast, Cape Coast.

Orozco, M. (2005). *Transnational engagement, remittances and their relationship to development in Latin America and the Caribbean*. Washington: Institute for the Study of International Migration, Georgetown University.

Oxford Business Group. (2011). The report: Ghana 2011. Retrieved from www. oxfordbusinessgroup.com/country/Ghana.

Smith, L. (2007). *Tied to migrants: Transnational influences on the economy of Accra, Ghana*. Leiden: African Studies Centre.

Taylor, L. (2009). *Return migrants in Ghana*. London: Institute for Public Policy Research.

Thomas-Hope, E. (1999). Return migration to Jamaica and its development potential. *International Migration*, *37*(1), 183–207. doi:10.1111/imig.1999.37.issue-1

Tiemoko, R. (2004). Migration, return and socio-economic change in West Africa: The role of family. *Population, Space and Place*, *10*, 155–174. doi:10.1002/(ISSN)1544-8452

Vertovec, S. (2009). *Transnationalism*. London: Routledge.

World Bank. (2014). Migrant remittances: Inflows and outflows: Ghana. Retrieved from http:www.worldbank.org

Wyman, M. (2005). In M. Harper (Ed.), *Emigrants homecomings: The return movement of emigrants, 1600–2000: Emigrants returning: The evolution of a tradition* (pp. 16–31). New York, NY: Manchester University Press.

Accidental Neoliberalism and the Performance of Management: Hierarchies in Export Agriculture on the Zimbabwean-South African Border

MAXIM BOLT*,**

*Department of African Studies and Anthropology, University of Birmingham, Birmingham, UK, **Wits Institute of Social and Economic Research, University of the Witwatersrand, Johannesburg, South Africa

ABSTRACT *South Africa's export farms have shifted from racialised paternalism to corporate managerialism. But how have workforce dynamics changed? This article offers an ethnographic perspective on agriculture on the transient Zimbabwean border. An 'actor-centred' approach examines the causes and extent of transformation. Who furthers managerial logics? Why? With what effects? White farmers emphasise impersonal, rationalised business for diverse reasons. What looks like part of a single global process of neoliberalisation is an accidental result. At the same time, foreign supermarket-funded development projects become subjected to logics of work-force paternalism. Managerialism itself has limited effect on labour arrangements. Workers' hierarchies and cross-border networks are built on different principles from global supply chains. From within each network, it is as if the other were invisible.*

Introduction

South Africa's settler agriculture, variously vilified or romanticised through its *boer*, colonial and apartheid histories, has seen important changes since apartheid began to crumble in the 1980s. Marketing boards intended to protect white farmer-landowners were largely dismantled, subsidies discontinued and commercial agriculture thrown onto the open market. Market liberalisation has pushed many growers into global supply chains, where profits are shored up by foreign exchange, but where supermarkets[1] have considerable power (see Mather & Greenberg, 2003). Farmers' khaki shirts are now emblazoned with the logos of export agents. Amidst a 'crisis of social reproduction' (for example von Holdt & Webster, 2005), a wave of casualisation has swept through the country's black farm workforces (Bernstein, 2013; Ewert & du Toit, 2005; Mather & Greenberg, 2003).

The wider context of change in agriculture is 'the current phase of neo-liberal restructuring' (Rutherford & Addison, 2007, p. 626). Market liberalisation has been accompanied by austere monetary policies (Bond, 2000), the outsourcing of state functions (for example Koelble & LiPuma, 2005), an emphasis on 'entrepreneurship' (Koelble, 2008), a 'rationality' of individual responsibility, and increasing financialisation of the economy (Marais, 2011). The transition from 'apartheid' to 'post-apartheid', from 'repression' to 'freedom', has been powerfully associated with those from 'state' to 'market', 'racial Fordism' to 'non-racial post-Fordism', and 'rigidity' to 'flexibility' (Hart, 2002, p. 25).

But what actually happens to labour arrangements on South African agricultural estates in the wake of globalising market liberalisation? There has been, broadly, a shift from 'paternalism' towards a corporate style of 'management', 'the idea that what farmers must do is not to *farm* but to *manage* [...] farming is no longer a "way of life" but a "business"' (du Toit, 1993, p. 325; italics original). The withdrawal of discretionary responsibilities not guaranteed by contracts or laws (Ewert & du Toit, 2005), and the shift to less socially embedded payment systems (Rutherford & Addison, 2007), appear to herald a whole new regime characterised by the abstraction and depersonalisation of employment obligations.

'Paternalism' appears a relatively coherent framework that can be replaced by or articulate with new labour regimes – even 'neoliberalism' (see for example Addison, 2006). But what this actually means is no simple matter. It is often difficult to distinguish paternalism from new regimes of management in practice. Farming areas have long been characterised by the fragmenting of black families in a mobile population (for example Waldman, 1996). Farmers' abrogation of responsibilities can coexist with senior black workers' continuing paternalist roles, belying any simple shift from paternalism to more atomised, depersonalised managerialism. In fact, recent changes in agriculture create *new* forms of authority within workforces. As farmers become more integrated into relations with 'capital upstream and downstream of farming' (Bernstein, 2007, p. 40), supermarkets establish development projects on farms for workers. These enable supermarkets to sell 'ethical' produce while tying farmers into supply chains. But such schemes also rely on senior-worker gatekeepers, for whom they become new potential sources of influence beyond working hours.

What all of this produces requires investigation. How, exactly, do recent changes shape employers' plans? How are employers' plans, in turn, realised in the everyday labour arrangements – the actual norms and relationships – into which workers are incorporated as a result of employment? This article presents the case study of Grootplaas,[2] a large citrus estate in a commercial farming area next to the Zimbabwean border, drawing on 17 months of ethnographic fieldwork (November 2006–April 2008) while resident in the workers' compound. Not claiming to characterise agricultural estates across the region (they are extremely diverse), the article raises cautionary questions about transformation following liberalisation. Neoliberalism sets the terms for larger-scale analyses of South Africa. But does this story account sufficiently for changes *at the level of workforce relationships and dependencies*? Corporate-style management itself is performed to further particular agendas. How far do its principles shape workers' networks and hierarchies?

A Transient Setting

On the banks of the Limpopo River – the border between South Africa and Zimbabwe – the dynamics of globalised export agriculture intersect with the fall-out of the Zimbabwean crisis. Since Zimbabwe's precipitous economic decline and political turbulence from 2000, countless people have climbed through the border fence in search of work. By 2009, Doctors Without Borders estimated that 3,000,000 had crossed (Doctors Without Borders, 2009), although large-scale undocumented migration means that assessments are open to question. Many were unemployed before they came, sometimes despite considerable education. Others left jobs whose remuneration was quickly eroded by one of the world's highest ever levels of hyperinflation – around 150,000 per cent by 2008 (Shaw, 2008).[3] Others again have fled persecution as supporters of the political opposition. An extraordinarily diverse population – in terms of regional, ethnic and class-based origin – has sought unskilled farm employment in recent years, under conditions of extreme vulnerability (Rutherford & Addison, 2007; Rutherford, 2008). Gangs along the border known as *magumaguma* rob and rape those crossing the river, and some arrive on the farms relieved of essential belongings.

Moreover, during the period of fieldwork, police deportation raids were frequent and aggressive. Seasonal workers would often avoid their rooms in the labour compounds, where they might be discovered, instead braving freezing winter nights in the bush. For farmers, this made for working populations that could be hired and fired with ease; that lacked freedom of movement beyond the farms; and that could even be denounced to the police just before month-end to avoid payment (see Human Rights Watch, 2006). On the other hand, farmers saw the paperwork required to replace deported workers as a considerable inconvenience, especially since deportees generally returned to their jobs within days, after climbing back through the border fence.

This description of transience and vulnerability sounds exceptional. But farmers in northern South Africa have long relied on cross-border migrants who faced crisis at home (Bolt, 2015; Werbner, 1991) and coercive, highly exploitative conditions as they sought work (Bradford, 1993; Murray, 1995; van Onselen, 1976). Today, farmers across the country – and especially near borders – respond to market liberalisation by capitalising on a floating reserve of migrant labour (Johnston, 2007). The experiences of farm workers on the Limpopo River represent not so much an exception as an extreme case of a wider historical and contemporary trend.

But there is more to workers' experiences than these conditions of vulnerability, or than the short contracts that leave their futures uncertain. During the five-month harvest each year, 450-odd recruits are put to work as pickers in the orchards (mostly men) and graders and packers in the packshed (women). They join Grootplaas's 140-strong permanent workforce, and enter a social world built on established relationships and hierarchies. The permanently employed have work permits and stable incomes, and some even acquire South African identity cards. By constructing furniture, front steps and yards, they have transformed their bare cells in the compound into provisional homes. They establish live-in, domestic relationships with women who come to the farm to find work, and for whom such relationships represent a form of integration into the relative stability of farm life.

Wages are meagre, and remittance to kin in Zimbabwe competes with the costs of compound life. And yet, for migrants seeking work, incorporation into the border farms means that living from one day to the next (see Day, Papataxiarchis, & Stewart, 1998) is mitigated by possibilities for planning. Forms of camaraderie developed in work teams extend into the compound. Labour arrangements shape not only work time, but also life on the farm more broadly. The resulting hierarchies can themselves produce exploitation among workers. Yet, like in other residential labour forces in southern Africa (for example Moodie & Ndatshe, 1994), senior workers are assessed through shared notions of ethical responsibility.

In such a world, how should we understand corporate managerialism and its effects?

Neoliberalism on the Ground?

Market liberalisation, and the wider transformations in South Africa noted earlier, make it tempting to regard recent changes on farms as part of neoliberalism's ascendance. Neoliberalism, as theory and class project, justifies the expansion of contractually defined market relations and free trade through a notion of individual entrepreneurial freedom (see Harvey, 2005). But it is not always clear what it means at the scale of everyday life. In South Africa (and elsewhere), it is held responsible for a wide range of phenomena (for example Comaroff & Comaroff, 2000; Geschiere & Nyamnjoh, 2000; Oomen, 2005). Neoliberalism becomes 'a kind of global meta-culture, characteristic of our newly de-regulated, insecure, and speculative times' (Ferguson, 2010, p. 171).

One approach is to focus on the creation of dispositions well suited to liberalised markets. 'The "responsibilised" citizen comes to operate as a miniature firm, responding to incentives, rationally assessing risks, and prudently choosing from among different courses of action' (Ferguson, 2010, p. 172). Ferguson argues that such a focus on neoliberal 'rationalities' is misplaced in African contexts. Neoliberalism as 'art of government', transplanted from research on Europe, is merely confused with 'a crude battering open of Third World markets' (Ferguson, 2010, p. 173). Yet in southern African agriculture, where white farmers historically promoted a paternalist form of 'domestic government' (Rutherford, 2001), matters may be less clear-cut. It is indeed important to understand not only market liberalisation, but also the forms of sociality produced by a corresponding shift towards corporate managerialism.

This paper takes such forms of sociality as its focus. Nevertheless, it argues that doing so does not expose a monolithic neoliberal rationality. Understanding farmers' 'government' over land and labour today means more than exploring how neoliberal places, people and regimes are constituted, or specifying the articulation between paternalism and neoliberalism. After all, the extraction of value by employers in liberalised markets often relies on – or even encourages the resurgence of – older forms of exchange and dependency (see Cross, 2010; Mollona, 2005).

On South African farms, particular people promote principles often associated with neoliberalism, with particular agendas in mind, and with particular effects. 'The perceptions and interpretations of the actors concerned' (Arce & Long, 1993, p. 179) are paramount. Taking key individuals as the brokers of wider social processes enables a variegated picture, especially apposite in the racialised settings of southern African settler agriculture. On farms, like on the region's mines, senior black employees form the interface between white employers and black labour, in systems that extend into all aspects of life. As Epstein (1958) showed for the Zambian Copperbelt, such 'intercalary' figures negotiate their positions through idioms of authority that have more than one source, and which may conflict. This invites a focus on the idioms of labour relations that pertain on the ground – here, paternalism and corporate-style management. Such models are not simply imports from elsewhere. They become products of the labour setting itself, intertwined with the agendas of both employers and powerful workers.

What follows explores how and why farmers present themselves as corporate businessmen; who takes up corporatising measures in the workforce itself; and how these play into hierarchies and the ethics of authority among workers. The next section turns to the white farmer whose vision sets the parameters of life at Grootplaas.

Accidental Neoliberalism: The View from the Office

Talking to Willem, who runs Grootplaas Estates, one certainly has the impression of a corporatising shift in the everyday reality of South African agriculture. The 40-something son-in-law of Grootplaas's founder, Willem is one member of a four-man family partnership. Unlike some older farmers, he draws a sharp separation between work and home life. He speaks of restricting his responsibilities as employer to the office. Claiming that he has only a limited grasp of dynamics within the workforce and the 'cultural' bases of disputes among workers, he underscores his reluctance to intervene in non-work matters. His concern is that he could be held accountable for decisions he might make without a full appreciation of their implications. Willem casts himself in contrast to an established ideal of paternalism, to which his father-in-law and other older whites on the estates aspire. According to this model, white farmers rule over their black 'people'. Relying on their cultural understanding, they intervene in non-work matters, and provide for workers and dependents through discretionary gifts and favours.

Willem is keen to present his farm in the idiom of corporate management, in which his limited responsibility for workers' welfare combines with a downplaying of racial distinction. During a meeting in his office (older farmers would meet at their houses), he set out the Grootplaas labour hierarchy. The idioms he employed were revealing. He first described the company's four 'shareholders' – Willem himself, his father-in-law Koos, and two of Koos' sons. He then moved on to senior employees: there is the (white) workshop foreman and mechanic, and Andre, the production manager, who handles everything to do with growing the fruit. Also part of 'management' are Michael, the black personnel manager; Marula, the black general manager; and the black packshed manager. These three sit on 'the management side of the table' in discussions with workers, and are salaried. The roles of the black 'managers' he listed would more usually be described on farms as clerk, senior foreman and packshed foreman. In this depiction, South African farm hierarchies are built around an opposition between management and labour, not white and black.

The reasons for this presentation are complex. For many South Africans after apartheid's demise in 1994, white landowners became an unwanted vestige of the old era. The racialised paternalism that had framed many farmers' aspirations meant that they had enormous personal power and responsibility over black workers in the total worlds of their 'little republics' (as farms have often been labelled in South Africa). Indeed, contrary to the ideal of fatherly protection, actual arrangements were often far from benign, and deeply coercive (see van Onselen, 1992) – one reason why farmers long relied on vulnerable migrant labour. State institutions and foreign supermarkets now speak the language of Black Economic Empowerment, pushing farmers to reform. In response, many have attempted to present themselves as the executives of deracialised businesses, subject to the same economic pressures as other enterprises. Here, as elsewhere (for example Vialles, 1994), a 'modern', sanitised, technologised depiction effaces the distinctiveness of a long-demonised form of production, creating generic industry. The context is ever-greater integration into international markets. Farmers' lives appear similar to the past: khaki outfits, weekend hunting, and lush-gardened farmhouses that emphasise a rural idyll. Yet their enterprises take them and their produce as far as the consumer marketplaces of Europe, the Middle East, China and Japan, as they extend their distribution networks. Willem went further and dispatched his son to Belgium to gain experience among international export agents.

Alongside the concern to establish distance from the past through corporate performance is the concern to remain flexible in the face of an uncertain future. Farmers such as those at Grootplaas participate in a buyer's market, but they have done well out of South Africa's agricultural liberalisation. The aeroplanes that they use to fly between estates testify to their success, under conditions that proved destructive for others along the Zimbabwean border. Some border farmers seek to expand further. A more acute concern is South African land reform (see also Hall, Wisborg, Shirinda, & Zamchiya, 2013) – a long, drawn out process that offers restitution for black South Africans who can demonstrate that their land was expropriated since 1913.[4] The whole border region is under claim, and the outcome is uncertain. Farmers strategise to ensure that they hold portfolios of estates and businesses – security in diversity – and increasingly talk of their farms in terms of pragmatic business calculations (Bolt, 2013). All of this encourages them to downplay established obligations.

Meanwhile, a leaner, more individualised form of agriculture is a response to legal changes. Post-apartheid legislation offered farm workers protections they had historically been denied. They, like domestic workers, were exempt from standard labour law. The new measures include minimum wages and working standards, and in theory increase transparency in how workers are paid. A common complaint by farmers is that they interfere with the mutual understanding between employers and workers, reducing relationships to bare wage-employment (see also Ewert & du Toit, 2005). Some consequently declare themselves unable or unwilling to continue as their workers' fatherly protectors. Before my arrival at Grootplaas, workers had demanded itemised pay sheets, listing money docked for housing and electricity. This was to replace a generic 'costs' deduction that assumed the legitimacy of payment 'in kind'. Willem had informed his employees that they would lose out from such a change. He would now be confined, he warned, to offering only the kind of assistance to his workers that could be articulated on a pay sheet. The implication was that what he did for his workers amounted to far more than what was deducted for 'costs'.

Agriculture-specific changes intersect with shifts in South Africa's political economy more generally. In the years before the fieldwork on which this paper draws, between 2000 and 2007, the labour market participation rate hovered between 55 per cent and 60 per cent.[5] South Africa, like many other countries, has seen a visible shift since the 1970s from a 'labour-scarce' society to a 'labour-surplus' one, itself the result of economic restructuring and consequent reduced demand for unskilled labour. Ties of paternalistic dependence between employers and workforces, forged under conditions of labour scarcity, are now being decisively broken (Ferguson, 2013).

The picture here is far more complicated than a story of neoliberalisation would suggest. While the results of farmers' strategies look neoliberal, the causes are diverse. Farmers attempt to efface a vilified past, address the vagaries of post-apartheid land reform, and respond to the South African government's enforcement of rights. As they face manifold pressures, they respond by means of a repertoire of corporate styles (including new terminology) and practices (including strategic, even short-term, business investments). As shown below, the promotion of non-manual, managerial black workers is central. Hart (2008) argues that particular historical processes always exceed their neoliberal characteristics – there are always other causes. But the point here is further reaching. What looks like neoliberalism at Grootplaas, and on other similar South African farms, is in large part an effect of non-neoliberal processes. It is accidental neoliberalism.[6]

Taking a more specific focus on a managerial style of labour relations foregrounds further complexity. Farmers' self-presentations – here exemplified by Willem – do not capture the messy reality of running an estate. This is for two reasons. Firstly, a rhetoric of pastoral concern continues, albeit more quietly. Willem claims that he has been unable to sustain his threats of more limited services to his workforce. He stills sees himself as protector of his 'people' when it comes to negotiating with police deportation raids. Farmers continue to provide transport. Their cast-offs and the carcasses from hunting expeditions end up in labour compounds as gifts for workers. Employees are given leave to return to Zimbabwe at a moment's notice if the occasion demands, and they are rewarded for good service by employment into old age. And Willem does occasionally resolve serious disputes among workers, as well as hold tribunals when employees are to be disciplined. To a large degree, measures to corporatise have people *off* the farm – South African officials, British supermarkets, or EUREPGAP[7] inspectors – as their audience. Secondly, where farmers do attempt to create added distance between themselves and their workforces, the effect is that hierarchies among workers are left unaltered, or are even reinforced. Farmers have national and international business networks; workers, meanwhile, have cross-border networks, described below. These are mutually dependent, but they operate according to completely different logics. From within each network, it is as if the other were invisible.

Examining how corporate principles are carried into the workforce itself, the following section shifts the focus to the centre of the labour compound. It begins with a meeting about supermarket-funded development, one dimension of the global value chains that now shape South African agriculture.

Debating Development in the Compound

The meeting was to be on a Saturday afternoon, at the end of the five-and-a-half day working week, and few were enthusiastic. Coming out of his house, Michael, Grootplaas's black personnel manager, stopped a worker who was walking past with his family and sent him to gather an audience. Slowly, residents made their way to the compound's central hall – a concrete-floored area with a corrugated metal roof, two open sides, a hatch to the compound shop and, opposite, the wire cage in which the new, supermarket foundation-funded 'games room' was located.

The agenda was a review of projects undertaken at the farm by the foundation.[8] Paid for not only by the supermarket that initiated it, but also producers, exporters and importers, the foundation is intended to address a history of extreme inequality experienced by farm labourers in South Africa. Its crèches, literacy centres, games rooms and football equipment represent attempts to engage holistically in workers' lives, in similar vein to paternalist ideals. But, focusing on the farms from which the supermarket buys fruit, this intervention places a new emphasis on 'empowerment' and the development of 'skills'.

Michael, as personnel manager, had recently been selected by Grootplaas's white farmers to represent the farm, and had subsequently been chosen by the foundation as a 'beneficiary' member of its Board of Directors. This meant attending meetings across South Africa. As a beneficiary director, Michael also assessed applications for project funds from other farms selling their produce to the supermarket. His education and administrative occupation at the farm made Michael an obvious gatekeeper with the British supermarket fund. He represented less the vision of the stereotyped, downtrodden farm worker than that of what farm workers could become. As he made his way to the hall to address his co-residents, Michael clutched a wad of applications that he had recently assessed. But, far from showing his co-workers their own future, these files stood as a symbol of his *difference* – of the administrative responsibility that made him Grootplaas's only black non-manual worker, and of his status well beyond the remoteness of the farm.

Thirty-five men took their places on benches in a rough semi-circle, and a group of eight women sat together on the floor by the shop. Michael took his place on another bench, facing the crowd. He was flanked by people who, in different ways, reinforced his role. On one side sat the member of the Workers' Committee who had officially called the meeting at Michael's behest. On the other, two employees took notes: Benjamin, the A-level-educated storeman and sometime clerk, and Ruth, a former teacher who ran the foundation-funded crèche. Like Michael, both derived status from their non-agricultural backgrounds.

Michael stood and, wielding the application forms that he had approved, chronicled the foundation's progress. The games room was coming along, and Willem had supported a plan to set aside a piece of land for workers to farm together, keeping the proceeds. Despite the apparently good news, this prompted heated objections from the audience about the implications of such a project. What about irrigation and transport costs? This came from Marula, the farm's black foreman, who had driven up in his *bakkie*[9] after the start of the meeting and asserted his own authority by seating himself on Michael's bench. Would such costs be born by the farmer or the foundation? Michael could only point to a similar scheme that had been successful in the Eastern Cape, hundreds of miles away. The farm's senior driver, preoccupied by his infant son, demanded: what if someone were to be fired – what would happen to his or her share? Was the scheme just to be a way to secure free labour? More protestations flew across the hall: no one had asked for this scheme; Michael should have consulted workers before going to Willem. No one had requested a games room either; what had been demanded were uniforms and equipment for football and netball. And would it cost money to use the new pool table, football tables and juke box? Michael hesitated, before shifting the conversation to the foundation-funded Adult Literacy Centre. He exhorted the audience to attend more diligently, but the response was further objection: it was those running the centre who were to blame for its gradual decline. Soon Marula left, shaking his head. Others followed, and the meeting petered out.

Why, given the long history of farmers' broad intervention into workers' lives – including education, games rooms and livelihood opportunities beyond the wage – were these schemes marginalised or rejected? The answer does not lie in their associations with global value chains or liberalised markets per se. Rather, such intervention reinforced the rise of a newly influential worker, and thereby came to embody a new model of authority in the workforce. Michael is well suited as a representative of the farm, fitting both the farmer's performance of progress and the supermarket foundation's stated goal of development. But this leaves Michael at odds with established forms of sociality and hierarchy. In unpicking why the meeting disintegrated, it is therefore worth starting with Michael himself.

The Performance of Corporate Management

Michael came to the farm in 1997, when Zimbabwe's economy was beginning to suffer but before the exponential increase in emigration. Like many more recent Zimbabweans, he lacks a lifelong farm background and is keen to avoid having people draw the conclusion that he has sunk to the level of farm labourer, an occupation so demonised in Zimbabwe that many farms there historically employed Malawians or Mozambicans (Rutherford, 2001). He characterises his past in terms of an education-centred narrative, marked by the accumulation of formal qualifications: O-levels, and diploma courses in Personnel Management, Office Management and Admin, Computers, and Modern Management. His parents hailed from a town in southern Zimbabwe. But he was sent to a rural, church-run primary school to avoid distractions, before attending an urban secondary school. At 18 he entered the army for 15 years, finishing as an administrator/supervisor. After a brief stint driving a taxi he had bought, he visited his now-deceased brother at Grootplaas and found employment. As he recounts his arrival, he had to hide his true, highly skilled nature from workers to avoid hostile attention. Only when he was told there was no permanent labouring job available did he reveal his qualifications and secure himself a 'management' position.

Each work day just before seven o'clock in the morning, Michael cycles into the office at the farm's workshop. He wears a collared shirt, often white, tucked into a belted pair of dark trousers, and is armed with his 3G Technology mobile phone despite the lack of reception across much of the farm. His office is dominated by a collection of grey, chest-high filing cabinets containing records of present and recent workers. On the opposite side of the room is a door leading to where whites work: Willem, his wife, brother-in-law and the secretary (the daughter of a neighbouring farmer). Michael and Benjamin (the workshop storeman who helps him with paperwork) rarely go through the door, especially uninvited. They work in close proximity to farmers and administrators. But they are overwhelmingly confined to responding to rather than initiating interactions. Nevertheless, such proximity ensures their easy access to the farmers in the eyes of other workers.

Michael's primary responsibility for much of the year is renewing permits. He maintains the paperwork and occasionally travels to Beitbridge border post to negotiate with both the Zimbabwean and South African sides. Doing so requires not only knowledge of the various documents, but also the relationships and expertise to negotiate the bureaucracies at Beitbridge. This is of vital importance in a heavily policed border area, where Zimbabweans without papers risk deportation. Further enhancing Michael's reputation, the job involves a high degree of literacy. This both resonates with a widespread valorisation of formal school education – itself the result of Zimbabwe's colonial and postcolonial class history – and harks back to some workers' happier days in higher-status work than agricultural labour.

Michael sits at a particular interface between white and black, especially during the harvest. Enlisting the help of other workers, he moves the filing cabinets to the packshed and takes on a greater range of responsibilities. He assembles a small team of workers who tend also to have non-farm backgrounds. Gerald, for example, is a general worker for much of the time but, like Benjamin, his A-levels mean that he is useful for any administration that needs doing. Relying on his team to look after matters in the office, Michael takes new recruits to Beitbridge to arrange their visas. Throughout the harvest he handles paperwork for fruit-buyers, and prints destination labels for the fruit pallets, work he refers to as 'data input'. The computer and buyer paperwork are in Willem's own office at the packshed. So what other workers see is Michael, dressed in an official-looking white coat and wielding a clipboard, spending hours each day in a room with their distant employer.

The figure of the corporate-style, non-manual black worker is replicated on other farms. On the estate next to Grootplaas, for example, a black employee who handles paperwork also acts as receptionist, attired in a shirt, tie and pressed trousers. On each farm, such a figure is an intermediary between white farmers and black workers – but an unusual one. More typical are the farm's foremen, with the senior foreman at their head. At Grootplaas, this is Marula.

Effectively a supervisor of supervisors, Marula spends his days touring around in his *bakkie*, keeping an eye on the various work teams around the estate. Like his counterparts on other estates, his role is to extend the labour hierarchy – and, by implication, the farmers' gaze – over a wide area, as he moves about the farm. His job is to have a broad understanding of the whole estate. By doing favours along the way – giving a lift, sharing a cigarette – he maintains both a superior and sympathetic position, a fatherly figure in the workforce. Meanwhile, as the radio on his *bakkie* crackles constantly with communication between the farm's vehicles and the office, he brings with him the institutional weight of the white employers.

Marula's role as lynchpin, necessary because of a rigid black/white separation, is intrinsic to the racial micropolitics of farms. Whites on the farm rarely enter the compound; it is Marula who usually gathers workers, including for emergency jobs in the evenings, at night or over weekends. Generally, supervisory employees direct the wider labour force. These are Marula himself; two more junior, specialised foremen; and Andre, the white production manager. Willem, the white farmer, who spends much of his time around the offices, represents a distant authority. He is more a last resort for complaints or appeals for leave than a direct overseer of labour.

Michael shares Marula's proximity to the white bosses, but this closeness is of a different kind. Michael is not a lynchpin in the hierarchy in the sense of a daily avenue of communication between bosses and workers. His position confines him to narrower spaces of work-related responsibility.

Consequently, he relies on formal channels to emphasise his seniority. One is his ability to hire and fire through explicit, private appeal to Willem. Another lies in the paperwork itself. Faced with large numbers of workers who need permits, he can exercise a degree of choice in whose he processes, and when. Especially during the harvest, when there are hundreds of recruits and many never receive legal documents, handling paperwork confers a great deal of power, at least over those who lack connections, influence or authority of their own.

Compound residents see Michael as an influential, high-status figure, whose pay overtook even Marula's. Since Michael's work is highly unusual in the black workforce, it is known that Willem sees him as indispensible and hears his complaints. Marula is more central to the day-to-day labour process involving most workers. Meanwhile Michael's authority comes from his responsibility for records to which others lack access, through interactions with a powerful boss that, behind the doors of offices, others are unable to observe.

It is not only because of his skills in administration that Michael is indispensible. He also enables a particular presentation of export-oriented agriculture in the twenty-first century: a production-oriented business, not the oft romanticised or vilified popular image of farming. Within this understanding, Michael is key. For, as previously noted, he is the one black employee who is not a manual labourer. Willem is keen to promote him as evidence of Grootplaas's managerial outlook. In conversations with me, he was careful to underline Michael's organisational importance, something he did not do in the case of Marula or other senior supervisory figures. Michael's directorship at the British supermarket development foundation lent Willem's assertions greater plausibility, giving a new reality to the figure of black manager, and underlining Grootplaas's willingness to adapt. This, of course, is the context in which Michael came to be convening the meeting described earlier.

However, Michael's privileged treatment by Willem has stark limitations. A non-racial, managerial version of farming barely extends beyond the office. Despite Willem's rhetoric, Grootplaas is run according to highly racialised conceptions of proper pay, accommodation and modes of interaction. Revealingly, when Willem described the farm's labour hierarchy, he listed white before black managers. With Michael, Willem adopts a commanding tone he would not use with whites: words slowly articulated and a hard, monotonous edge to his voice. Whereas with Andre, the white production manager, he discusses progress in the orchards over an afternoon cup of tea in the tearoom, with Michael his interaction is kept strictly to the office. In this regard, Michael remains unambiguously a black worker, separated by the racial divide that has him live in the compound, not a security fence-encircled farmhouse. When he stood before other workers in the compound hall, as representative of a distant supermarket foundation, this tension – non-manual, managerial figure versus worker in the compound – was underscored.

Michael's role reveals the limitations of non-racial corporatisation at Grootplaas. But what of the other side of the managerial model – the narrowing of obligations and dependences to the language of contracts and the market? Michael asserts a distinctly corporate position among other employees – one that rejects established forms of hierarchy. Turning to his place on the farm beyond work time illuminates the place of such managerial norms amidst established structures of authority and responsibility.

Managerialism Marginalised: Elders, Networks and Workforce Hierarchy

To understand Grootplaas's workforce hierarchy, and how it extends beyond wage work, it is useful to begin at the court (TshiVenda: *khoro*) where disputes are heard. The elders who pass judgment are among the oldest of the senior workers – most in their late 40s – and many are those who become picking supervisors during the harvest. Two high-ranking workers, although considered good candidates, are excluded because of their youth (one is in his 20s; the other is 44). Yet age alone does not determine membership. The *khoro* is dominated by Venda from the border area. The one exception is a well-established Shona worker, included because he 'speaks well' (assesses situations fairly and expresses his opinions convincingly, albeit in ChiShona).

Marula acts as *musanda* (headman). The *khoro* is located in the yard of his dwelling, itself a focal point of the compound. As the longest serving and most established black worker, he has adapted two two-room senior workers' houses into his own chiefly enclosure. Underneath a tree, Marula has built a seating area for the *khoro* and for drinking by nailing together several benches, with a second row of lower benches for busier occasions.

When there are disputes, compound residents approach an elder, who convenes the *khoro*. An example will elucidate how the tribunals work. On one occasion, a mother approached a long-standing senior worker because a man had insulted her after seducing her daughter. The elder led the hearing. As the accused sat in the middle of a tight semi-circle, the mother positioned herself at the end and, standing, recounted the events. She had found the young man in bed with her daughter in a compound room. Rather than respectfully acknowledging her, the man had simply attempted to hide under the sheet. When she drew back (having seen him), and waited outside, he had simply walked off. He had done something similar on a second occasion. Speaking at length, slowly and with a sense of drama, her narrative culminated with the man's final insult. Drunk one night, he had broken into her room, assuming her to have locked her daughter in to protect her chastity. Throwing a broken padlock on the ground in front of her as evidence, she screamed a threat to call the police. The elder who had convened the meeting interjected and quickly promised to resolve the situation at the *khoro*.

Each weighing in with a short speech, the six elders present discussed what to do about this case of unfulfilled responsibility tempered by insubordination. The mood shifted rapidly back and forth between relaxed joking and dramatic anger. Marula sat back, checking his phone and even leaving to take a call. But this only served to add gravitas to his words when he did intercede, late in the proceedings: a man should be able to bear the consequences of his actions. The culprit and the daughter remained quiet, the former attempting nervously to read the situation. Eventually, he was threatened with the prospect of marriage, although it was clear that he could not afford to look after either the daughter or the child she already had. He was ordered simply to stay away from her.

This description of a hearing at the *khoro* conveys the nature of authority in the compound. Here is a court with circumscribed power. The man's sister, who had publicly insulted the woman's mother, refused to turn up to the *khoro* at all. Enforcement is far from straightforward. The elder who convened the meeting threatened to take the case to a village council in Zimbabwe – there at least, he said, a court would beat the culprit with *sjamboks*.[10] But Grootplaas's *khoro* had never turned to the greater power of headmen across the border. Like the mother's threat to call the police over the broken lock, this possibility remained conjectural.

And yet, despite its clear limitations, such keeping of the peace is an important part of farm life. Grootplaas's seasonal workers, especially, are often far from the mundane regulation of home, subject to the indignities of overcrowding and police deportation raids. Actually achieving a degree of stability on the border means establishing connections to senior figures – connections that are often fragile. It is important not to paint core workers simply as benign figures. The compound's rules are overwhelmingly established and enforced by permanently employed men. While elders stake their claims to seniority and respect on notions of proper authority, there is little redress beyond them. This is especially the case for women. Cases of sexual violence may simply be argued between aggrieved men: the accused and the boyfriend.[11] Moreover, for men who have experienced middle-class decline in the Zimbabwean crisis, the rough camaraderie involved in building relationships means compromising norms of behaviour that connect them to their past lives – actual or imagined (Bolt, 2010). Nevertheless, such ties bring recruits under the protection of influential figures. They increase the likelihood of receiving a work permit, and offer the stable residential base – at least for a while – to establish informal businesses, such as selling cigarettes, snacks or marijuana to other workers (Bolt, 2012).

The labour hierarchy here offers some sense of order, however provisional. And this order, in turn, depends on the place of senior workers in networks along and across the border. In the *khoro* case just described – a minor offence – threats to take matters across the border appear far-fetched. But they served to remind the culprit that he and his sister, the mother and daughter, and many of the elders all hail from the same group of villages. In fact, these threats were quietly followed by another, made plausible by precisely these informal but apparent connections: to summon the young woman's brothers from towns to the south, and leave matters to them. Shared origins among the core of the workforce countermand the transience of a migrant-labour setting. The most established permanent workers have several kin in the compound, and on other farms along the Limpopo. Marula himself was born on a nearby estate, his father and brothers also foremen in their time, and he has a number of children and other dependents on the border estates. The authority of the *khoro* draws on idioms shared with Zimbabwean villages, as well as on webs of kinship that span the border. Networks among workers underpin labour force cohesion, and therefore buttress the networks of global distribution in which the white farmers are implicated. But, in everyday terms, they have minimal impact on each other.

The *khoro* is where a model of compound authority is most explicitly performed. In this model, senior workers are not merely workers, but rather wise, older men with experience and responsibility. Beyond the *khoro*, the elders fulfil similar roles: taking in newcomers who require shelter; speaking for them in disputes; reprimanding residents for misdeeds. Marula himself regularly patrols the compound, on foot or in his *bakkie*, keeping an eye on things. At other times, he waits in his yard, as workers bring him beer and news. Senior workers establish themselves by building up retinues of dependents. New recruits quickly learn the relationships and the forms of self-presentation that constitute the farm hierarchy.

How, then, does Michael's notion of corporate, managerial authority fit into all this? Around the same age as Marula, he is old enough to sit on the *khoro*, and his TshiVenda is good enough, despite his Ndebele origins. But he is not invited to join, and he gives the institution a wide berth. This is because of the elders' opinions of his role as personnel manager, and his self-understanding as a corporate figure. Michael is seen to be too interested in his own meetings, where he is able to address people alone. Moreover, he is always '*waya-waya*' – rushing around on his own business in an apparently secretive manner. The papers under his arm are for his eyes only. They enable him to deliver news, not debate it, as at the supermarket development meeting. This runs against the grain of the publicly deliberative authority of the *khoro*. Just as significantly, the kind of managerial authority that Michael embodies calls into question the image of senior workers as wise elders. Through the lens of managerialism, Marula and his circle are simply lifelong farm workers, lacking education or access to a wider world beyond agriculture. No wonder then that, as Michael recounted the supermarket foundation's latest successes, Marula positioned himself next to his rival, pushed the meeting into critical debate, and shifted the focus of discussion from project goals and accomplishments to the specifics of farm life.

Unsurprisingly, Michael rejects the prerogative of the *khoro* to pass judgment. He has, in fact, approached the elders for help in the past (even reportedly appearing before the *khoro*). On one occasion, police at a roadblock found him to be in possession of a fraudulent South African passport and arrested him. Marula and another senior worker found Willem, who successfully intervened on his behalf. Yet Michael maintains that farm workers, lacking qualifications or official sanction, have no place making or enforcing laws. Real authority comes from outside, and it is the police and the army who should keep the peace.

Michael's life in the compound reflects his attitude towards the elders and their *khoro*. Whereas the status of Marula and his supervisors is buttressed by appeals for assistance and judgement, Michael sees his responsibilities rather differently. He is known in the compound to tell others to look after themselves: 'you've got your job, I've got mine'. Matters are of course more complicated. Michael does form personal relations with and helps particular people. When impressed by a newcomer's education, he may act to ensure that they are offered employment in the packshed, amounting to indoor work with higher pay. But, reflecting a more sharply bounded notion of occupational authority, Michael's assistance to others in the compound is confined to dispensing highly individualised favours.

While Marula's well-visited house suggests an extension of family life into the compound, the appearance of Michael's senior-worker house underlines his privacy. The outside is strikingly unadorned: a bare yard marked by a high hedge, containing only a low table for washing up, a disused vegetable garden, and a crumbling mud-and-pole shed built by a previous occupant. Even in comparison to most other senior workers, Michael's yard looks basic, even neglected. This is not the case inside the house. Unlike other residents, he has bought a double bed and sprung mattress, and owns not only a large television but also hi-fi separates and floor-standing speakers.[12] With these he entertains guests, either watching the television or listening to music through the door, or (unusual in the compound) sitting inside. Michael's privacy limits discussion of his non-work past. Keen to highlight his professional success, he keeps details about the rest of his life to himself. For example, though he has several adult and school-going children, I was long into fieldwork before I even heard mention of them.

Michael speaks proudly of his position as 'manager of this organisation', employing distinctly corporate language. But he is also aware that his job can be framed as little more than that of a farm labourer – in the eyes of some, he is simply a clerk. This is a feeling augmented by the contrast between his own fate and that of his younger brother, a registered tour guide living in Midrand outside Johannesburg. For those, like Michael, who are disappointed with their fates but have attained a senior post on the border farms, a managerial idiom can serve to maintain a sense of self-respect. Benjamin, the storeman/clerk with whom Michael works, feels a similar ambiguity.

This is one way of dealing with a problem faced by an increasing number of Zimbabweans: how to assert their histories of education and class aspiration, now lost due to economic collapse at home and consequent geographical dislocation. Seasonal workers with higher status backgrounds and non-Venda origins assert their difference in ways that mirror Michael's. They refer to management books to criticise work dynamics and the dominant notions of authority and responsibility in the workforce. They characterise themselves through education and etiquette. And they tell stories of home that emphasise access to commodities like cars. The few couples granted their own accommodation invite guests inside their rooms rather than socialise in public. No doubt Michael feels all the more acutely the need to be not 'just' a farm labourer as he seeks out and engages the best educated of the new arrivals. His style is impressive to some with middle-class aspirations. But they are seasonal recruits who move on. And in any case, Michael remains too much of a permanent fixture at the farm for the most elite of seasonal workers to identify with him.

Meanwhile, a reaction to this same influx of relatively well-educated Zimbabweans buttresses Marula's position within the more influential permanent workforce. He has accrued widespread respect and status among permanent workers, especially TshiVenda speakers like him, after long years working his way up from shepherd to foreman. Marula and his elders are increasingly faced with recruits who draw on alternative bases of status to which they lack access: education, urban sophistication, even non-Venda-ness. But this makes their centrality and superiority within the world of the farm all the more important. Farm hierarchy is given new meaning as it confronts assertions of superiority based on personal histories far from the farming area.

While Marula's lifestyle is intended to place him at the centre of residents' existence, Michael's marks his managerial seclusion and sophistication – his difference from mere farm workers. Idioms of management and paternalism are played out even in workers' living spaces. But the managerial model is valued only by Michael and a few other residents. And the mode of sociality it promotes – with its sharp distinctions between manager and rank-and-file and between work and leisure-time responsibilities – leaves him isolated. Michael's situation is all the more difficult because he has incompatible goals. He presents himself in terms of managerial distance but, immersed in a world of paternalist hierarchy, he is nevertheless keen to assert his importance in farm dwellers' non-work lives. This is the contradiction of a managerial model in a residential farm workforce like Grootplaas's. Drawing a sharp distinction between work and leisure time, Michael turns to alternative pastoral roles, consistent with his self-understanding, which he has accrued through the interventions of the supermarket development foundation.

The supermarket foundation-funded Adult Literacy Centre – 'the School' – has offered one possibility. Certificates, accredited by a well-known South African educational institution, were issued on completion of computer-based courses in English reading and writing. Appointed senior facilitator, Michael provided guidance, oversaw work sessions, marked homework and chased up course participants, enabling him to extend an educated style of authority into the compound. He even provoked Marula, by offering to teach him English. However, attendance wavered, no one completed a course, and the programme was eventually discontinued – a decline evident in Michael's meeting and its accusatory references to the School. With few ways out of farm employment, workers see such qualifications as pointless. Michael's teaching responsibility appeared similarly peripheral.

The supermarket foundation, and the role of beneficiary director, has appeared to offer Michael fresh possibilities as quasi-paternal dispenser of wealth. But these efforts have met with limited success. As in his work for the School, workers have seen Michael as too keen to underline his difference and distance from others. His model of authority is seen as incommensurable with the established, generalised responsibilities that come with seniority in the workforce. He is regarded as secretive with important information, making decisions about workers' welfare without consulting them. It is in part because of his failure to find a central position in compound life that Michael asserts his status through stark seclusion – a bounded sense of responsibility, consonant with neoliberal ideals of individual independence.

Conclusion

Starting from actors' projects, perspectives and motivations, this paper has examined exactly what happens to corporate managerial norms in a workforce, and how they intersect with other models of hierarchy. It has traced the plans of the Grootplaas farmer, the tensions built into these plans, and their limited realisation through the key figure in the workforce who actually stands for managerialism. This approach has highlighted two points: the limits of neoliberal transformation as an analytical lens, and the limits to change in labour arrangements more generally.

Firstly, farmers like Willem emphasise depersonalised 'business' and individual responsibility in their language and behaviour. But in fact, a repertoire of corporate idioms serves to address various perceived ills. What looks like neoliberalism is often accidental – the product of unintended consequences. Secondly, corporate 'management' is actually performed in limited, partial ways. Willem's performance is really to an audience off the farm, whereas he is unable to live up to these norms as employer. Instead, he places much of the onus on his 'personnel manager', who is caught between the status and imagined possibilities of corporatised agriculture and the everyday centrality of paternalist hierarchies and kinship networks in the workforce. In the coming years, the fragility and changeability of this strategy will be underlined. Long after my departure from the farm, Michael will be found to have used his role as work-permit broker to embezzle funds. Marginalised, with reduced pay and responsibilities, his status through the supermarket foundation will also disappear, along with Grootplaas's contract with the supermarket itself.

A single case study cannot generalise about change on South African farms. This article's aim has rather been to question any simple narrative. Change in labour regimes does not land in workforces from above. In a period of uncertainty in agriculture, different visions of farming – an established paternalist model and a corporate managerial one – are taken seriously for different reasons. Two visions of agriculture not only coexist, but also actively constitute each other. By illustrating the complexities of dynamics within one workforce, the article cautions against extrapolations from macro- to micro-level analysis, and against the postulation of far-reaching logics of neoliberalism or transformation. It is imperative to investigate how norms that develop in global supply chains intersect with those that govern networks of workers, and understand how key actors mediate between them.

Acknowledgements

For comments on earlier drafts of this article, the author wishes to thank Neville Bolt, Matthew Engelke, Jane Guyer, Jason Hickel, Jessica Jacobson, Deborah James, Geert de Neve, Jonathan Parry, participants of the economic anthropology writing group at the London School of

Economics (LSE), and participants of the departmental research seminars in the anthropology departments of the LSE, the University of Sussex and Brunel University. Thanks also to Keith Breckenridge for discussion about the article's central themes.

Disclosure statement

No potential conflict of interest was reported by the author.

Funding

Research was funded by the Economic and Social Research Council (PTA-031-2005-00006) during a PhD at the LSE.

Notes

1. As well as EUREPGAP, a European regulatory scheme for retailers.
2. All names are pseudonyms. The present tense, intended to capture immediacy not stasis, refers to the period of fieldwork.
3. Zimbabwe's hyperinflation ended in 2009 with the official adoption of the US Dollar, South African Rand and Botswana Pula, altering the significance of cross-border migration, although not its overall importance.
4. The year of South Africa's defining Natives Land Act, which allocated 8 per cent of land to black South Africans.
5. Stats SA estimates for adults aged 15–64. <http://www.statssa.gov.za/PublicationsHTML/P0210September2000,2001,2002,2003,2004,2005,2006,2007/html/P0210September2000,2001,2002,2003,2004,2005,2006,2007.html> (accessed 2 Dec. 2009).
6. Thanks to Keith Breckenridge for suggesting this term.
7. See endnote 1.
8. The name of the supermarket and foundation are omitted to maintain anonymity.
9. Pick-up truck.
10. Whips.
11. Reportedly, this is also often the case in rural Zimbabwe.
12. Unlike Marula's investments, most of Michael's are potentially mobile. In the last few years, Michael began buying building materials, to establish a (now-complete) home next to his brother's (mother's sister's son's) house in Beitbridge District in Zimbabwe. Marula, unlike the majority of workers, has nowhere else to go except his mother's house in Musina town 60 km away.

References

Addison, L. (2006). *Frontier farm labour: A study of neoliberal restructuring and Zimbabwean migrant farm workers in Limpopo Province, South Africa* (unpublished master's thesis). Carleton University, Ottawa, ON.

Arce, A., & Long, N. (1993). Bridging two worlds: An ethnography of bureaucrat-peasant relations in western Mexico. In M. Hobart (Ed.), *An anthropological critique of development: The growth of ignorance* (pp. 197–208). London: Routledge.

Bernstein, H. (2007). Agrarian questions of capital and labour: Some theory about land reform (and a periodisation). In L. Ntsebeza & R. Hall (Eds.), *The land question in South Africa: The challenge of transformation and redistribution* (pp. 27–59). Cape Town: HSRC Press.

Bernstein, H. (2013). Commercial agriculture in South Africa since 1994: 'Natural, simply capitalism'. *Journal of Agrarian Change, 13*, 23–46. doi:10.1111/joac.2013.13.issue-1

Bolt, M. (2010). Camaraderie and its discontents: Class consciousness, ethnicity and divergent masculinities among Zimbabwean migrant farmworkers in South Africa. *Journal of Southern African Studies, 36*, 377–393. doi:10.1080/03057070.2010.485790

Bolt, M. (2012). Waged entrepreneurs, policed informality: Work, the regulation of space and the economy of the Zimbabwean-South African border. *Africa, 82*, 111–130. doi:10.1017/S0001972011000751

Bolt, M. (2013). Producing permanence: Employment, domesticity and the flexible future on a South African border farm. *Economy and Society, 42*, 197–225. doi:10.1080/03085147.2012.733606

Bolt, M. (2015). *Zimbabwe's migrants and South Africa's border farms: The roots of impermanence.* Cambridge: Cambridge University Press.

Bond, P. (2000). *Elite transition: From apartheid to neoliberalism in South Africa.* London: Pluto Press.

Bradford, H. (1993). Getting away with murder: 'Mealie kings', the state and foreigners in the Eastern Transvaal, c.1918–1950. In P. Bonner, P. Delius, & D. Posel (Eds.), *Apartheid's genesis, 1935–1962* (pp. 96–125). Braamfontein: Ravan Press.

Comaroff, J., & Comaroff, J. L. (2000). Millennial capitalism: First thoughts on a second coming. *Public Culture, 12*, 291–343. doi:10.1215/08992363-12-2-291

Cross, J. (2010). Neoliberalism as unexceptional: Economic zones and the everyday precariousness of working life in south India. *Critique of Anthropology, 30*, 355–373. doi:10.1177/0308275X10372467

Day, S., Papataxiarchis, E., & Stewart, M. (1998). Consider the lilies of the field. In S. Day, E. Papataxiarchis, & M. Stewart (Eds.), *Lilies of the field: Marginal people who live for the moment* (pp. 1–24). Boulder, CO: Westview Press.

Doctors Without Borders. (2009, February 17). Beyond cholera: Zimbabwe's worsening crisis. Retrieved from http://doctorswithoutborders.org/publications/article.cfm?id=3408&cat=special-report

du Toit, A. (1993). The micro-politics of paternalism: The discourses of management and resistance on South African fruit and wine farms. *Journal of Southern African Studies, 19*, 314–336. doi:10.1080/03057079308708362

Epstein, A. L. (1958). *Politics in an urban African community*. Manchester: Manchester University Press.

Ewert, J., & du Toit, A. (2005). A deepening divide in the countryside: Restructuring and rural livelihoods in the South African wine industry. *Journal of Southern African Studies, 31*, 315–332. doi:10.1080/03057070500109524

Ferguson, J. (2010). The uses of neoliberalism. *Antipode, 41*(s1), 166–184. doi:10.1111/anti.2010.41.issue-s1

Ferguson, J. (2013). Declarations of dependence: Labour, personhood, and welfare in southern Africa. *Journal of the Royal Anthropological Institute N.S., 19*, 223–242. doi:10.1111/jrai.2013.19.issue-2

Geschiere, P., & Nyamnjoh, F. (2000). Capitalism and autochthony: The seesaw of mobility and belonging. *Public Culture, 12*, 423–452. doi:10.1215/08992363-12-2-423

Hall, R., Wisborg, P., Shirinda, S., & Zamchiya, P. (2013). Farm workers and farm dwellers in Limpopo Province, South Africa. *Journal of Agrarian Change, 13*, 47–70. doi:10.1111/joac.2013.13.issue-1

Hart, G. (2002). *Disabling globalisation: Places of power in post-apartheid South Africa*. Berkeley, CA: University of California Press.

Hart, G. (2008). The provocations of neoliberalism: Contesting the nation and liberation after apartheid. *Antipode, 40*, 678–705. doi:10.1111/anti.2008.40.issue-4

Harvey, D. (2005). *A brief history of neoliberalism*. Oxford: Oxford University Press.

Human Rights Watch. (2006). *Unprotected migrants: Zimbabweans in South Africa's Limpopo Province*. New York, NY: Human Rights Watch.

Johnston, D. (2007). Who needs immigrant farm workers? A South African case study. *Journal of Agrarian Change, 7*, 494–525. doi:10.1111/joac.2007.7.issue-4

Koelble, T. A. (2008). Market and society. In N. Shepherd & S. L. Robins (Eds.), *New South African keywords*. Athens, OH: Ohio University Press.

Koelble, T. A., & LiPuma, E. (2005). Traditional leaders & democracy: Cultural politics in the age of globalisation. In S. L. Robins (Ed.), *Limits to liberation after apartheid: Citizenship, governance & culture*. Oxford: James Currey.

Marais, H. (2011). *South Africa pushed to the limit: The political economy of change*. London: Zed Books.

Mather, C., & Greenberg, S. (2003). Market liberalisation in post-apartheid South Africa: The restructuring of citrus exports after 'deregulation'. *Journal of Southern African Studies, 29*, 393–412. doi:10.1080/03057070306210

Mollona, M. (2005). Factory, family and neighbourhood: The political economy of informal labour in Sheffield. *Journal of the Royal Anthropological Institute N.S., 11*, 527–548. doi:10.1111/jrai.2005.11.issue-3

Moodie, T. D., & Ndatshe, V. (1994). *Going for gold: Men, mines, and migration*. Berkeley, CA: University of California Press.

Murray, M. (1995). Blackbirding at 'Crooks' Corner': Illicit labour recruitment in the Northeastern Transvaal 1910–1940. *Journal of Southern African Studies, 21*, 373–397. doi:10.1080/03057079508708453

Oomen, B. (2005). *Chiefs in South Africa: Law, power and culture in the post-apartheid era*. Oxford: James Currey.

Rutherford, B. (2001). *Working on the margins: Black workers, white farmers in postcolonial Zimbabwe*. London: Zed Books.

Rutherford, B. (2008). An unsettled belonging: Zimbabwean farm workers in Limpopo Province, South Africa. *Journal of Contemporary African Studies, 26*, 401–415. doi:10.1080/02589000802481973

Rutherford, B., & Addison, L. (2007). Zimbabwean farm workers in northern South Africa. *Review of African Political Economy, 34*, 619–635. doi:10.1080/03056240701819491

Shaw, A. (2008, February 22). Zimbabwe inflation passes 100,000%, officials say. *The Guardian*. Retrieved from http://www.theguardian.com/world/2008/feb/22/zimbabwe

van Onselen, C. (1976). *Chibaro: African mine labour in Southern Rhodesia 1900–1933*. London: Pluto Press.

van Onselen, C. (1992). The social and economic underpinning of paternalism and violence on the maize farms of the South-Western Transvaal. *Journal of Historical Sociology, 5*, 127–160. doi:10.1111/j.1467-6443.1992.tb00159.x

Vialles, N. (1994). *Animal into edible*. Cambridge: Cambridge University Press.

von Holdt, K., & Webster, E. (2005). Work restructuring and the crisis of social reproduction: A southern perspective. In E. Webster & K. von Holdt (Eds.), *Beyond the apartheid workplace: Studies in transition* (pp. 3–40). Scottsville: University of KwaZulu-Natal Press.

Waldman, L. (1996). Monkey in a spiderweb: The dynamics of farmer control and paternalism. *African Studies, 55*, 62–86. doi:10.1080/00020189608707840

Werbner, R. (1991). *Tears of the dead: The social biography of an African family*. Edinburgh: Edinburgh University Press.

Resilient Labour: Workplace Regimes, Globalisation and Enclave Development in Swaziland

VITO LATERZA
Centre for African Studies, University of Cape Town, Cape Town, South Africa

ABSTRACT *Are new forms of foreign investment in Africa having a major impact on local workers? Are they significantly altering labour practices and conditions? I explore these questions with reference to Swaziland and the ethnography of labour relations in a Christian company town. A comparative perspective looking at the South African regional economy shows that the legacy of apartheid enclave development casts a shadow over workers' futures. Economic dualism, characterised by cheap labour drawn from an ever expanding informal sector and reinforced by social, political and institutional factors, tends to neutralise the possibility of inclusive economic growth driven by foreign capital.*

African Globalisation and its Discontents

The term 'globalisation' has long become embedded in local and international imaginaries. The term is commonly used to refer to the process of increasing integration of economies and societies around the world, encompassing all spheres of economic, cultural, environmental and social relations. In Africa, this process has intensified during the 1980s, spearheaded by the Structural Adjustment Programmes imposed by the IMF and World Bank. Their loans were made conditional to wide-ranging fiscal and economic reforms, including a drastic reduction of public budgets to cut debt and opening up of the national economies to foreign investors. These policies were hailed as a panacea for African economic problems and a new era of growth and prosperity. It is now clear that the benefits of globalisation for the vast majority of the people in the continent are actually minimal or non-existent (Ayenagbo et al., 2012). African economies continue to be characterised by sharp income inequalities, low wages and inadequate infrastructure and social service provision.

This linear narrative of the phenomenon, however, does not do justice to the variety of outcomes and configurations on the ground. First, globalisation is not a linear process leading to one single integrated world system as mainstream economics and some development discourses want us to believe (Cooper, 2001, p. 189). In this sense, it is more of an ideal framework superimposed over local realities, than the inevitable direction of world history. The expansion of the penetration of foreign capital is highly uneven, both within and across African countries (Cooper, 2001, p. 190). The dominance of foreign capital is not something new, and has been going on for centuries. For the African context, its history is rooted in the laissez faire capitalism of the nineteenth and early twentieth centuries and the more structured top–down large-scale enterprise development of late colonialism from the World War II period onwards (Hart & Padayachee, 2013, pp. 58–59).

Recently, high growth rates in sub-Saharan Africa resulted from a new wave of foreign investment to African countries, much of it from the BRICS countries – especially China and South Africa. This raises a number of questions which are crucial to understand these trends and their impact on the lives of African workers. Does the latest wave of investment show genuinely new features? Is it a radical break from the colonial and post-independence paradigms? To what extent do local and historical factors influence the trajectories of change brought about by changes in investors, donor funding and global market structures? Do the recent configurations of global capital help people on the ground move out of poverty and underdevelopment as mainstream free market narratives seem to suggest?

A focus on labour offers a particularly productive way to tackle these questions. Through wage labour, a large number of people enter into contact with foreign capital and the structures of transnational markets. Interactions and conflicts between workers and capital constitute a privileged standpoint through which we can evaluate the multiple trajectories of the phenomena commonly subsumed under the rubric of globalisation.

The aim of my article is to attempt some partial answers through a focus on the historical and institutional context of labour in Swaziland, with specific reference to the ethnographic case study of a Swazi company town where I carried out fieldwork in 2007–2008. Previously an asbestos mine, Enkopolwani has recently been redeveloped as a social enterprise by a group of (mostly) white Southern African and North American Christian businessmen and missionaries. For profit economic activities like timber logging and harvesting, production of planks, agricultural production and tourism were conducted hand-in-hand with the development of foster homes for Swazi orphans.

Enkopolwani's insertion into new configurations of local and global networks of donors makes it an ideal case study to explore issues of continuity and change in the relationship between foreign capital and labour. The primary emphasis is on a critical interrogation of notions of 'innovation' and 'change' advocated by recent reconfigurations of capital through a consideration of the resilience of certain features of previous workplace regimes – for instance, paternalism, informality and racial difference as ways of organising workplace relations. These recurrent features connect the contemporary system with the colonial and postcolonial past. The analysis will consider how these elements adapt and transform in response to changes in foreign investment.

I situate the genesis and reproduction of paternalism within the wider context of enclave development in the South African regional economy. Swaziland had been integrated into the South African regional economy from the early twentieth century, first through mass labour migration to the South African mining economy, and then through increasing penetration of South African capital in the Swazi economy. Here I draw on recent re-elaborations of Lewis's (1954, 1977) theory of economic dualism (Fields, 2004; Hart & Padayachee, 2013; Mhone, 2001) and briefly revisit the notion of articulation of modes of production (Hall, 1980; Wolpe, 1972, 1980).

Economic dualism developed historically through colonial rule: the formal sector, dominated by white capital, grew as an 'enclave' surrounded by the subsistence economy in the rural areas where Swazis farmed under customary land tenure controlled by the traditional authorities led by the Paramount Chief (the title the British gave to the Swazi king). The pre-existing mode of production, with its reciprocal non-market relations, coexisted hand-in-hand with the growing formal sector. The low wages of the formal sector and the systematic discrimination of African workers inhibited the gradual integration of the vast majority of the population into the formal economy. At independence racial discrimination was formally abolished. Yet, the dualism between the informal sector and the formal economy remained. The Paramount Chief became king and absolute ruler of the country, a system still in place today. The royal family and those closely connected to it began to broker deals with foreign capital, thus enabling only a tiny local bourgeoisie to share the benefits of enclave development with foreign capitalists.

Today the formal sector is dominated by South African investment, Swazi migration to South Africa remains high, and the economic ties between the two countries strong: more than 90 per cent of all imports come from South Africa and 60 per cent of all exports are to South Africa (Central Intelligence Agency [CIA], 2013). Given the development of the Swazi economy as a periphery of the South African regional economy, there are major similarities between workplace regimes in the two countries.

A study of the Economic Globalisation Index in 25 African countries reports Swaziland as the most globalised in the set (Ayenagbo et al., 2012, using data from Lockwood & Redoano, 2005). At the same time, the rule of the monarchy employs an ideology of traditionalism that gives customary law and land tenure prominence and conceives the king as the 'guardian of tradition', placing emphasis on social conservatism and preservation of heritage. Working at the intersection between two systems, the monarchy plays the dual role of keen ally of capital in the formal sector and overseer of the customary tenure system in the rural areas. Royalist idioms and practices are at the same time 'global' and 'traditional'.

The next section of the article will provide a brief overview of the history and political economy of labour in Swaziland, providing the necessary context for the development of the enclave economy. After this, I will consider the microsociological dimensions of enclave development at the workplace level, with specific reference to my ethnography of labour relations in Enkopolwani.

I will then briefly link the context of the Swazi case study to developments in contemporary workplace regimes in South Africa. The final section will expand on the notion of enclave economies and its relevance for the understanding of contemporary workplace regimes in the South African regional economy, followed by some concluding remarks about the resilience of inequality and exclusion in the current era of flexible capitalism.

Capitalism, Colonialism, Globalisation: A Brief Outline of the Political Economy of Swazi Labour

The establishment of British colonial rule in the early 1900s marked the rapid integration of Swazis into the growing regional South African economy and their subjugation to an unjust economic system that alienated natural resources and extracted labour from them for the benefit of Western capital and white settlers. Swazi rural dwellers were squeezed onto one-third of the country under the customary rule of chiefs and the traditionalist royal aristocracy headed by the Swazi 'Paramount Chief' – but still regarded as king by Swazi commoners. The remaining two-thirds were assigned as title deed land to white settlers and big capital (Crush, 1980).

Imposition of a hut and poll tax in the customary areas forced homesteads to seek cash, obtained primarily through migrant wage labour. Many Swazis found themselves as tenants on white farms, with no land rights. Others sought wage labour in the towns, the local mines and farms. Most migrants moved to the better-paying South African mines, plantations and large infrastructure projects in the Rand and in Natal.

The urban areas were under white control. Swazis did not have access to credit and, with the exception of a few overcrowded townships, could not buy land on the private market. Hotels, public facilities, public transport were all segregated by race (Dlamini, 2007). The subsistence economy in the customary areas was under threat, but continued to provide a substantial contribution to homestead livelihoods. Desertion rates in labour contracts were very high and migrant male labour was hired on short-term contracts. Men came back to their rural homesteads after a few months of work in the towns to participate in agricultural activities there. Most migrant workers never became a full proletariat, and continued to move back and forth between the formal sector and the customary system. Wages were very low (lower in Swaziland than in South Africa), working conditions harsh, and workers suffered frequent verbal and physical abuse (Crush, 1987).

The pre-existing monarchic structures – which oversaw all local chiefs – lost overall political control of the country, but maintained substantial powers over Swazi rural dwellers. In collusion with colonial rule, the monarchy actively manipulated the ideology of tradition to maintain its influence over Swazis (MacMillan, 1985). While conflicts and tensions with the colonial government were high, royals and chiefs quickly realised that the colonial system was there to stay. Traditional authorities had to find avenues of collaboration to keep their power base. One such area of collaboration was over the control of labour. Royal aristocracy sent their *tindvuna* (plural of 'supervisor' in SiSwati) to South African mines in the Rand with a high presence of Swazis to maintain social control over workers (Crush, 1987). The same system was replicated in large workplaces in Swaziland. In the 1950s and 1960s, the years preceding independence, a conscious alliance between white settlers and the royal aristocracy emerged to counter the rise of black progressive movements. The latter advocated non-racialism and strongly opposed any form of racial discrimination, including the racist system of workers' exploitation. The royal aristocracy was trying to contain any workerist democratic tendencies, in order to perpetuate traditional rule after independence. Royals, white settlers and big capital shared a common enemy: unions, workers' protests and political mobilisation along class lines (Simelane, 2003, pp. 180–182).

In the wake of independence, finally secured in 1968, the black progressives were marginalised and the British attempt to lead a transition towards multi-party democracy was quickly neutralised. Five years after independence, King Sobhuza II suspended the constitution and banned political parties. The structure of the colonial economy was not radically altered. White settlers and foreign capital – now increasingly South African – continued to play a prominent role in the domestic economy (Daniel, 1982). Their dominant position was maintained as long as they did not threaten Sobhuza's political hegemony.

The programmes initiated in the late colonial period to buy back land for the Swazi nation went on, but the transfer of the newly acquired land benefited few. Many people in royal circles became capitalist agricultural producers, taking control of the newly acquired land, and a small black middle class fostered by the indigenisation and rapid expansion of the state bureaucracy was able to accumulate some land and wealth. Large-scale capital investments from South African and British capital continued, with royal elites getting a direct stake through the royal investment fund Tibiyo Taka Ngwane (Tibiyo from now onwards). In principle the returned land and the capitalist investments were held by the King 'in trust for the nation'. In practice royal elites accumulated wealth for themselves, excluding the vast majority of the population from any substantial gain (Levin, 1997; Simelane, 2002). Wages remained very low and the land mass available to commoners in the customary system did not significantly increase.

Dependence on South Africa grew and the vast presence of South African capital was a major contributing factor in keeping the main features of the apartheid workplace regime in Swazi post-colonial workplaces. The *indvuna* system was transformed in a formal works council system chaired by management and with a king's appointee in 'representation' of Swazi workers' interests (Levin, 1997, p. 88). Trade unions – which, unlike political parties, remained legal after 1973 – channelled the discontent of exploited Swazis. The monarchy made it clear that it was not sympathetic to labour demands and the government proved generally hostile against unions. Unions managed to gain recognition in many companies and challenge the works council system, but threats to their effectiveness abounded. Throughout the 1970s and the 1980s, workplaces remained under the firm control of whites and foreigners, with middle and top management positions largely occupied by whites.

Despite the fall of apartheid rule in South Africa and the opening up of the South African economy in the 1990s, this scenario did not substantially change in the last two decades. The current ruler, King Mswati III, followed in the footsteps of his father, Sobhuza II. The monarchy continues to build partnerships with foreign capital and royal elite accumulation benefits from cheap labour drawn from the rural and urban informal sectors. The most successful example of this enduring alliance is the sugar industry, where the two major players, the Royal Swaziland Sugar Corporation and Ubombo Sugar, are joint ventures between Tibiyo and South African multinationals.

Following the impetus from post-apartheid South Africa, localisation of management in the private sector has made some headway in recent years. The number of black Swazis in lower and middle management has substantially increased. But whites and foreigners of other racial and ethnic groups still occupy a highly disproportionate amount of top management positions.

At the same time, the national economy continues to be characterised by high unemployment (41% in 2010), under-employment in the subsistence and informal sectors, very low wages and harsh working conditions. Tati's (2004) work explores the question of the persistence of certain elements of the political economy of labour through a review of labour market data about Swazi workers in the national and Southern African labour markets for three decades, from 1973 to 2003. While much has changed in terms of regional and global structures of capital investment, patterns of labour use in Swaziland have not been significantly transformed by these changes. Economic policy is dictated by multinational capital, and labour remains in a subordinate position. The supply of migrant labour to South Africa under highly exploitative conditions continues to play a major role in the Swazi political economy. Openness to global capitalism reinforces the dominant trend towards appallingly low wages in the domestic economy, with a new wave of unskilled female labour force drawn from the homestead economy. The development of agri-business is supported by further land alienation, used as a means of labour extraction from rural homesteads. In summary, the dominant features of the colonial and post-colonial economy 'are reproduced through relations of production that give prominence to the evolving interests of multinational capital and local elites and leadership' (Tati, 2004, p. 2).

The rapid growth of the textile and clothing industry in the early 2000s sadly exemplifies these trends. The growth was spurred by the opening of Taiwanese-owned factories taking advantage of the inclusion of Swaziland in the African Growth Opportunity Act, which gave preferential access to the US markets for apparel goods, at a time when the South African rand – to which the Swazi currency is tied – was weak against the US dollar. This new wave of investment created 40,000 new manufacturing jobs – most of them young women – in a stagnating economy with a small industrial workforce (Simelane, 2008). The Swazi government effectively closed an eye on the numerous reports of malpractice, including harsh working conditions, poor health and safety, reports of verbal and physical abuse of workers, and breach of minimum wage regulations (Bezuidenhout & Jeppesen, 2011; Simelane, 2008). By 2011, the workforce was reduced to 18,000 after several years of decline escalated by the end of the Multi-Fibre Agreement and a strong rand (Bezuidenhout & Jeppesen, 2011).[1]

With rising population pressures, the HIV/AIDS pandemic, and a looming sovereign debt crisis, the basic living conditions of most Swazis have not improved; on the contrary, they are rapidly worsening; 88.4 per cent of the population lives on 5 US dollars a day or less.[2] The state lags behind in the provision of basic services like access to drinking water and electricity, especially in the rural areas, and has not offered any substantial protection from the devastating impact of cheap labour in the form of social grants. There are no unemployment benefits and the social pension for the elderly is minuscule. Access to land under customary tenure remains the only form of 'welfare state' for most Swazis, who cannot afford to buy land in the private market. Seventy-eight per cent of Swazis reside in a rural area under chief's rule, and those residing in urban areas or company compounds continue to maintain strong links with a rural homestead. While it is true that subsistence farming is experiencing a long-term decline, maize production and livestock rearing constitute important economic activities for many Swazis to supplement their meagre wages. A large number of informal economic activities also take place at the intersection between rural and urban, and customary land constitutes a valuable resource that can be used for other purposes beyond farming – for instance, building accommodation for rental to commuting workers near the main towns.

In this section I have outlined the historical and institutional context that influences contemporary workplace regimes in Swaziland. The next section will provide an analysis of some of the micro-sociological dimensions of labour relations in Enkopolwani, a Christian company town in the north-west of Swaziland. While this social enterprise is inserted into new configurations of global capital working at the intersection between charity and business, the workplace regime established by the missionaries presents the familiar local features that perpetuate the exclusion of workers from the benefits of economic development.

Race, Inequality and Exclusion in a Christian Company Town

From November 2007 to December 2008, I conducted long-term ethnographic fieldwork in Enkopolwani,[3] a Christian company town in Swaziland and in the past one of the biggest mining operations in Southern Africa.[4] It has recently been redeveloped by a group of (mostly) white Southern African and North American Pentecostal Christian missionaries and businessmen as a sustainable social business project under the aegis of not-for-profit company Enkopolwani Ministries Swaziland (EMS from now onwards). The primary mission of providing care for orphans was conducted in tandem with the production of wealth from activities such as timber logging, plank production and other economic enterprises (that is, tourist lodge, livestock and agriculture, honey harvesting, bakery, mechanics workshop, carpentry workshop, bottled water production). The company vision was to use profits from the economic activities to sustain the running of the town, its social services and its wide-ranging orphan care programme. In practice, EMS was strongly reliant on donor funding, from a mix of secular and Christian donors based in North America, Europe and Southern Africa.

Enkopolwani was located 2 km from a quiet border post leading to South Africa and 16 km from a small urban centre in the north-west of Swaziland. The steep slopes and the heavy rains made it a tough place for maize farming, the main subsistence crop in Swaziland. The adjacent area under customary land tenure, Lapha, was not a prosperous rural area relative to the rest of Swaziland. People there were heavily reliant on employment in Enkopolwani or remittances from relatives who left for the bigger urban centres of Swaziland and South Africa.

The company town infrastructure was built along mountain slopes. The workers' residences, the management houses, the old club areas, and several other infrastructures were all left over from the mining times. Chrysotile asbestos was being extracted since the late 1920s, after obtaining a mineral concession to mine on 'native area n.3', one of the customary areas designated by the British (Crush, 1992). Major infrastructural development had gained momentum in the 1950s, when the asbestos multinational giant that ran the operations acquired title deed over the Enkopolwani area. Besides the town infrastructure, the main asset left from the mining times was 2,200 hectares of forest, populated by pine and eucalyptus.

A Global Encounter

The genesis of the EMS sprang from an interesting encounter of global and local forces. The last decades of globalisation have corresponded to the fast spread of charismatic and Pentecostal Christian churches throughout Africa, but also in Asia and Latin America (Coleman, 2000; Robbins, 2004). International links with similar churches in North America have also grown in importance. With the exception of a small foster home for girls run by Anglican nuns, all other missionaries in Enkopolwani were 'born again' Christians – a popular term for Pentecostals. The main EMS church service was a non-denominational charismatic service. In line with Pentecostal practice, prominence was given to the spontaneous movement of the Holy Spirit acknowledged as a crucial driving force in everyday life, and the main tool through which God and Jesus manifested themselves in the material world. All life in the secular realm centred around the divine presence of the Trinity, and all work done by 'proper' Christians was in preparation for the realisation of the 'Kingdom of God'. This was a millenarian movement actively working within a paradigm where the end of the world and judgement day were believed to be imminent.

The white Southern African business missionaries, mostly from Swaziland and South Africa, and with a strong presence of Afrikaners, were part of a wider trend in neighbouring South Africa. After the end of apartheid, many Afrikaners and other white South Africans have converted to Pentecostal movements, moving away from more traditional denominations like the Dutch Reformed Church. The Southern African missionaries were thus seeking to reconstruct themselves in a post-apartheid world, a transition marked by the conscious rejection of racism (Chipkin & Leatt, 2011). The Calvinist business ethics was carried forward from their previous ideologies and the mixing of business and Christian service seemed a natural choice for many. A number of the top managers had previously run businesses or worked as lower or middle management in mines and other business settings in the region.

Adrian, a successful born again Canadian businessman, decided in his middle age that time had come to fully dedicate himself to put his business skills at the service of God. In the process of touring the world in search for the right place and the right project, he connected with a white Swazi Christian eye surgeon he had met at a development conference in Asia. The eye surgeon linked Adrian with Alan, Marc and Dan in Swaziland.

Alan was a charismatic local white pastor running a successful retreat for street kids near the Swazi capital. Marc was a Swazi of Afrikaner descent who had grown up on his family farm in southern Swaziland and had his own brick-making business in central Swaziland. Dan, also a Swazi of Afrikaner descent, and Marc grew up as neighbours in the same area; they both became born again and looked up to Alan as their spiritual leader. Dan was the biggest independent timber operator in Swaziland, running several sawmills. Before the establishment of the EMS, he had partnered with another local businessman, and together they owned Enkopolwani, bought at a bargain price in 2004 after the company town went into liquidation following the demise of the mine. Dan had started a sawmill there, but soon after Dan's partner, Stephen, was looking for a way out. Stephen's secular vision for a sustainable business town built around arts and crafts died away for lack of capital investment. Adrian's vision now had legs, and he teamed up with Alan, Marc and Dan to create the EMS. Dan donated his share of the company and the EMS bought out Stephen's share. In May 2006, the EMS had formally acquired the Enkopolwani property. All four became founding directors of the EMS, and Marc was appointed as managing director.

On the surface, the project presented many innovations rooted in the discourses and practices of globalisation. For one, neoliberal ideologies and mission service were coming together in a new trend referred to in the missiology literature as 'business as mission' (Steffen & Barnett, 2006). One way for EMS Christians to fulfil their role and follow the message of Jesus was to serve the community by putting their business skills at the service of God. As good 'global' Christians, they could now harness the power of markets to alleviate poverty and spread the gospel.

Adrian, the Canadian businessman and chairperson of the board of directors, played a crucial role in channelling donor funds, and brought crucial skills from Canada in the areas of PR and business development. The project had a pretty slick image from the beginning, with a strong internet presence, and a sophisticated model that linked the business side with the charity activities. The rhetoric of top managers was strongly influenced by this. The ultimate goal was ambitious: EMS missionaries were grooming the most neglected and vulnerable people in Swaziland – orphans whose number was on the rise due to the HIV/AIDS crisis – to become the future leaders of Africa. At the same time, the rest of the community would not be ignored, as adult men and women could find employment opportunities in the business activities. There was no pressure to convert for adult workers, not least because the emphasis of the Christian mission was focused on orphans – most of them in their early years of childhood when they arrived in Enkopolwani. In practice, Adrian's free market vision for a Christian and better future for all quickly 'localised' in ways that he and the Canadian directors, missionaries and volunteers failed to predict.

In the previous business partnership that bought the town in 2004, Dan had set up a timber sawmill as one of the core revenue-generating projects. The timber business grew organically, without any major change in structures of employment and management since the Christian management took over. Timber processing and timber harvesting were integrated into Dan's private business structures, without clear boundaries between the EMS not-for-profit activities and Dan's for-profit business. Some of the EMS top managers were paid by Dan's private company, and bank loans to the EMS were given with Dan's private business acting as guarantor.

To make things more complicated, workers labouring in the EMS profit-making economic activities were not employed by the EMS. A labour broker was used as an intermediary, and all employees working in the business activities – around 410 at the end of 2008 – were formally employed by Malindzisa and Sons. The labour broker was the same broker who employed workers in Dan's private timber business.[5]

Paternalism, Informality and the Racial Division of Labour

Despite the globalising rhetoric and the social mission, the EMS workplace regime showed many continuities with other exploitative workplaces in Swaziland. EMS benefited from the low wages holding in the wider national economy and did not alter the general pattern of cheap labour and harsh working and living conditions holding in other comparable workplaces in the timber industry and other sectors.

Wages were very low, about half of those offered by other multinational timber companies operating in Swaziland. At the end of 2008, most EMS workers earned 35 emalangeni a day.[6] Working conditions in the main sawmill (the largest workplace) were dismal, with major health and safety issues and a high number of work accidents (Laterza, Forrester, & Mususa, 2013). Material conditions in the smaller workplaces were somewhat better.

When queried about the apparent contradiction between the Christian vision of the company and the workers' salary packages, top managers did not see this as an anomaly, but rather as a necessary consequence of the local labour market conditions. After all, these business missionaries saw the 'free market' as a God-given tool to lift people from poverty, and would not question its exploitative structures. This ideology conveniently rationalised the persistence of inequality and systematic exclusion of workers from the benefits of economic development, and obscured the historical legacy of colonialism and apartheid. Racist arguments about the lack of a proper work ethic and laziness were often used as justifications for Swazi workers' impossibility to improve their material and social conditions. According to the missionaries, everybody in Enkopolwani had been given a choice by God to join the community of believers as equals, however workers' 'culture' made the exercise of this choice difficult. Despite the effort at reconstructing a post-apartheid identity as non-racist Christians, Southern African top managers maintained their racist views to make sense of inequality and underdevelopment, and their continued privilege vis-à-vis Swazi workers.

The spatial arrangement of the town was another major factor in perpetuating the geography of exclusion that characterised the formal and informal segregation of (black) workers from (mostly white) management. Workers were given free accommodation in the workers' village, the compound previously occupied by miners and their families in the heyday of the asbestos mine. These houses had not been properly maintained for over two decades – in 1991 the multinational asbestos giant had sold out the mine and a number of short-term speculators entered the scene, with no interest in the preservation of the town infrastructure. Many of these houses did not have working toilets, and there was no electricity in most of the compound. The workers' village was clearly separated from the management houses, which were previously occupied by mine managers and had been renovated by the EMS. The spatial segregation of the mining town had been replicated – with one substantial difference. Many of the management houses were reused as foster homes for orphans, geographically separated by forests and the main town roads from the workers' village. Here too the segregation was not accidental: the missionaries made it clear that workers had to be kept as far away from orphans as possible. 'Children's protection' arguments were frequently used to justify this arrangement.

The generally poor level of workers' accommodation was also inserted into the general geography of rural–urban relations inherited from the colonial period. Virtually all workers had relevant ties with rural areas under customary tenure across Swaziland, many from the neighbouring Lapha. They went home every end of the month, engaging in substantial exchanges of cash, gifts and other goods with their rural kin. In many cases, subsistence maize farming and livestock rearing contributed to household needs, complementing the limited amount of goods and cash made available through wages. Cash remittances were also used to buy fertilisers, and more entrepreneurial workers and families were able to reinvest small amounts of cash in productive informal businesses, ranging from transport to the opening of grocery shops in rural locations or the sale of maize or other crops in local markets. These activities were sustained by a mix of market ideologies and local idioms and practices of reciprocity which emphasised mutual obligations and questioned the legitimacy of private property and individualistic accumulation. These wider social and economic relations that cut across wage labour were for most workers more important than the job itself. The labour turnover was high, and many workers moved as soon as they found better opportunities through their social networks.

Not dissimilar from the colonial and early postcolonial period, paternalism was the dominant feature of labour relations. Work regimes were set unilaterally and informally by top managers, and adjusted to the situation on a personalistic basis. There was no formal voice mechanism, except for a regular meeting with the labour broker where a representative from each workplace would be present – vaguely resembling a works council. The labour broker was known for his disdain of any formal bargaining or negotiation, and rarely listened to workers' concerns. There was no recognised union and unions were not welcome. Workers sought employment through their kinship and rural networks. When top managers needed specific skills, they would rely on their trusted supervisors to recommend relevant people. These supervisors were often perceived by workers as management 'spies'. Talented workers were ignored by management and promotions were rarely based on merit. Salary increases were often given to workers who showed the right dose of subservience to management rule. At the time of fieldwork, only two managers with substantial decision-making powers were black Swazis.

Despite some slick company organograms, there was no clear management structure that made top managers accountable to the company or responsible for the enforcement of specific standards of fairness and transparency. Incidents and disputes were sorted out on an ad hoc basis by the labour broker. Workers had no room for redress because they could not easily access the government labour office in the nearby town and did not have the finances to bring their grievances to the labour courts.

Workers felt that they were not treated any better than in most other workplaces they experienced in the country or South Africa. They pointed out that very much like in colonial times, the *belungu* ('whites') were in control of the place and they were not good employers. Tensions erupted in a wildcat strike in 2008, which led to only marginal gains and no substantial change in labour practices. In 2011 and 2012, two forest fires were intentionally caused by disgruntled workers. By then workers had lost hope in meaningful dialogue with management as a way to address their concerns.

The 'Localisation' of Enkopolwani

The contradictions between the globalising Christian rhetoric of development and the resilience of local practices were reflected in the relationship between the Canadian directors and the white Southern African directors and top managers. The Canadians wanted the EMS to develop better management structures and increase transparency, accountability and sustainable planning for the future.

A major point of conflict between the two groups was over the presence of black managers. Canadians felt that an almost all-white management was not a good sign of engagement with the community and the local context, and made the EMS vulnerable to strong criticism from donors and the international community. Despite the differences, both groups converged on their unquestioned acceptance of the 'free market' to determine workers' wages.

These conflicts culminated in 2011 in the temporary withdrawal of new funding commitments from the Canadians, then reversed the year after. In October 2012 another confrontation led to the resignation of Adrian. The visionary founding father from Canada was now out of the picture. Other Canadian directors stayed, but it was clear that the process of 'localisation' of the EMS had gone further than anybody expected.

The Post-Apartheid Workplace Regime

The basic structures of paternalism and informality that characterised workplace relations in Enkopolwani are dominant in other Swazi workplaces as well – though the almost all-white management and the high degree of racial discrimination in Enkopolwani are not necessarily the norm. Whites and expats of other racial or ethnic groups continue to play a disproportionately influential role in an economy dominated by foreign capital. The only choice left for workers when they are ill-treated is to look for better patrons, who still offer wages within a range set by a distorted and exploitative formal labour market. With weakened unions and a hostile state, workers have no other structures to protect their interests.

Similar findings are reported from many South African contemporary workplaces in different sectors of the economy (that is Barchiesi, 2011; Bernstein, 2013; Bezuidenhout, 2004; Connor,

2013; Du Toit & Ewert, 2002; Du Toit, 2005; Ewert & Hamman, 1999; Hart, 2002; Von Holdt, 2003; Webster & Von Holdt, 2005). This is not surprising, given the strong influence of South African capital and the integration of Swaziland into the South African economy.

In a study of the engineering industry in South Africa, Swaziland and Zimbabwe, Bezuidenhout (2004) provides a clear conceptual framework to compare some of these post-apartheid trends with previous workplace regimes. According to Bezuidenhout, many elements of the apartheid workplace regime prevail, with some changes, in the engineering industry in South Africa and Swaziland – and to a lesser extent in Zimbabwe (2004, p. 20). Bezuidenhout improves and modifies Von Holdt's (2003) insights on the 'neo-apartheid workplace regime'. Bezuidenhout calls it more aptly the 'post-apartheid workplace regime'. This workplace regime emerges from the ruins of the apartheid workplace order, which had as its defining features:

> (i) a racial division of labour, (ii) a racial structure of power supplemented by attempts to incorporate a colonial construction of 'ethnicity' in supervision, (iii) a system of migrant labour, (iv) the racial segregation of facilities, and (v) a location of workplaces in a bifurcated industrial geography. (Bezuidenhout, 2004, p. 4)

These defining features persist, albeit in a restructured form. There is no systematic racial division of labour enforced by the state through discriminatory regulation anymore. Yet, akin to the findings from the Enkopolwani case study, white managers play a prominent role in most of these companies. Black management is often in the minority, and in most cases subordinate to top management positions occupied by whites and expats of other racial and ethnic groups. Following Burawoy's (1972) study of localisation in postcolonial Zambian mines, Bezuidenhout refers to this phenomenon as the 'upward floating colour bar': a greater number of black managers are appointed, replacing whites at lower and middle level, but whites continue to occupy prominent positions at the top.

The data show that an informal wage colour bar still holds. Whites often earn more than blacks even where they occupy the same job grade or skill level. Increasing numbers of casual workers and top management manipulation of the threat of closure due to global competition tend to perpetuate many aspects of the racial structure of power that was legitimised by the apartheid dispensation.

The empowering effect of trade unions protected by progressive labour legislation is majorly curtailed by these trends. The segregation by racial group of industry facilities is officially banned and opposed in principle by management. In practice, the fact that management includes a disproportionate amount of whites and other non-blacks in its ranks sustains workers' perception that the segregation of facilities by rank is informed by a racial logic. This kind of spatial segregation is also resonant with the findings of my Swazi case study.

Migrant labour is a central feature of the contemporary political economy of labour as it used to be in the past. The vulnerability of internal and foreign migrants plays in the hand of capital and is a threat to the improvement of workers' welfare. The legacy of the industrial geography of colonialism is very much alive today (Bezuidenhout, 2004, pp. 17–19). This geography created stark separations between the rural and the urban and regulated flows between the two, moulding the rural areas into a vast reserve of cheap labour for the cities (Mamdani, 1996). Although the legal discriminatory practices that enforced these separations are a thing of the past, the interactions between these two systems continue to work in a logic of hierarchy and dependence. Capital can easily relocate to the peripheries of the South African regional economy, like Swaziland and Lesotho, to take advantage of weak labour rights and cheaper wages, thus curtailing the positive effects of improved labour legislation and workers' rights in post-apartheid South Africa (Bezuidenhout, 2004, p. 18).

Bezuidenhout's insights provide us with a viable conceptual framework to make sense of workplace relations in Enkopolwani. All the features analysed above apply to Enkopolwani in one way or another, from the ongoing racial inequalities in management structures and living and working conditions, to the bifurcated industrial geography that allows for the continued availability of cheap labour from rural areas.

Enclave Development and the Evolution of the South African Regional Economy

How do we make sense of the resilience of the main features of the apartheid workplace regime in the post-apartheid South African regional economy? The answer lies in the historical roots of exploitation and marginalisation of workers in the formal sector. The following words by Nobel-Prize winning West Indian economist W.A. Lewis on the development of the formal economy show striking resemblances with the contemporary situation:

> What we have is not one island of expanding capitalist employment, surrounded by a vast sea of subsistence workers, but rather a number of such tiny islands . . . We find a few industries highly capitalized, such as mining or electric power, side by side with the most primitive techniques; a few high class shops, surrounded by masses of old style traders; a few highly capitalized plantations, surrounded by a sea of peasants. (Lewis, 1954, p. 147, in Fields, 2004, p. 3)

According to Lewis's (1954, 1977) theory of economic dualism, this is the basic starting point for all modern economies around the world. The evolution of this system has been uneven and produced very different outcomes around the world, resulting in the unequal hierarchy of developed and underdeveloped countries. In developed economies, the initial dualism is sustained by unlimited supplies of labour, due to the lower productivity of the subsistence sector and the availability of masses of potential workers willing to work in the formal sector for a wage slightly above subsistence levels. As the formal sector expands, the informal sector increases its productivity and its wages – the assumption here is that marginal productivity of labour in the informal sector is zero or negative. Wages in the formal sector begin to rise attracting ever more workers from the informal sector, until the unlimited supply of labour is exhausted (Fields, 2004, p. 8). As wages rise, workers have more spending power and start to benefit from the redistribution of wealth. By increasing consumption, they become active agents of economic development, driving demand for more goods, in a virtuous circle that benefits both capitalists and workers-citizens. The tax base increases and the financial viability of the state grows accordingly. Improvements in public services and welfare provisions further strengthen citizens' participation in the economy, positively impacting on economic growth (Mhone, 2001, p. 14–15).

In the South African regional economy, the evolution of a racist colonial order enforced systematic barriers between the formal and the subsistence sectors, thus inhibiting the possibility for a growing internal market with better outcomes for African workers. Strict controls on mobility between rural and urban areas, the reinvention of customary rule in rural areas, and the systematic exclusion of migrant workers from access to credit, individual property rights, comprehensive labour rights and substantial welfare provisions in health and education, all contributed to perpetuate enclave development in a formal labour market characterised by very low wages and harsh working conditions (cf. Feinstein, 2005). There are, of course, differences in degrees between Swaziland and South Africa, not least the level of state control and regime brutality in enforcing this dualism that occurred at the peak of apartheid in South Africa. One major historical difference was the amount of land reserved for African occupation. While Swazis were confined to one-third of the whole country, African groups in South Africa received a much worse deal, and by 1936 they were relegated to 13.5 per cent of all land.

As Harold Wolpe's landmark theory of the articulation of modes of production shows (Hall, 1980; Wolpe, 1972, 1980), race was central to this project, both during the segregation years of British rule and in the systematic assault on black livelihoods brought about by the apartheid state since 1948. Race became the primary ideological conduit of class differentiation, and black people were exploited as cheap labour to the benefit of white capital and the white working classes. The existence of rural areas under customary rule was key in keeping the cost of labour below subsistence. In effect, the communal relations of production pre-dating colonialism and apartheid continued, but in a transformed form, and were subjugated in a relation of dependence to the dominant mode of production – industrial capitalism initially driven by growth in the mining sector, subsequently expanding to manufacturing as well. The degree of dispossession and gradual dissolution of the subsistence mode of production was variable. The distribution and productive capacity of rural land under customary tenure were highly uneven across different areas (Simkins, 1981), as was the impact of the forced relocation campaigns carried out by the apartheid regime to push substantial numbers of Africans into the artificially crafted ethnic 'homelands' – also known as bantustans – mapped around the rural areas previously earmarked for African occupation.

Lewis's (1977) explanation of the evolution of the international economic order well complements Wolpe's insights, and offers us a broader perspective that pre-dates the institutionalisation of racism by way of state policies. The enormous differentials between salaries for white workers and managers and black workers were at the heart of the largely unregulated mineral revolution of the late nineteenth century. They were caused, among other things, by mass migration from Europe towards temperate countries like South Africa – these also included the United States, Canada, Argentina, Chile, Australia and New Zealand (Lewis, 1977, pp. 14–20). Due to higher productivity of agriculture in Europe, white workers fetched much higher wages, as they would only move to South Africa if incentivised by higher-than-European wages and the resulting settler lifestyles that continued throughout the twentieth century until the present day (Hart & Padayachee, 2013, p. 59). The pre-existing economic dualism was aggravated and reinforced by a racist political system that privileged whites over the local population in all spheres of economic, social and political life, but the seeds of it were present before the full development of colonial and apartheid racism.

Conclusion: Workers' Welfare and the Paradoxes of Globalisation

This analysis has two important implications. Firstly, enclave development was already integral to the first wave of globalisation of capital experienced between the late nineteenth century and the beginning of the twentieth century. There are many more continuities between past and present that some recent discourses on 'innovation' and 'change' tend to acknowledge. Secondly, there are strong material reasons for the perpetuation of enclave development in the post-apartheid South African regional economy that go beyond the impact of changes in the legal and institutional framework. Formal racial discrimination in South Africa and Swaziland are things of the past, and, at least in the South African context, labour legislation has made huge leaps forward in terms of workers' protection. Despite this, the basic structures of the economy have not changed. The racial composition of capital has, to some extent. It now includes the emerging black elites from the post-apartheid order – and the royal elites in alliance with foreign capital in Swaziland – and different nationalities of foreign investors beyond Europe and North America. The bulk of the black African population is tied to an underdeveloped informal sector (now not only rural, but increasingly located in the urban areas) and has little or no prospect of moving out of poverty.

Do the basic insights of the economic dualism paradigm still make sense in a market landscape increasingly characterised by a long-term decline of formal sector employment and increasing casualisation? Is dualism disappearing due to the gradual dissolution of alternative livelihoods sustained by rural areas under customary tenure as Wolpe predicted? There is some evidence that rural dependency and deagrarianisation are increasing, recently sustained in South Africa by an extensive system of modest social grants that somewhat mitigates the negative effects of the lack of employment opportunities in the formal sector (Bryceson, 2002; Eastwood, Kirsten, & Lipton, 2006). It is true that subsistence farming is on a trajectory of long-term decline, both in South Africa and in Swaziland. Despite this, 75 per cent of Swazis are involved in subsistence farming (Freedom House, 2013). Even in South Africa, where land alienation was much more pronounced than in Swaziland, there are currently about 4 million people involved in subsistence agriculture (Altman et al., 2009). Furthermore, ideological and organisational elements of the subsistence mode of production continue to infuse a vibrant informal sector cutting across rural and urban spaces. Here people mix reciprocal relations and market idioms to produce alternative economies that partially subvert the structural constraints imposed by unequal growth. Land under customary tenure is used as a valuable resource for other economic activities beyond farming and ranching – see, for instance, the growth of vernacular land markets (Chimhowu & Woodhouse, 2006). Wholesale dispossession has not quite happened in the way it had been predicted by Wolpe's (1972, 1980) 'linear proletarianisation' thesis, and the informal sector continues to sustain a large number of people, even more so now that formal sector employment levels are down and casualisation on the rise.

In spite of all the hype about globalisation and the manifold positive changes that it is supposed to bring about for the wider populace, most workers in the South African regional economy continue to struggle at the margins of a system that does not provide any realistic avenue for advancement and a decent livelihood. Opportunities for positive change, then, need to be sought elsewhere, outside the neo-liberal paradigm that advocates opening up of African economies to international investors as a miraculous solution to underdevelopment.

The reasons for the resilience of labour practices historically associated with the apartheid and colonial era are rooted in the enclave development of the South African regional economy. Economic dualism helps us understand how the separation and interdependence of the formal and the informal sectors came about and why it persists in the current situation. The analytical discussion in this article has been confined to economic frameworks. However, in order to craft effective policy interventions to improve workers' position, we will need to shift our analytical focus towards the social, political and institutional factors that are contributing to the perpetuation of enclave development and its devastating socio-economic effects.

A more comprehensive theory that takes into account social, political and institutional factors is needed. Enclave development is a real property of social and political relations in workplaces. Enclaves operate in geographic configurations that mediate the relationship between global capital and local labour relations (cf. Bezuidenhout, 2004; Sidaway, 2007). The case study of a Christian company town presented here provides some insight into the micro-sociology of enclave development. The harsh realities of labour in Enkopolwani suggest that until the institutional, ideological and geographic barriers inhibiting the gradual integration of the informal sector into the formal economy are addressed, new configurations of foreign investment will fail to produce substantial improvements in workers' lives.

Acknowledgements

This research would not have been possible without generous support from the Economic and Social Research Council, award no. PTA-031-2005-00040. An earlier version of this article was presented on 29 June 2013 at the Fifth European Conference on African Studies in a panel on labour and globalisation in Africa. I am grateful to the panel convenors Laura Mann and Mark Graham for providing such an opportunity, and the panel speakers for offering useful feedback. I would also like to thank Harri Englund, Keith Hart, Kate Meagher, Patience Mususa and Max Bolt for their invaluable input. The data I have used in this article will be made available on request to bona fide researchers.

Disclosure statement

No potential conflict of interest was reported by the author.

Notes

1. The industry is likely to experience further decline as the US government decided to exclude Swaziland from AGOA effective from January 2015, after pressure from unions and pro-democracy groups focusing the attention on the poor workers' and human rights record of the country.
2. These data were extracted from a query to the World DataBank Poverty and Inequality database and refers to the year 2010. Retrieved 10 October 2013 from http://databank.worldbank.org/data/views/variableSelection/selectvariables.aspx?source=poverty-and-inequality-database

3. All real names of places, people and organisations in this section (pp. 5–9) have been anonymised to protect research participants.
4. This was part of 23 months of doctoral field research carried out in Swaziland from 2007 to 2008. I am grateful to the Economic and Social Research Council (UK) for providing full funding for this project. I carried out several brief follow up visits in Enkopolwani after that, and have remained in touch with key collaborators and research participants there.
5. Labour brokers are a common feature of the private sector in Swaziland and South Africa. Companies use them so that they are not legally responsible for any dispute with their employees.
6. In August 2008, 35 emalangeni (Swazi currency) would have been roughly equivalent to US$4.55 per day.

References

Altman, M., Hart, T., & Jacobs, P. (2009). Household food security status in South Africa. *Agrekon*, *48*, 345–361. doi:10.1080/03031853.2009.9523831

Ayenagbo, K., Rongcheng, W., Wengjing, W., Nguhi, S., Kimatu, J. N., & Patrick, J. M. (2012). The impact of globalization on African countries economic development. *African Journal of Business Management*, *6*, 11057–11076.

Barchiesi, F. (2011). *Precarious liberation: Workers, the state, and contested social citizenship in postapartheid South Africa*. Albany, NY: State University of New York Press.

Bernstein, H. (2013). Commercial agriculture in South Africa: 'natural, simply capitalism'. *Journal of Agrarian Change*, *13*, 23–46. doi:10.1111/joac.12011

Bezuidenhout, A. (2004). *Post-colonial workplace regimes in the engineering industry in South Africa, Swaziland and Zimbabwe* (LSE Crisis States Programme Working Paper n.53).

Bezuidenhout, A., & Jeppesen, S. (2011). Between market, state and society: Labour codes of conduct in the southern African garment industry. *Development Southern Africa*, *28*, 653–668. doi:10.1080/0376835X.2011.623923

Bryceson, D. F. (2002). The scramble in Africa: Reorienting rural livelihoods. *World Development*, *30*, 725–739. doi:10.1016/S0305-750X(02)00006-2

Burawoy, M. (1972). *The colour of class on the copper mines: From African advancement to Zambianization*. Lusaka: Institute for African Studies.

Central Intelligence Agency. (2013, September 25). *The world factbook: Swaziland*. Washington, DC: Author. Retrieved 7 October 2013 from https://www.cia.gov/library/publications/the-world-factbook/geos/wz.html

Chimhowu, A., & Woodhouse, P. (2006). Customary vs private property rights? Dynamics and trajectories of vernacular land markets in sub-Saharan Africa. *Journal of Agrarian Change*, *6*, 346–371. doi:10.1111/joac.2006.6.issue-3

Chipkin, I., & Leatt, A. (2011). Religion and revival in post-apartheid South Africa. *Focus*, *62*, 39–46.

Coleman, S. (2000). *The globalisation of charismatic Christianity: Spreading the gospel of prosperity*. Cambridge: Cambridge University Press.

Connor, T. (2013). Borders of mutuality, frontiers of resistance: Paternalism and working identities of farm labourers in the Sundays River Valley, South Africa. *African Studies*, *72*, 375–398. doi:10.1080/00020184.2013.851466

Cooper, F. (2001). What is the concept of globalization good for? An African historian's perspective. *African Affairs*, *100*, 189–213. doi:10.1093/afraf/100.399.189

Crush, J. (1980). The colonial division of space: The significance of the Swaziland land partition. *The International Journal of African Historical Studies*, *13*, 71–86. doi:10.2307/218373

Crush, J. (1987). *The struggle for Swazi labour, 1890-1920*. Kingston: McGill-Queen's University Press.

Crush, J. (1992). The construction of compound authority: Drinking at Havelock, 1938–1944. In J. Crush & C. Ambler (Eds.), *Liquor and labor in southern Africa* (pp. 367–394). Athens: Ohio University Press.

Daniel, J. (1982). The political economy of colonial and post-colonial Swaziland. *South African Labour Bulletin*, *7*, 90–113.

Dlamini, N. (2007). *The legal abolition of racial discrimination and its aftermath: The case of Swaziland, 1945–1973* (Unpublished doctoral dissertation). University of the Witwatersrand, Johannesburg.

Du Toit, A. (2005). *Forgotten by the highway: Globalisation, adverse incorporation and chronic poverty in a commercial farming district* (CSSR Working Paper n.101).

Du Toit, A., & Ewert, J. (2002). Myths of globalisation: Private regulation and farm worker livelihoods on Western Cape farms. *Transformation*, *50*, 77–104. doi:10.1353/trn.2003.0010

Eastwood, R., Kirsten, J., & Lipton, M. (2006). Premature deagriculturalisation? Land inequality and rural dependency in Limpopo province, South Africa. *Journal of Development Studies*, *42*, 1325–1349. doi:10.1080/00220380600930614

Ewert, J., & Hamman, J. (1999). Why paternalism survives: Globalization, democratization and labour on South African wine farms. *Sociologia Ruralis*, *39*, 202–221. doi:10.1111/soru.1999.39.issue-2

Feinstein, C. (2005). *An economic history of South Africa: Conquest, discrimination and development*. Cambridge: Cambridge University Press.

Fields, G. S. (2004, September 14). Dualism in the labor market: A perspective on the Lewis model after half a century. Cornell University, ILR School. Retrieved from http://digitalcommons.ilr.cornell.edu/articles/268/

Freedom House. (2013). *Swaziland: A failed feudal state*. Washington, DC: Freedom House. Retrieved August 6, 2014, from http://www.freedomhouse.org/sites/default/files/Swaziland-%20A%20Failed%20Feudal%20State%2019%20September%202013.pdf

Hall, S. (1980). Race, articulation and societies structured in dominance. In UNESCO, *Sociological theories: Race and colonialism* (pp. 305–345). Paris: UNESCO.

Hart, G. (2002). *Disabling globalization: Places of power in post-apartheid South Africa*. Durban: University of Natal Press.

Hart, K., & Padayachee, V. (2013). A history of South African capitalism in national and global perspective. *Transformation*, *81–82*, 55–85. doi:10.1353/trn.2013.0004

Laterza, V., Forrester, B., & Mususa, P. (2013). Bringing wood to life: Lines, flows and materials in a Swazi sawmill. In T. Ingold & G. Palsson (Eds.), *Biosocial becomings: Integrating social and biological anthropology* (pp. 162–190). Cambride: Cambridge University Press.

Levin, R. (1997). *When the sleeping grass awakens: Land and power in Swaziland*. Johannesburg: Witwatersrand University Press.

Lewis, W. A. (1954). Economic development with unlimited supplies of labour. *The Manchester School*, *22*, 139–191. doi:10.1111/j.1467-9957.1954.tb00021.x

Lewis, W. A. (1977). *The evolution of the international economic order*. Princeton: Princeton University Press.

Lockwood, B., & Redoano, M. (2005). *The CSGR globalisation index: An introductory guide* (CSGR Working Paper n.155).

MacMillan, H. (1985). Swaziland: Decolonisation and the triumph of tradition. *The Journal of Modern African Studies*, *23*, 643–666. doi:10.1017/S0022278X00055014

Mamdani, M. (1996). *Citizen and subject: Contemporary Africa and the legacy of late colonialism*. London: James Currey.

Mhone, G. C. Z. (2001). *Enclavity and constrained labour absorptive capacity in southern African economies*. United Nations Research Institute for Social Development. Retrieved August 6, 2014 from http://www.unrisd.org/80256B3C005BCCF9/%28httpPublications%29/B81999299E53F9ECC1256BC90047A536?OpenDocument

Robbins, J. (2004). The globalization of Pentecostal and charismatic Christianity. *Annual Review of Anthropology*, *33*, 117–143. doi:10.1146/annurev.anthro.32.061002.093421

Sidaway, J. D. (2007). Enclave space: A new metageography of development? *Area*, *39*, 331–339. doi:10.1111/area.2007.39.issue-3

Simelane, H. S. (2002). The state, landlords and the squatter problem in post-colonial Swaziland. *Canadian Journal of African Studies*, *36*, 329–354. doi:10.2307/4107208

Simelane, H. S. (2003). *Colonialism and economic change in Swaziland, 1940-1960*. Manzini: JAN Publishing Centre.

Simelane, X. (2008). Textiles and employee relations in Swaziland. *Employee Relations*, *30*, 452–465. doi:10.1108/01425450810879402

Simkins, C. (1981). Agricultural production in the African reserves of South Africa, 1918-1969. *Journal of Southern African Studies*, *7*, 256–283. doi:10.1080/03057078108708028

Steffen, T., & Barnett, M. (2006). *Business as mission: From impoverished to empowered*. Pasadena: William Carey Library.

Tati, G. (2004). *Swaziland: In the pursuit of economic liberalisation and growth. How is poverty reproduced at the micro-level under changing labour market regimes?* Paper presented at the African Development and Poverty Reduction: The Macro-Micro Linkage conference, Somerset West, South Africa, October 13–15.

Von Holdt, K. (2003). *Transition from below: Forging trade unionism and workplace change in South Africa*. Pietermaritzburg: University of Natal Press.

Webster, E., & Von Holdt, K. (Eds.). (2005). *Beyond the apartheid workplace: Studies in transition*. Scottsville: University of KwaZulu-Natal Press.

Wolpe, H. (1972). Capitalism and cheap labour in South Africa. *Economy and Society*, *1*, 425–456. doi:10.1080/03085147200000023

Wolpe, H. (Ed.). (1980). *The articulation of modes of production: Essays from 'Economy and Society'*. London: Routledge & Kegan Paul.

Index

Note: **Boldface** page numbers refer to figures and tables, n denotes endnotes

For Product Safety Concerns and Information please contact our EU representative GPSR@taylorandfrancis.com Taylor & Francis Verlag GmbH, Kaufingerstraße 24, 80331 München, Germany

Batch number: 10732736

Printed by Printforce, the Netherlands